SO-ADW-997

UW Library BOOK SALE

Intervention Without Intervening?

The OAS Defense and Promotion of Democracy in the Americas

Andrew F. Cooper
and
Thomas Legler

INTERVENTION WITHOUT INTERVENING?
© Andrew F. Cooper and Thomas Legler, 2006.

All rights reserved. No part of this book may be used or reproduced in any manner whatsoever without written permission except in the case of brief quotations embodied in critical articles or reviews.

First published in 2006 by
PALGRAVE MACMILLAN™ ·
175 Fifth Avenue, New York, N.Y. 10010 and
Houndmills, Basingstoke, Hampshire, England RG21 6XS
Companies and representatives throughout the world

PALGRAVE MACMILLAN is the global academic imprint of the Palgrave Macmillan division of St. Martin's Press, LLC and of Palgrave Macmillan Ltd. Macmillan® is a registered trademark in the United States, United Kingdom and other countries. Palgrave is a registered trademark in the European Union and other countries.

ISBN 13: 978–1–4039–6751–0
ISBN 10: 1–4039–6751–2

Library of Congress Cataloging-in-Publication Data is available from the Library of Congress.

A catalogue record for this book is available from the British Library.

Design by Newgen Imaging Systems (P) Ltd., Chennai, India.

First edition: August 2006

10 9 8 7 6 5 4 3 2 1

Printed in the United States of America.

CONTENTS

ACKNOWLEDGMENTS

This book has been a collaborative endeavor between two researchers with very different backgrounds: one a student of International Relations and Comparative Foreign Policy (Andrew Cooper) and the other a student of Latin American Politics and Development (Thomas Legler). Our connection was a shared sense that many of our commonplace understandings concerning how multilateral actors operated to defend and promote democracy required revision. Indeed, when we started this project in 2000, it appeared that we were on the cusp of an exciting advance in this arena from both normative and institutional perspectives. Through a wider conceptual lens, pro-democracy activity envisaged a sea change in breaking free from the constraints of the Cold War era when regime form mattered much less than ideological alignment in inter-state relations and when "defending democracy" was often the pretext for military intervention of a coercive nature. Through a narrower lens, the OAS held the capacity to become an international pioneer in the evolution of a regional democratic solidarity paradigm.

Our conclusions suggest that the advances on the democracy agenda should not be exaggerated. A shift from what we highlight as club to networked multilateralism has been held back by a variety of factors, not the least of which is the hold of national sovereignty or more specifically what we term executive sovereignty. At the same time, however, the impact of an evolving mode of multilateralism both on the ground and in terms of scholarship cannot be ignored. At the heart of our analysis is a focus on two compelling episodes of OAS action to defend democracy precipitated by political crises. The first that unfolded in 2000 in Peru was brought on by Alberto Fujimori's electoral transgressions and the second, in Venezuela, was catalyzed by the attempt to overthrow Hugo Chávez in April 2002. The lessons learned from the Peruvian experience gave the impetus to the landmark Inter-American Democratic Charter.

Venezuela's crisis in turn presented the first test case of the new charter. In both these instances, the OAS adopted an innovative third-party mediation role that facilitated dialogue among polarized domestic political elites. This approach, which we call "intervention without intervening," forms the overarching theme of the book.

Comparatively we believe the insights gained from the OAS experience stretch far wider than the two case studies on which we concentrate. In the Americas there are a host of other illustrations of fragile democracies where this model could be deployed. Indeed, the OAS finds itself once again promoting intra-elite democratic dialogue, currently in Nicaragua and Ecuador. Beyond the Western Hemisphere, the obvious question that needs to be posed is whether this model can be replicated in some form or other in the repertoire of other multilateral institutions.

Theoretically, the book tackles head-on the challenge of bridging the traditional divide between International Relations and Comparative Politics. Our study of the OAS underlines the need for conceptual tools that allow scholars to take into more nuanced consideration the internationalization and transnationalization of democratization processes in their analysis, that is, the heightened involvement of cross-border networks of state, inter-governmental, and non-state actors in processes of "domestic" political change. In order to try to overcome this problem we offer an "inter-action" approach that bridges the gap in a dynamic, agency-oriented fashion.

We have accumulated an enormous number of debts in the pursuit of this project. Andrew Cooper was facilitated in its early stages of research by the award of a Canada-U.S. Fulbright fellowship, in the Western Hemisphere Program at the Paul H. Nitze School of Advanced International Studies, Johns Hopkins University, Washington, DC. During that time he enjoyed the intellectual stimulation of Riordan Roett, Charles Doran, Carol Wise, Isabel Studer Noguez, and Chris Sands. At SAIS, he also had the opportunity to use a graduate seminar as a sounding board for the project. On top of the Fulbright fellowship financial support came from a variety of sources that included the Social Sciences and Humanities Research Council of Canada, El Colegio de México, the University of Waterloo, and the project on "Middle States and Regionalism in the Americas" under the direction of Gordon Mace and Louis Bélanger at the Université Laval.

Tom Legler is also indebted to Gordon Mace and Louis Bélanger for their support through the aforementioned project. His research also benefited from a Human Security Fellowship from the Canadian Consortium on Human Security, a fellowship that he held at the Centre for Global

Studies, University of Victoria. He owes special thanks there to Gordon Smith. Mount Allison University provided generous support through a faculty start-up grant, a Bell Grant, as well as a Social Sciences and Humanities Research Council of Canada (SSHRC) internal research grant. He also received a SSHRC Standard Research Grant for a project entitled "Democratization as a Transnational Phenomenon." Tom Legler gained enormous insights into Peruvian political life as an elections observer for Common Borders in the April 2001 presidential elections and similarly for Venezuela as a Carter Center monitor during the 2003–2004 presidential recall referendum process.

For this book, in addition to processing a huge amount of stimulating written material, we conducted interviews with more than one hundred diplomats, politicians, bureaucrats, civil society leaders, and scholars. We interviewed a number of these individuals more than once. We have intentionally kept the identity of the interviewees anonymous. In our efforts to reconstruct the events surrounding the OAS-facilitated, intra-elite dialogue processes in Peru and Venezuela, our interviewing took us on repeat occasions to Ottawa, Washington, DC, Lima, and Caracas.

In the course of the project, we were helped by the expertise and contacts of a large number of academics and practitioners. Scholars who shared their insights with us included Carmen Rosa Balba, Dexter Boniface, Maxwell Cameron, Ralph Espach, Sharon Lean, Barry Levitt, Raúl Benítez Manaut, Robert Pastor, Wilma Petrash, Pablo Policzer, Jennifer McCoy, Yasmine Shamsie, Peter Smith, Brian Tomlin, Arturo Valenzuela, and Cuadros.

One of the methodological tips we picked up along the way was how useful our Canadian diplomatic representatives can be in facilitating interviews with high ranking officials abroad. We are grateful to the staff of the Canadian Permanent Mission to the OAS in Washington, DC, and the Canadian embassies in Lima and Caracas for helping to set up key interviews for which our own cold call efforts would likely have had little success.

Practitioners (or former practitioners) who were particularly helpful to our research included Lloyd Axworthy, Carlos Carbacho, Francisco Diez, Graeme Clark, Paul Durand, Bruce Friedman, John Graham, Fernando Jaramillo, Sofía Macher, Don Mackay, Peter Quilter, Manuel Rodríguez, Rafael Roncagliolo, Étienne Savoie, Jorge Santistevan, Diego García Sayán, Tom Shannon, Michael Shifter, Eduardo Stein, Jorge Valero, Catherine Vézina, and Renata Wielgosz.

The support of Peter Boehm, Elizabeth Spehar, and Jean-Philippe Thérien is especially appreciated. All of them followed this project from start to finish and provided enormously valuable input along the way.

This book started before Andrew Cooper took on the position of associate director at The Centre for International Governance Innovation (CIGI). However, his hybrid role between the worlds of academia and think tanks served to complement our attempt to straddle the conceptual/practical divide. As per other activities more directly related to the work of CIGI, this project benefited from the enormous enthusiasm of John English, CIGI's executive director, as well as its research and administrative personnel. Kelly Jackson, the project officer at CIGI for the Complex Diplomacy Program, not only helped to edit the manuscript but facilitated a final author's meeting. She also acted as a liaision with the press. Koren Thomson and Emily Shephard at Mount Allison University and Jennifer Jones at CIGI provided additional support in preparing the manuscript.

Both of the authors wish to thank a number of journals for the granting of permission to use material that was originally published in article form. These articles include "The OAS Democratic Solidarity Paradigm: Questions of Collective and National Leadership," by Andrew F. Cooper and Thomas Legler, *Latin American Politics and Society* (formerly *Journal of Interamerican Studies and World Affairs*), 43, 1 Spring 2001, 103–126; "A Model for the Future? The OAS in Peru," by Andrew F. Cooper and Thomas Legler, *Journal of Democracy*, 12, October 4, 2001, 123–136; and "The Making of the Inter-Democratic Charter: A Case of Complex Multilateralism," by Andrew F. Cooper, *International Studies Perspectives*, 5, February 1, 2004, 92–113.

For turning the project into book form we would like to express appreciation for the efforts of Anthony Wahl, senior editor at Palgrave Macmillan, Heather Van Dusen, associate editor, and the team at Newgen, India.

Moving from the professional to the personal, this book is the culmination of a rewarding collaboration and close friendship between the two authors. Methodologically, joint research trips to the field and tandem interviewing enhanced our research wonderfully. In addition to our complimentary fields of expertise, working together made our interviews more thorough and our post-interview debriefings over coffee or dinner that much more insightful. To the individualistic skeptics of collaborative research in the social sciences and the humanities, we offer our experience as testimony to how it can work.

As in all our endeavors we were supported by our spouses, who even if not specialists in the same field could fully understand why we took this project so seriously! It is to Sarah and Roanne that we dedicate this book.

CHAPTER ONE

The Multilateral-Democracy Nexus: An Overview

That there is an expanse of connections between multilateral institutions—and multilateral processes—with the defense and promotion of democracy in different parts of the world is increasingly apparent. A wide range of international organizations, most notably the European Union (EU), the G7/8, the Organization of American States, the Commonwealth, and international financial institutions such as the IMF and the World Bank have attached political conditionalities focused on democratic accountability and good governance to economic assistance. In a similar vein, the United Nations (UN) has been increasingly occupied in projects devoted to the promotion of democracy. A host of civil society groups and non-governmental organizations (NGOs) have dedicated their time and energy to a wide variety of democracy assistance initiatives.

As has been manifested recently in Ukraine, a high degree of involvement by multilateral actors such as the Organization for Security and Cooperation in Europe (OSCE) and the Council of Europe can have a positive influence on the outcome of elections. In the Ukraine, the presence of some 12,500 observers on top of the weight of the foreign observer presence and the international attention obliged national authorities to annul fraudulent presidential elections and hold new ones. In contrast, in places such as Zimbabwe, persistent multilateral efforts led by the Commonwealth have had little success in preventing or helping rectify the erosion of democracy. Because of both its quantitative span and qualitative implications, this nexus between multilateralism and democracy deserves much closer attention than it has received up to now.

In recent decades there has been a flurry of pro-democracy activity through the OAS. In the context of the restoration of representative democracy in the Americas during the late 1970s and the 1980s as well as at the end of the Cold War, the OAS developed a set of principles and diplomatic tools for collectively defending democracy when any of its member states found itself in political crisis. Over the course of the 1990s and the new millennium, the OAS intervened in defense of democracy in Peru, Paraguay, Guatemala, Haiti, Venezuela, Bolivia, and Ecuador. Through its Unit for the Promotion of Democracy (now called the Department for the Promotion of Democracy), it also organized 85 electoral observation missions since 1990. Richard Bloomfield has termed these OAS pro-democracy principles, tools, and activities a col-lective-defense-of-democracy regime. Former Secretary-General César Gaviria called them a democratic solidarity paradigm.[1]

Amidst all of this activity, obtaining a nuanced appreciation of multilateral promotion of democracy is a demanding task. How has the multilateralism-democracy nexus evolved over time? What is the evolv-ing nature and impact of the OAS defense and promotion of democracy? Have OAS efforts ultimately reinforced the status quo or have they helped to strengthen democracy in a sustained fashion? We find that where the OAS has responded to threats to democracy, the institutional and cultural dimensions of multilateralism must be taken seriously as influences on its ability to defend or promote democracy. As we outline in detail below, the OAS has been subject to an ongoing internal tension between an older, club-style of multilateralism and a newer networked form of multilateralism. Practically, the outcome of this struggle within the organization has enormous repercussions in terms of the OAS's ability to respond in a timely and effective manner to political crises in the region. In our analysis, we reconstruct and assess key moments in the political crises of Peru and Venezuela, in which the nexus between multilateralism and democracy appears crucial. We situate our case studies within the overall evolution of the OAS democratic solidarity paradigm during the past two decades. For as Ellen Lutz and Kathryn Sikkink note, temporal considerations are paramount: "The clearest variation in the amount of international pressure was not between counties or scenarios, but over time."[2]

In teasing out these complexities, we explore the nexus through three axes. The first axis surveys the pivotal site for democratic transition rang-ing from an externally dominant domain to an exclusively domestic realm. Although often portrayed in stark either-or terms, the use of this axis allows some detailed exploration of the range of activity in between.

A second axis traces the mode of intervention utilized by external actors in promoting democracy. Following Tesón,[3] intervention is taken to be an effort to influence other states that can take three forms. *Soft* intervention is captured in diplomatic discussion, examination, and recommendatory action.[4] *Hard* intervention entails the use of coercive diplomatic measures, such as economic sanctions. *Forcible* intervention means the use of force, such as military invasion. The third and final axis widens the parameters of discussion from domain and modes to an assessment of consequences. That is, the multilateralism-democracy nexus can be associated with either longer-term normative and institutional developments or with far more immediate and tangible impacts relating to alterations in the rules of the political game on a country-specific basis.

Reflective of this matrix, we are interested in the entire ambit of democratization as it pertains to the life of multilateral institutions and mechanisms. The book as conceived is an enterprise that by its mix of ambitious conceptualization and case-study details lends itself to comparative examination. Yet, if located in a manner that encourages universal application, our work concentrates on the smaller regional world of the Western Hemisphere and the OAS. This focus reflects our own interests and expertise. But this focused canvass also allows us to address what one recent review of the existing literature has suggested is a huge gap in the study of the relationship between international organizations and democratization, the lack of "cross-national empirical studies" exploring the manner by which this relationship has played out. In contrast to works that focus primarily on secondary sources,[5] our book relies extensively on field research based on numerous interviews with key actors involved in the nexus between multilateralism and democracy. By looking closely at a set of geographically clustered cases—with apparent similarities as well as differences—this task is made more compatible and easier to comprehend.

Locating the Pivotal Site of Democratic Transition

Alternative schools of thought have given very different weight to the externally and domestically directed dimensions of democratization. At one end of the spectrum lies what can be termed the external reengineering scenario in which democracy is imposed from outside without much consideration for the history, the culture, or the intricacies of domestic political processes. The most compelling illustration of this scenario is the case of Japan in the aftermath of World War II. Under the leadership of General Douglas MacArthur the U.S. occupation forces drew up and implemented a plan to transform the Japanese political system and resocialize its people. The imposition of a new political architecture enshrined in what came to be known as the MacArthur Constitution was explicitly designed as a blueprint to prevent the revival of militarization and to strengthen the fabric of democracy.

At the other end of the spectrum are the cases of democratization considered to be outcomes exclusively confined to the internal attributes and dynamics contained within the domestic political system. The consensus view on these cases has been that democratization was induced not through outside-in forces but via a rearrangement of the institutional architecture triggered and delivered by an autonomous national process. Post-Franco Spain is an oft-cited example as is the transition in South Africa.

Of the two phenomena it has been the internal conceptualization that has been traditionally dominant. The mantra of democratization studies was established in the mid-1980s by Phillip Schmitter who argued that: "[One] of the firmest conclusions that emerged . . . was that transitions from authoritarian rule and immediate prospects for political democracy were largely to be explained in terms of national forces and calculations. External actors tended to play an indirect and usually marginal role."[6]

On a similar note, in his initial appraisal of the "International Aspects of Democratization," Laurence Whitehead held to the standard formulation: "In all the peacetime cases considered here internal forces were of primary importance in determining the course and outcome of the transition attempt, and international factors played only a secondary role . . . the international setting provided a mildly supportive (or destructive) background which was often taken for granted and which seldom intruded too conspicuously on an essentially domestic drama."[7]

Various leading path dependency theorists shared this domestic-centered or "nativist" analytical tendency. The paths they identified were determined exclusively from internal variables. Terry Lynn Karl, for instance, observed that Latin American countries democratized despite an unfavorable external environment, such as decreasing export earnings, debt crises, and a unilateral-oriented U.S. foreign policy.[8] Accordingly, the modes of transition to democracy that she identified were the outcome of the interaction of two domestic factors: transition strategies (compromise or force) and relative actor strength (elite ascendant and mass ascendant). In a similar vein, Gerardo Munck and Carol Skalnik Leff juxtaposed two key endogenous variables in identifying various modes of transition: the strategy of the agent of change (confrontation versus accommodation) and the identity of the agent of change (incumbent versus counter-elite).[9]

Through this set of lenses the externally dominant cases were viewed as the exceptions that proved the rule. A case such as Japan only came about through a massive shock to the system. In structural terms large scale warfare was superceded by unconditional surrender, extensive destruction, and long-term occupation. In terms of agency the United States took on a sustained project of political reconstruction. A command and control order was not only deemed to be efficient but legitimate. Although domestic actors could be consulted, it was the outside actors that remained instrumental in setting the timetable and the rules.

Over time, though, the either-or categorization has dissipated. An advance in this regard was found in the work of Karen Remmer, who made one of the first concerted attempts to integrate internal and external factors in the analysis of democratization across Latin America.[10] According to Remmer, how incumbent Latin American elites responded to the external economic shocks of the 1970s had an important bearing on key relationships between governments and business communities, often leading to alienation and eventually authoritarian regime breakdown. Remmer also provided an important distinction between the international political and economic environments. Whereas the international economic environment helped precipitate regime change during the 1970s and 1980s, the international political environment of the Cold War at the time was definitely not conducive to democratization. Only with the decline—and then the end—of superpower rivalry did the international political climate become more favorable for democratic consolidation. Nonetheless, following the logic that international influences were mediated through domestic structures, Remmer's core variables remained domestic: the relationship between the government and the business community and the structure of military rule in each country.

In their own path dependence approach, Juan Linz and Alfred Stepan provided additional improvement in terms of integrating international factors into the study of democratization. They identified three sets of international influences: foreign policies, zeitgeist or spirit of the times, and international diffusion effects. In an analogous fashion to Remmer, they conceived international factors largely as contextual. In other words, in terms of agency versus structure, international influences for them remained clearly more structural in nature. For them there continued to be little or no role for international agents of change. The key agents of transition and consolidation that they identified were exclusively domestic: the leadership of the prior regime and the agents who initiated and controlled the transition.[11] Ultimately then, their perspective did not represent a significant departure from other path dependence approaches that accorded primacy to domestic causal factors and only an indirect role to international variables.

Yet the proliferation in recent decades of international actors involved in the defense and promotion of democracy has provided a sound reason to conceptualize the international dimensions of democratization, not solely as contextual or structural but also as agency-based. In a sharp break from their earlier assertions about the primacy of domestic causality, the more recent work by both Schmitter and Whitehead provides the most sophisticated attempt yet to incorporate external considerations into the study of democratization.[12] In contrast to the long-standing "nativist" assumption within much of the comparative politics literature, Whitehead alerts us to the fact that some two-thirds of the democracies that existed in 1990 were brought about at least partially by some form of external imposition. Indeed, in very few cases could regime change truly be considered a purely domestic attribute or dynamic. On this important point, Whitehead writes: "it may be artificial to dichotomize the analysis into domestic and international elements. Although there will always be some purely domestic and some exclusively international factors involved, most of the analysis will contain a tangle of both elements. In the contemporary world there is no such thing as democratization in one country, and perhaps there never was."[13]

Moreover, the need for bridging the historical divide between comparative politics and international relations is accentuated when some empirical snapshots are added to this conceptual overview. For the blending of the international dimension provides a much richer and accurate mix even in a variety of cases that have been taken to be classic examples of "made at home" processes in operation. The presence of a vital connection between external developments and political change in Spain—via pressure from Western Europe (through a combination of European Community, national state, and transnational societal forces)—has been widely commented on.[14]

The need to include external as well as internal factors in democratization analyses intrudes even in other more recent European cases commonly taken to be the most domestic-oriented in nature. To the extent that the German Democratic Republic (GDR) became absorbed into the Federal Republic of Germany (FRG), the case of German reunification appears to be the most one-sided illustration of a "made at home" process. Yet, when looked at in a comprehensive manner, this case remains not only "deviant" but highly complex. Not only did an important contagion effect within Eastern Europe (as a "flow of messages and images" penetrated the GDR from reformist countries in Eastern Europe, most notably Poland to Hungary) influence the German case,[15] but the external projection and impact of the West German/European mass media and various non-governmental actors, together with attitudes of the big powers (not only the West but the Soviet Union/Russia), need to be factored-into any comprehensive account. A similar complexity shines through a wider cross section of other cases on a global basis. The case of the Philippines is best known for its 1986 demonstration of "people power." But the role of the downfall of the Marcos regime hinged as much on a decisive (albeit late) shift in its external support as on the massive display of popular resistance. In the analysis of one close observer of the Philippines situation, ". . . important interventions" by the United States and Europe ". . . were effective in encouraging an autocratic leader who had lost legitimacy to leave office and in preventing military coups."[16]

The external dimension is equally salient in gaining accurate insights into the case of the transition to democracy in South Africa. This argument does not discount the role of the "domestic" negotiations between the Nationalist government and the African National Congress (ANC) in facilitating the transition process. What it points to is the supplementary effect on this "pacted" outcome of the presence of a number of international pressure points including changes in the international financial environment (with the decision of Chase Manhattan and other banks not to roll over loans in 1985) even prior to the introduction of very different ideological/geopolitical conditions associated with the end of the Cold War.[17]

Resituating the Pressure Points of Intervention

It is one thing to take into account external sources as catalysts for democratization. It is another thing to detect how and when these pressure points have been applied. This is especially true along the unilateral/multilateral continuum. As noted above the classic case of democratization pushed forward through an outside in trajectory—Japan after World War II—highlighted the unilateral dimension in which an occupying force dictated the process of transformation in a national political system. Again, as reflected in the Japanese case, it is one actor—the United States—that dominated the process of democratization. Although other external forces were present, most notably other allied powers such as the United Kingdom or Australia, they played a subsidiary role.

In more recent times much of the orientation for externally projected democratization has tilted toward the multilateral pole of activity. This ascendancy has been associated above all with the release of the disciplines of the Cold War. Until the end of the era of superpower competition, there was little or no room for a wide range of activist democratic promotion activities bursting out from the confines of ideological competition. Support for an expansion of liberal democracy (or for that matter socialist solidarity) might be mooted in declaratory terms but in practice priority was given to geostrategic/economic containment. The test in this regard, as Schmitter well recognized, was the ability of the OAS as well as other national and transnational actors to pursue effectively the principle of collective action to promote and defend democracy in the region of the Americas. As Schmitter notes, "Were it to become effective, the entire international context of democratization would be radically transformed."[18]

On both sides of the post–1945 bipolar divide, this order allowed little room for extensive multilateral activity promoting democracy. The status quo was managed and heavily policed—with the acquiescence of the other side. With respect to the Eastern bloc it was not until the evolution of the Helsinki network that "democracy" entered into the agenda.[19] And even then realists in the Western camp discounted this process as a distraction or even a counterproductive component in the overall relationship between the superpowers. With respect to the intra-West dimension, a number of very positive initiatives took place to bring peripheral actors in Europe into the fold of the democratic community as illustrated by the case of Portugal as well as Spain. Yet outside the European case the dictum remained quite clear—that it was better to have an authoritarian leader/government in place than risk an erosion in stability.[20] Diplomatic work was directed to propping up "friends" (however unpalatable and tarnished) rather than to voicing concern about the state of affairs in terms of human rights and democracy promotion.

This recipe accenting stability rather than justice was heavily emphasized in the Americas, the U.S.'s own strategic and economic backyard. The Cold War architecture effectively tied this region to the anticommunist coalition under U.S. leadership, but with no claims of equal footing, such as those found in the case of the Western European allies of the United States. Under a military system of "collective security" that was considerably less structured than one managed through NATO, the role of the Latin American armed forces was subordinated on issues of "hemispheric defense" and directed toward "internal security."[21]

It has been in the Americas, therefore, that the situating and then resituating of the unilateral/multilateral pressure points have been very dramatic. Throughout the Cold War years it was in its own immediate region or neighborhood that many of the central characteristics of the main strategic doctrine shaping U.S. behavior took shape. As Anthony Payne has depicted this impulse: "What was new and vital about US relations with the Americas in the Cold War years was the way in which the United States perceived its own standing as a hegemonic power and its associated credibility in the eyes of both its enemies and allies in all parts of the world to be dependent in some measure on its capacity to maintain and demonstrate control of its own hemispheric community—its 'backyard'."[22]

Unchecked as the dominant power of the region the United States had almost complete leeway to develop its own ideological brand. States—such as Canada—with some tradition of acting as diplomatic moderators of U.S. zealousness—made themselves unavailable. Alternative perspectives—as a response to the imposed disciplines—were forced (or perceived) to become the polar opposite, as exemplified by the extreme form of estrangement and polarization between Cuba and the United States. Indeed, in what proved to be its last gasp, this ideological struggle became increasingly bitter as the conflict between the leftist (pro-Castro and pro-Soviet Union) Sandinista government of Nicaragua and the anti-Sandinista rebel forces known as "Contras" (financed by the U.S. government and operating out of Honduras and Costa Rica) greatly intensified in the mid-1980s. In addition, there remained the lingering conflicts between leftist guerrillas and the governments of El Salvador and Guatemala.

In terms of application there was little or no space for dissent from the approach of the United States. If countries of the Americas moved off the line they were brought back in the fold through coercive means—even if that meant subverting democratic principles. The justification provided for such actions (explicitly stated in the so-called Mann Doctrine formulated in 1964) was the putative rise in the presence and influence of Soviet Union in the region. The best-known early illustration of this coercive approach in action came with the U.S. campaign to replace Guatemala's leftist President Jacobo Arbenz in 1954. Another later example, of course, came with U.S. efforts to destabilize the democratically elected Salvador Allende government in Chile, leading up to a coup staged by Augusto Pinochet and the Chilean army on September 11, 1973.

Another key feature was that the low priority given to the promotion of democracy in the region was of the consideration given not only to "friends" (with authoritarian governments) but to countries such as Mexico with which the United States was not in agreement. So long as this category of country did not step out of line on core issues they were given freedom to operate as they wanted. Domestically, in the late 1960s and early 1970s, Mexican governments could wage their own versions of "dirty wars," including the Mexico City student massacre in 1968. Internationally, Mexico (along with Canada) could maintain, for example, both diplomatic and economic relations with Cuba despite the U.S. blanket embargo. Party of the Institutional Revolution (PRI) administrations in Mexico not only expressed some solidarity with the Castro regime, but furthermore several Mexican presidents (starting with President Luis Echeverría and continuing with José López Portillo and the three successor presidents), akin to Pierre Trudeau of Canada in 1976, made visits to Cuba during their tenures in office.[23]

What aroused a response on the part of the United States was not the authoritarian nature of the regime or even some notable deviations on foreign policy but rather fear of any fundamental alteration in the political status quo in Mexico. This bottom line was made most explicit in 1988 when the first Bush administration reiterated its support for the ruling PRI against the challenge of the leftist Revolutionary Democratic Party (PRD)—notwithstanding abundant evidence that president-elect Carlos Salinas had won (or stolen) the July 1988 election in the context of wholesale electoral irregularities.[24] As Lutz and Sikkink note, the OAS Inter-American Commission on Human Rights (IACHR) took on its first three Mexican-related cases involving alleged electoral irregularity highlighted by the National Action Party (PAN): "Refuting the Mexican government's claim that the IACHR was barred by the OAS Charter from addressing electoral issues, the commission recommended that the Mexican government reform its internal electoral law."[25]

The final—and for the purposes of this book the most intriguing—characteristic of the evolution in external pressure points is the adaptive change in the role of the OAS in response to the changed nexus of multilateralism and democracy. Throughout the Cold War era the image of the OAS was debased in no uncertain terms by those on both sides of the ideological divide. After he found that dealing with the OAS was an awkward experience, when moving to deploy the so-called Inter-American Peace Force (IAPF) with respect to the Dominican Republic crisis in 1965, U.S. President Lyndon Baines Johnson dismissed the organization as one that: "couldn't pour piss out of a boot if the instructions were written on the heel."[26] As might be expected, Fidel Castro adopted an even more critical outlook toward the organization. Frozen out of the OAS since the early 1960s, Castro referred to the organization as a "putrid, revolting den of corruption," a "disgusting, discredited cesspool," a "ministry of colonies of the United States," to which Cuba would only return if the "imperialists and their puppets were kicked out first." Relations with other Latin American countries, Cuba's leader added, could only be restored if OAS sanctions were rejected, if these countries had a revolution, and if they condemned U.S. crimes against Cuba as well.[27]

There is a good deal to back up at least some of these extremely negative reviews, even when the pithy rhetoric is taken away. Buttressing the perspective of President Johnson and other U.S. officials, the OAS could be taken to task for a number of serious ongoing institutional dysfunctions. Even if the OAS had found the will to take some creative actions it had little capability to do so. The skill-set of its personnel was compromised by the use of the OAS as a place to "retire" former high-ranking state officials and by various forms of nepotism and cronyism. Its resources were constrained by tight budget restrictions.

From Castro's perspective the image of the OAS as being in the pocket of the United States—or at least the shadow instrument of its power—evolved out of a number of instances. In the Cuban case, most directly, the United States sought legitimization of its embargo through the imposition of a collective "quarantine" on Cuba. Subsequent to a vote at the OAS conference at Punta del Este, Uruguay at the end of January 1962, Cuba was expelled from the body. The 1954 Guatemala case points to a similar conclusion, as the OAS became thoroughly implicated in the toppling of President Arbenz. At the Caracas meeting of the OAS in March 1954, featuring a robust speech by Secretary of State John Foster Dulles and the positive endorsements by representatives from the Somoza, Trujillo, and Batista dictatorships, the OAS voted 17 to 1 on a U.S.-sponsored resolution to condemn communism in Guatemala (with only Guatemala dissenting and Mexico and Argentina abstaining).

Still, amidst all these charges, some evidence of a more positive picture emerges even in these polarized ideological years. Albeit weak in capacity the OAS in some of these well-rehearsed cases tried to be more assertive in checking U.S. actions than one might have thought. Notwithstanding the vote on communism at the Caracas conference, the OAS failed to endorse multilateral intervention against the Arbenz government. Furthermore, the OAS proposed a fact-finding mission to evaluate the Guatemala situation on the ground. Unfortunately, for its lingering claims to credibility, however, the implementation of this mission was delayed by various forms of obstruction. First it was held up by the refusal of the Arbenz regime to agree to its mobilization. Then it was stymied by the actions of the U.S. government to prevent it from reaching Guatemala City. By the time it reached its destination, the coup—and all the evidence of American involvement—had disappeared.[28]

The legitimacy function performed by the OAS also worked across a wide spectrum. In its interventions in the Americas the United States preferred to cover its actions with the sanction of the OAS. It is important to note that during the 1962 Cuban Missile Crisis the United States devoted considerable attention to obtaining OAS approval for a blockade as a means both to legalize and to legitimize U.S. actions. Indeed, one of the fundamental reasons for the United States not intervening with direct military force was its lack of credibility with the OAS. A similar dynamic took hold in the case of the 1965 Dominican Republic intervention, in the aftermath of a military coup. Although a number of important states voted against this intervention (Mexico, Uruguay, Chile, Ecuador, and Peru with Venezuela abstaining), six countries volunteered to participate in the IAPF (Brazil, Honduras, Nicaragua, El Salvador, Paraguay, and Costa Rica). A Brazilian general was named commander, with his deputy being the commander of U.S. forces in the Dominican Republic. On top of the deployment of this military force, more constructive diplomatic action came through the establishment of an OAS special three-person commission that eventually proved successful in allowing a provisional government to be established.

Leaping forward to the post–Cold War era, the issue is not so much whether the OAS role has been reshaped in terms of the nexus between multilateralism and democratization. There is widespread agreement that as an agent of collective action in the defense and the promotion of democracy the organization has come to matter in an unprecedented manner. The issues that need to be investigated in greater depth are those pertaining to why this transition in performance has taken place together with an assessment of the actual degree of operational change undertaken.

In asking why such a substantive breakthrough has occurred the role of the United States is again crucial. Whatever the global circumstances the United States will never be just another state in the Americas.

Nonetheless, the end of the Cold War—and the absence of a Communist threat, real or imaginary—has altered its main game. Although concerns about terrorism abound both from within and without the Hemisphere, the disciplinary impulse of the United States as the policeman of the region has been fundamentally altered. Even though the United States still perceives Cuba to be a toxic presence in the neighborhood, its level of tolerance in terms of the types of democratically elected governments it deems to be acceptable has been expanded. This is not to say that all the longstanding gaps and flaws in the U.S. approach to democracy have disappeared. Some critics charge that one form of discipline has been substituted for another. Rather than the geopolitical/strategic order favored by—and imposed by—the United States in the past over leftwing/socialist regimes, the parameters of behavior are now shaped and bounded by the acceleration of an embedded corporate culture imposed by the market and consumerism together with the lending/surveillance mechanisms managed by the International Financial Institutions (IFIs). No less than anywhere else in the world, national control has been further lost in the Americas, with states losing autonomy to the forces of finance operating through the processes of the globalized market economy.

From another perspective, the image of a more benign United States is misleading for other reasons. Despite the popular overtones of the U.S. support for democracy in the region this change in image is more cosmetic than real. If the United States has refrained for the most part from direct intervention, it is just as interested—and as actively involved—in maintaining the rules of the game as it sees fit in the Americas.[29] States and their leaders, such as Hugo Chávez in Venezuela, when they step beyond the limits of what the United States deems acceptable (via their diplomatic connections with Cuba and other pariah states and/or threat to property rights) are brought to task.

Yet, amidst these lingering challenges, until very recently some consensus existed that the relationship between the United States and the Americas has improved considerably in the aftermath of the Cold War. OAS members no longer felt that U.S. intervention was directed toward them. U.S. culture, including respect for its system of government, enjoyed unprecedented popularity and acceptance in the region.[30] Rather than the longstanding problems linked with the United States paying too much scrutiny to the region's affairs, the problem became one of U.S. neglect and disinterest. Starting in the Clinton years and intensified during the administration of George W. Bush, the thrust of the posture of the United States toward the region became more uneven and ambivalent. On specific questions the United States confirmed its willingness to seek improvements in the inter-American democratic paradigm (as we will see later with respect to both state-specific episodes and the creation of the Inter-American Democratic Charter). At other times, the United States adopted a problematic combination of passive/ aggressive tactics, swinging between neglect and bursts of democracy à la carte filtered through the lens of national interest.

This image of greater complexity has been accentuated by the erosion of the image of the United States as a stereotypical unitary actor. With a redefinition of the stakes involved and the absence of a common enemy, one of the side effects of the end of the Cold War has been a fragmentation of bureaucratic interests. Although where one sat or stood administratively had always been of importance, the sense of competition between not only the Pentagon and the State Department but also the intelligence services and drug enforcement officials became far more complicated and intense.

The flip side of this process was the rise of non-state actors to a different plane of involvement and status. To be sure, NGOs have long been on the scene in the various aspects of the politics and policies relating to the Americas. Nevertheless, the trajectory of their activity became transfigured in the post–Cold War years. Some of the NGOs that had focused their efforts on opposing the U.S. state in its involvement within the region—most notably in Central America during the 1980s—began to turn their labor to democracy promotion. This focus allowed them to work with and inter-act in a more cooperative manner with the U.S. government.

If widening the source of U.S. bureaucratic engagement, the end of the Cold War also expanded the range of participation for other actors. In terms of agency, for countries such as Canada, the region of the Americas no longer appeared to be the backyard of the United States and accordingly as an area with few rewards and considerable problems. With the shock of the new world order, the neighborhood appeared in a different light as one full of diplomatic and some economic promise. For others such as Argentina, Brazil and Chile (and later Mexico), at the regional level they could proclaim and make use of their new profile as democratic states. In terms of trajectory, some forms of collective endeavor were encouraged by the United States because as Abraham Lowenthal suggests, "multilateral programs are more likely to be effective over time than bilateral ones."[31]

The Uneven Trajectory of the Response by the OAS to Structural Change

Following the assumptions of the larger body of literature, it might have been expected that the OAS would be ripe for a quick if not instant transformation to make the nexus between multilateralism and democratization the centerpiece of its activities. After all, the regional site appears to be particularly amenable to making this connection. Pridham points to this phenomenon by reference to the creation by the European Community "of an ambience with significant potential for influencing internal change."[32] So does Whitehead: "the importance of such international dimensions of democratization seems much clearer at [the] regional level than at the world-wide level of analysis."[33]

A number of factors are understood as contributing to this generalized connection between regional institutions and processes of democratization. Small memberships allow for a very different pattern of inter-action and socialization than do much larger units as in the UN. Learning, leadership, and resources can all be concentrated in an issue-specific fashion.

As elaborated in the next chapter, the OAS moved a long way in terms of embracing democratization at the declaratory level and its mode of operation also morphed considerably in the immediate aftermath of the end of the Cold War. Yet, the response of the OAS cannot be considered to be unidirectional and systematic. While taking some big strides forward there were also signs of inertia and even regression at times.

To understand both the movement to advance the democracy agenda and its limitations, the OAS has to be positioned as an in-between or hybrid institution with respect to the reshaping of multilateralism. In the aftermath of the wave of democratic transitions, the OAS was willing and able to find some space for alternative forms of leadership and agenda-promotion. Motivated by their own domestic experiences of democratization,[34] a number of states were ready to project their newfound democratic principles through their foreign policy and to take on different and more ambitious roles promoting democratization at the regional level. Viewed as a club where membership came with obligations as well as rights—democracy became a valued measure of performance.

Amidst this progress, there were also restrictions on moving too fast and too far. Though eager to bandwagon with the United States and

Canada on democratization, most states in the region also desired to counterbalance U.S. influence. Memories of U.S. unilateral intervention were still too raw. The principle of sovereignty remained ingrained as a defensive mechanism.[35]

The cautious side of the OAS drew it back into compliance with the tenets of old multilateralism as laid out by John Ruggie and James Caporaso. The central concern within these generalized principles of conduct are the relationships of the members of an institution with one another.[36] The focus is therefore tilted toward continuity as opposed to change. As a club full of relatively weak members at least in international terms this response is a logical one, in that it reduces the room and opportunity for interference or meddling by the dominant actor in the region. To reinforce the notion of both organizational equality as well as constraint, the institutional culture—or rules of conduct—that developed in the OAS accorded significant weight to consensual decision-making. No one actor would be able any longer to get its way however large its muscle.

In combination these ingredients of old multilateralism channeled the OAS toward a safety-first, organizational maintenance approach. In style the onus was on diplomatic opaqueness, with great consideration for protocol and doing things by the book. In substance, the stress was on cautious problem solving (or what has become known as fire-fighting) governed by an instinct to contain rather than expand the agenda.[37]

Though in many ways the hold of this form of old multilateralism—or what we refer to as club multilateralism—became entrenched with structural change through the 1990s,[38] vibrant pressures directed at the OAS nudged it to take on many of the trappings of a new kind of multilateralism as well. Part of the supply side for this modification came inevitably from the NGO community. As suggested above, the NGOs discerned the end of the Cold War as a great opportunity to expand their access to the decision-making process. What they discovered, though, was an environment that still remained unreceptive to them. Indeed, in a variety of ways, the transition had been accompanied by a backlash against non-state actors. The OAS argued more convincingly as a club of democracies—than as an institution full of dictatorships and military regimes—that as long as its decisions were made in an inter-governmental forum, it had a solid legitimacy. Under this mantra, the OAS did not consider it necessary to question the more or less closed nature of its decision-making structures, or to think about the inclusion of civil society organizations within its debates.

Interestingly, club multilateralism has been both reinforced and challenged as states in the inter-American system have shifted from authoritarianism to democracy. On the one hand, the recent regional wave of democratic transitions with its democracy and human rights norm cascade has exposed the inter-American system to pressures for expanding the participation of non-state actors in multilateralism. Even legislative actors, such as the Parliamentary Confederation of the Americas, have pushed for greater influence in inter-American affairs. On the other hand, the new democratic footing of states in the Americas with elected leaders has paradoxically reinforced and legitimized the continuity of executive sovereignty, that is, the externally recognized supreme authority of heads of state and government as well as their diplomatic representatives. Perversely, this reinforces the club style of multilateralism that pre-dated the onset of democratization in the Americas.

Paralleling the societal calls from below came additional pressure from above for forms of new, complex[39]—or what we term networked—multilateralism to be incorporated into the workings of the OAS.[40] One source pushing for change came from within the OAS itself. Although the structural weaknesses of the OAS can be elaborated upon at some length, sustained reference to these deficiencies should not block from view the progress made by way of institutional reform. César Gaviria, the secretary-general of the OAS during 1994–2004, must take a good deal of credit for this turnaround. Intellectually, Gaviria took the lead in promoting an inter-American "paradigm of democratic solidarity."[41] Bureaucratically, Gaviria injected some new blood into the organization. Instead of accepting the notion that the OAS was the preserve of the older generation, Gaviria surrounded himself with a "kindergarten" of talented younger advisors. Operationally, he was willing to bend the restrictions of club multilateralism vis-à-vis the use of his "good offices" to defend and promote democracy through various actions, including issuing frequent press statements on situations of concern in the region, fact-finding missions to trouble spots, and third-party mediation or rather facilitation as the OAS has come to term it.

A more generalized indication of the intent and ability of the OAS to do things differently came in relation to the role of its Unit for the Promotion of Democracy (UPD). Since its creation in 1990, the UPD (now the Department for the Promotion of Democracy) has organized a number of electoral monitoring missions as well as a variety of assistance and education programs designed to strengthen democracy. If for the most part this work has been done in a low-key, technically oriented fashion, it has potential for support in forms of new multilateralism.

Another source of encouragement for new or networked multilateralism came from the dominant actor in the hemisphere. In the post–Cold

War the United States was placed in a situation where it could not simply impose its will on others. It possessed too much baggage from its past unilateralist forays to be an effective catalyst for collective action. What it found necessary, therefore, was to substitute diplomatic skill for muscle. The United States possesses the maximum leverage on a bilateral basis among the countries of the Americas. Together with a wealth of experience and knowledge on democratic institution building, the United States also continues to hold the crucial function of chief financier of democratic development. Therefore, how the United States reacts to each case of democratic advancement and backtracking will be a prime determinant of the future condition of the democratic solidarity agenda.

A third source of commitment to expressions of transformed multilateralism was the presence of other countries constituting a diverse but active pro-democracy lobby within the OAS. Many of these states were too small to possess much diplomatic weight or capacity in their own right. On a selective basis, nonetheless, even these countries could make a contribution as witnessed by the role of President Oscar Arias and Costa Rica in opening the way to democratic elections in Nicaragua in February 1990.[42]

A greater burden fell on states such as Chile, Brazil, and Argentina in one category of states and Canada in another. As emergent democracies the three major southern cone states put a huge emphasis on the international promotion of democracy in the mid-1980s to early 1990s. Argentina, after the election of Raúl Alfonsin in 1983, took the lead in these activities. Joining in this campaign, however, was Chilean President Patricio Aylwin (who came to office in 1990) and to a lesser extent President José Sarney in Brazil. As one commentator observed, these leaders. "shared similar preoccupations and goals [and] agreed to coordinate action on a series of international issues deemed important for domestic processes consolidation."[43]

Canada in particular had a number of constraints on its role in promoting democracy in the hemisphere of the Americas. Canada was a country that had traditionally kept the Americas off its mental-map and had only joined the OAS in 1990. Yet it also had strengths unavailable to other countries in the region. Canada had an activist diplomatic culture that could cultivate new multilateralism. Its state officials also had a well-deserved reputation for technical acumen and problem-solving ability.

Juxtaposed throughout this book then are these two variants of multilateralism. In form they differ with respect to their contours vis-à-vis democratization. The club style of multilateralism is essentially a top-down or vertical form that privileges and upholds the prerogatives of national executives and their diplomatic representatives. The dictates of sovereignty are buckled only when a specific problem or crisis demands a consensus among the members that some form of intervention is necessary. New multilateralism is very different in the sense that networks are built not only at the elite level but also in a far more extended and pluralistic fashion, with space for bottom-up as well as top-down engagement.

In terms of scope, club multilateralism is resolutely state-centric. While this narrows the coordination problem, it also creates the perception of a huge democratic deficit. Networked multilateralism encourages a heightened degree of mobilization by diverse actors, both state and non-state. Its challenge is to lessen the two-culture divide, where states and non-state actors run with very different agendas and approaches. NGOs, for example, may embarrass states by naming and shaming. In their concern with getting results, states may see the need to accept solutions that are possible even if they compromise principles.

In terms of intensity, club multilateralism favors the lowest common denominator or, if consensus is lacking, perhaps no action at all. As extant in the traditional diplomacy of the OAS, club multilateralism is slow-paced and extremely measured. Its activism is invariably a function of the established norm whereby the leaders of states targeted for OAS intervention must provide their consent for anything but the hardest forms of intervention. Accordingly, even pariah leaders enjoy membership privileges and are therefore able to hold up efforts to defend democracy collectively.

The appeal of networked multilateralism is in its intensity of activity, with speed as its mantra. The focus is not on what is possible but on what is seen to be right. Rapid (sometimes erratic) moves as well as the search for ad hoc routes to deliver results have become an essential component of its repertoire. A "just in time" quality is taken to be central to the success of any process based on this model.[44] Many civil society actors, such as the Carter Center-led Friends of the Democratic Charter initiative, advocate timely and effective intervention.[45]

Between Club and Networked Multilateralism

Defined as very different forms of social construction, the two faces of multilateralism aim at contrasting outcomes in the democratization process. Old or club multilateralism is for the most part content with democracy promotion that allows the status quo to be managed more effectively. Its central goal is to get the rules of the democratic game in order or smoothened out. There is very little appetite to get the OAS embedded in the national political process of any particular state. Initiatives are very much at the surface level, with little penetration inside the walls of the domestic system.

New or networked multilateralism is far more ambitious in its desire to effect change and in its prescriptive model. Its primary purpose is to design and implement institutional transformation at both the architectural and normative level. Unlike the pragmatic approach of the old multilateralism, new multilateralism wants to offer some elements of a principled approach. Far from being content to bounce off the outer shell of the sovereignty-protected system, new multilateralism wants to effect change within the corpus of the domestic political system. Although differing in the level of commitment to this approach, all the agents of networked multilateralism become in effect entrepreneurs of "norms in action" through which the pursuit of diplomatic activity goes hand in hand with normative development.[46]

For the advocates of networked multilateralism, the limitations of club multilateralism are situated in its inter-governmentalism, its club-like atmosphere and diplomatic culture, and its problem-solving style. Thoroughly embedded in the tight boundaries of a modernist framework, states are left with some degree of flexibility to look after the democratic agenda within these confines. For the proponents of old multilateralism it is precisely these restrictions that lend legitimacy to this system and allow it to work. The opening up of multilateralism in a post-modernist fashion to allow diversity has the danger of pulling the system in directions that some members may not only be uncomfortable with (especially pertaining to opportunities for undiplomatic behavior) but also find extremely difficult if not impossible to implement.

If socially constructed in very different ways, these two modes of multilateralism reveal signs not only of divergence but also of integration; they do not operate in completely separate worlds. Paralleling each other they inevitably become intertwined. Even state-centric officials seek out the approval of non-state actors and become involved and influenced by the processes of what Anne-Marie Slaughter terms trans-governmentalism.[47] They may also want to accelerate the pace of diplomatic activity. Even oppositional, "outsider" NGOs push for access to privileged, "insider" sites of inter-governmental negotiations.[48] They may as well take on a more technical and accommodative mindset. If still uneven, therefore, the different currents of multilateralism merge at least at the tactical level.

At the core of the thematic structure of this book is the notion that by looking more closely at the in-between or hybrid status of the OAS's club/networked multilateralism showcased through the democratization agenda, an essential element of transition in the Americas can be captured. This hybrid form combines elements of verticality and top-down diplomacy connected with old multilateralism and the horizontalness and informal bottom-up associational activity key to the ascendancy of new multilateralism. At the same time the contours between what is considered inside and outside of the domestic sphere become blurred. These conceptual operational boundaries are no longer fixed entities but are rather fluid and shifting.

Coming to terms with complex or hybrid multilateralism with respect to democratization in the Americas is an exciting project. However, it remains a multidimensional, overlapping, and contradictory one as well. The key element to applying the requisite roadmap—what we term intervention without intervening—is to engage and explain more thoroughly the "interactive processes" laid out by John Ikenberry and Michael Doyle.[49] This approach allows different literatures to speak to each other and practices to mix them however messily. The central question is no longer whether the international or the domestic is superior or subordinate in the democratization process but why and how these dimensions work in tandem or struggle at odds with each other on the ground.

Returning to our starting point, we appreciate that our approach is far more intricate than the standard more parsimonious interpretations of the democratization dynamic such as the one provided by Whitehead and Schmitter. Still, though their abovementioned international dimensions of democratization are heuristically neat, it must be mentioned that Whitehead and Schmitter do not provide us with a method for systematically ascertaining the relative significance of domestic and international causal factors or the way in which their combinations affect political outcomes. Their analysis permits us to categorize international factors, a staple of the comparative politics tradition, but its explanatory value is limited because of a lack of underpinning methodology. From their international dimensions we now have a better understanding of where to look but not how to look.

The challenge is not only to underline the importance of international factors but also to analyze the manner by which they intertwine with domestic factors to influence the course of political change, whether by reinforcing or altering the status quo. To appreciate fully the international/transnational character of political change,[50] we must put agency front and center.[51] In order to do so methodologically, we need to identify the main domestic, international, and transnational actors involved as well as undertake a meticulous deconstruction (or reconstruction) of how their actions are interlinked. This is what we call an "inter-action" approach.[52] In any process of democratization, actions occur at both the domestic and international levels across a wide continuum, some isolated and some intertwined. Interaction analysis permits us to determine the sequence of events: action, reaction, counteraction, coordinated and combined action, or coincidence. Utilizing this approach, therefore, we can ascertain whether international actors and actions have a direct or indirect role and whether their influence is ad hoc/episodic or sustained. An inter-action approach also helps explain the outcomes of political change, whether building added momentum toward a democratic solidarity paradigm or persistent resistance to these trends. Thus it is to this fundamental tension—at the core of our undertaking to trace the contours of the nexus between multilateralism and democracy—that we must turn to and explore in more depth.

CHAPTER TWO

The OAS Democratic Solidarity Paradigm: Agency Innovation and Structural Constraints

The OAS has been torn between an urge to innovate and to maintain the status quo in terms of democratization. Momentum in building a "right to democracy"[1] or a "collective defense of democracy" paradigm[2] was accelerated by the end of the Cold War and the wave of democratic transitions experienced throughout the Americas on a national basis. Yet the collective efforts of the OAS toward the building of democratic values continued to face a number of serious constraints. At an instrumental level, the means of translating the inter-American system of democratic solidarity into practice has been a daunting task. Club multilateralism proved effective in smoothing some crises, most notably that of Guatemala in 1993. In other cases the limitations of this paradigm were strongly evident. The Haitian experience revealed the difficulty in enforcing economic sanctions. In the case of Paraguay's crisis of 1996, the OAS response time was questioned and attention was drawn to its inadequate preventative and monitoring abilities.[3] The OAS has been criticized as well, in a more general context, for what has been called a "firefighter approach"[4]: focusing on extinguishing threats to democracy among nation states when they ignite rather than preventing crises before they flare up. At a more conceptual level, the OAS members' degree of commitment to collective initiatives to safeguard democracy underscores the conflicting foreign policy principles found in the region, most notably the perennial tension between support for pro-democracy collective interventions and the respect for non-intervention and state sovereignty.[5]

Against this dualistic background, featuring both a push to and a counter-pull against democratization, an important set of questions concerning the nature of leadership in the promotion of democracy within the inter-American system must be teased out in greater detail. Converting democratic values into action in the region requires decisive and sustained leadership at both the national and the collective level. Notwithstanding all the genuine progress made during the 1990s, hemispheric pro-democracy activism remains hindered by a significant leadership deficit. As argued in this chapter the source of this deficit derives from a number of factors: an imperfect and incomplete democratic solidarity doctrine, an ad hoc and ill-defined division of labor, scarce financial resources, and debilitating internal problems among potential regional leaders. After tracing the development and parameters of the inter-American system's pro-democracy doctrine, the impediments that constrain leadership are examined in some detail. The chapter concludes with a discussion of ways to move beyond these problems in order to buttress the promotion and defense of democracy in the Americas.

Toward a Democratic Solidarity Doctrine

The emergence of a democratic solidarity paradigm has been shaped by a gradual and uneven evolution. The original charter of the OAS had made "the effective exercise of representative democracy"[6] one of the guiding principles of hemispheric cooperation. However, from 1948 through to the late 1970s, this commitment was declaratory not operational. What progress took place came in a case-specific fashion. The first sign of a substantial move to some form of pro-democracy doctrine came in 1979 with the passage of a resolution condemning the human rights record of the Somoza regime in Nicaragua.[7] This resolution was a breakthrough in a number of ways. First of all, the resolution demonstrated a marked sense of collective commitment on the part of the OAS membership to become involved in the promotion of democracy on a state-specific basis. With the exception of the opposition expressed by the permanent representatives from Nicaragua and Paraguay, the OAS General Assembly rallied around the call for the immediate replacement of the Somoza regime by a freely elected democratic regime. Moreover, this action was taken even though many of the countries that voted in favor of the resolution were themselves guilty of gross human rights violations and dictatorships during that period. Secondly, the resolution adopted by the OAS established some important precedents. Not only did the resolution nudge the OAS toward setting an obligation to advance democracy in the Americas, it also sent a clear signal that the organization was prepared to denounce anti-democratic governments on at least a selective basis.[8] Implicitly, the resolution created an important new function for the OAS: a legitimizing (or de-legitimizing) mechanism for the region's governments.[9]

The Protocol of Cartagena de Indias, approved at the 14th Special Session of the OAS on December 5, 1985 in Colombia, raised the organization's obligations to advance democracy to an explicit purpose. This document amended the OAS Charter in order to add a new provision under Article 2 of Chapter I, "Nature and Purposes." The OAS Charter henceforth enshrined the regional obligation to "promote and consolidate representative democracy, with due respect for the principle of non-intervention."[10] Subsequent OAS declarations and action plans of the Miami and Santiago summits of head-of-states have reaffirmed and elaborated upon this duty.

While the Cartagena protocol elevated the external advancement of representative democracy in terms of the hierarchy of purpose of the inter-American system, it did not specify what types of action would be taken in pursuit of this goal. This disconnect between goals and means became obvious during the Panama crisis of 1989, a situation precipitated by the move on the part of Manuel Noriega to annul the elections held in that country. The OAS passed a resolution defending the Panamanian people's right to elect their leaders in a democratic fashion[11] and mounted a ministerial effort to mediate through a delegation headed by the foreign minister of Colombia. But it failed to undertake any effective action against Noriega's illegal government. The inability of the OAS to move from declaratory to operational practices contributed to the decision of the United States to launch an invasion of Panama on December 20, 1989 in order to install the victor in the May election, Guillermo Endara.[12]

With the Panama debacle imprinted on its collective memory, the OAS moved to correct this problem at the twenty-first session of the General Assembly held in Santiago, Chile in June 1991. In the declaration issued at this meeting, entitled the "Santiago Commitment to Democracy and the Renewal of the Inter-American System," the signatories pledged to adopt "efficacious, timely, and expeditious procedures to ensure the promotion and defense of representative democracy . . ."[13] The accompanying resolution, "Representative Democracy (1080)," went even further in this direction. In the event of any interruption of democratic government in the region, it instructed the secretary-general to convene immediately a meeting of the Permanent Council and to hold an ad hoc meeting of the ministers of foreign affairs and/or a special session of the General Assembly, all within the ten-day period following the occurrence of this type of crisis. It also authorized the ad hoc meeting of foreign ministers and/or the General Assembly to examine the events and "adopt any decisions deemed appropriate."[14]

With this shift in emphasis, the Santiago Commitment and Resolution 1080 added some crucial elements to the emerging pro-democracy doctrine. First of all, they contributed a new, automatic procedure to follow for organizing an external response to democratic breakdown. Secondly, these documents issued a license to the OAS to undertake a wide range of collective activity so long as these actions were approved by the foreign ministers of its member states and/or the General Assembly. Thirdly it underscored the principle of rapid response.

Subsequently, the OAS has assembled a more comprehensive tool kit to further its pro-democracy aims. Denouncing anti-democratic governments has been a traditional measure utilized by the organization, as witnessed by resolutions passed in the context of the interruption of democratic rule in Nicaragua (1979), Panama (1989), Haiti (1991), Peru (1992), and Guatemala (1993). This approach fit well with the diplomatic culture of the inter-American system, in that the practice of denying recognition to governments that come to power by force had been the motivation of the so-called Betancourt Doctrine (named after the former president of Venezuela). During the 1960s, Venezuela invoked the doctrine on numerous occasions, severing diplomatic ties with Argentina, Brazil, Cuba, Guatemala, Honduras, and Peru.[15]

With the Protocol of Washington the OAS added the threat of suspension of membership to its repertoire of punitive actions. Brought forward on December 14, 1992, this amendment to Article 9 of the OAS Charter stated that

> . . .[a] member of the Organization whose democratically constituted government has been overthrown by force may be suspended from the exercise of the right to participate in the sessions of the General Assembly, the Meeting of Consultation, the Councils of the Organization and the Specialized Conferences as well as in the commissions, working groups and any other bodies established . . .[16]

The OAS also created an institutional mechanism—the Unit for the Promotion of Democracy (UPD)—to help foster democratic development through the region. Brought to life in June 1990 through General Assembly Resolution 1063[17] and further refined through Permanent Council Resolution 572,[18] the UPD's mandate includes democratic institution-building; information generation, dissemination, and exchange on democracy; promoting democratic dialogue among experts and institutions in the hemisphere; and electoral observation and technical assistance.[19] Recently renamed the Department for the Promotion of Democracy (DPD), its activities encompass an impressive range of functional/geographic responsibilities. These tasks include furthering the peace process in Guatemala, reintegrating combatants in Nicaragua, the training and shaping of young democratic leaders, and the promotion of effective local government throughout the region. The DPD's work on external election monitoring has taken on a particular importance. Although widely accepted as giving the seal of approval of the OAS in terms of electoral process credibility, these missions have also become the focal point for backlashes against the perceived institutional intrusiveness of the OAS.

The parameters placed on the overall scope of OAS intervention have been defined through practice. In Resolution 1080, the provision to "adopt any decisions deemed appropriate" in the event of the overthrow of a democratic government has been interpreted and shaped via actions taken in the Haitian, Peruvian, Guatemalan, and Paraguayan crises. For example, the response to the Haitian case established a precedent for the use of economic sanctions, cooperation with the United Nations (UN), and UN-legitimized military force as acceptable measures to dislodge illegal governments.

In the 1993 Guatemala crisis the OAS secretary-general led fact-finding missions that served the purpose of demonstrating the organization's solidarity with an elected but fragile government. At the same time, though, these activities highlighted the features not of networked but of old club multilateralism. The Guatemala crisis was triggered by the attempt by President Jorge Serrano to mount an *autogolpe* or self-coup as an excuse to suspend basic rights, shut down Congress and the courts, and detain members of the opposition. These actions received almost universal condemnation in the Americas. However, it did not trigger any punishment by the OAS. What kudos the OAS received during the crisis was for what it did not do as opposed to an activist approach. After João Clemente Baena Soares, the OAS secretary-general, arrived on his fact-finding mission, he was presented with an easy way out of the crisis through the restoration of the status quo that had prevailed prior to the *autogolpe*. To his credit, Soares refused to make a deal on these lines. After laying down these parameters of club behavior the OAS secretary-general left it to the domestic political process to work out the details of who was in and who was out of the government. As two academics have described the situation: "By the time Baena Soares returned to Guatemala after briefing the OAS Foreign Ministers . . . Serrano was in exile and Vice President Gustavo Espina had been forced to resign because of his initial support for Serrano's *autogolpe*. Soon afterward [with a new untarnished President in place] Baena Soares congratulated the winner and returned to Washington."[20]

By amending the OAS Charter to allow for the suspension of anti-democratic governments, the Protocol of Washington contributed yet another defining aspect of the emerging democracy doctrine: representative democracy as a criterion for participation in the inter-American system. The text of the declarations on these questions is precise. The signatories are defined as democratically elected heads of state, and representative democracy named as the sole legitimate political system within the Americas.

The original precedent for representative democracy as a criterion for participation in the inter-American system had in fact been established with the expulsion of Cuba from OAS participation in 1962. However, the impact of this resolution was distorted on at least two counts. First of all, the decision to expel Cuba was adopted more for Cold War hemispheric security concerns than out of any genuine commitment to representative democracy. Second, the precedent was not upheld during the wave of authoritarian regimes that plagued Latin America during the 1960s and 1970s. Indeed the cynical expression "democracy for dictators" gained wide currency during these years as there was deemed to be a double standard between the coercive tactics applied to Cuba and the hands-off approach adopted toward right-wing/military regimes.

Although Cuba has continued to be treated as an exceptional case right up to the present, the growing consensus on democracy in the OAS has implied a significant revision of the notion of sovereignty vis-à-vis the inter-American system. In the spirit of the Calvo (1868) and Drago (1902) doctrines,[21] the OAS continues to pay heed to the traditional principles of equality among states, self-determination, and territorial inviolability. Article 19, under Chapter IV of the OAS Charter, "Fundamental Rights and Duties of States," states these guidelines clearly: "No State or group of States has the right to intervene, directly or indirectly, for any reason whatever, in the internal or external affairs of any other State. The foregoing principle prohibits not only armed force but also any other form of interference or attempted threat against the personality of the State or against its political, economic, and cultural elements."[22] Article 20 adds that. "[n]o State may use or encourage the use of coercive measures of an economic or political character in order to force the sovereign will of another State."[23]

The spirit of this traditional stance is challenged by many of the elements of the inter-American system's emerging democratic solidarity doctrine: the promotion and consolidation of representative democracy as a defining purpose of the OAS, the principle of collective intervention for democracy, a rapid response mechanism in the event of democratic breakdowns, and a collective action repertoire to deal with errant members. The notion of sovereignty itself has been fundamentally altered: territorial inviolability, non-intervention, and self-determination are rights reserved only for freely elected governments of the hemisphere.[24]

In practical terms, a great deal of unevenness can be found in the extension and application of the democratic solidarity doctrine. While the doctrine has been put into action in Haiti, Peru, Guatemala, and Paraguay, it is nonetheless deeply constrained. For example, there is no universally accepted definition of democracy in the inter-American system. Even after the 2001 Inter-American Democratic Charter established an ample list of essential elements and conditions for democracy in Articles 3–6, there is no consensus on a single, acceptable model. This lack of consensus is highlighted by the preamble to Resolution 1063 that created the UPD:

> . . . in the context of representative democracy, there is no political system or electoral method that is equally appropriate for all nations and their peoples and the efforts of the international community to shore up effectiveness of the principle of holding genuine and episodic elections should not cast any doubt on the sovereign right of each State to elect and develop their political, social, and cultural systems freely, whether or not they are to the liking of other states . . .[25]

Across national lines, there has not yet developed a tight consensus on the types of measures to be adopted against those who would overthrow democratic governments. The use of military force is especially contentious. Brazil, most notably, abstained from the UN Security Council vote on Resolution 940 that gave the go-ahead for the U.S.-military intervention in Haiti. Chile, Colombia, Ecuador, Peru, and Mexico, all refused to participate in the multinational force assembled for the purpose of restoring deposed President Aristide to power in Haiti in 1994.[26]

The Rio Group, whose members include the majority of Latin American states, is opposed to the use of military force to safeguard democracy.[27]

The paradox of U.S. structural power further exacerbates this sense of awkwardness. The success of the democratic solidarity doctrine rests on the willingness of the United States to be channeled into multilateral or plurilateral actions determined by the OAS. Yet, there are few signs that the United States has been reined in on a continuous or effective basis through these alternative means. Historically, the United States has adopted a policeman role for itself in the hemisphere on the basis of the Monroe Doctrine and the Roosevelt Corollary, which reversed Roosevelt's 1934 promise that the United States would not interfere in the domestic affairs of Latin America. This coercive role did not preclude some gaps in this mandate. A movement away from this approach was evident in both President John F. Kennedy's Alliance for Progress and President Jimmy Carter's embrace of "ideological pluralism" in the Americas (an opening that was crucial to the 1979 OAS actions against the Somoza regime in Nicaragua). Yet after these brief spells of permissiveness the unilateral impulse on the part of the United States took hold again. Kennedy's initiatives were closed by President Johnson's return to the doctrine of support for authoritarian pro-U.S. governments. Carter's flexible approach gave way to President Ronald Reagan's hard-line.

Questions of Collective and National Leadership

In addition to an incomplete and disputed democratic solidarity paradigm, the external promotion of democracy in the Americas suffers from a number of other deficiencies. As rehearsed above, inter-American activism is inhibited by an ill-defined division of responsibilities in terms of the pursuit of democracy, inadequate resources, and internal constraints on the performance of solidarity partners. Combined together, these problems highlight the need to pay more attention to the question of leadership. Despite progress on the conversion of the democracy agenda from declaratory to operational expression, and the presence of a number of potential candidates, a fully effective mode of leadership on this issue in the inter-American system has not been forthcoming.

Central to this dilemma is the overlapping institutional architecture found in the regional system. While the plan of action of the Miami Summit of the Americas established the OAS as the main organization for the defense and consolidation of democracy within the Americas, other sources of initiatives also have emerged. Indeed, there has been an impressive growth of other bodies that can play significant roles in the process of reform and change. In addition to the OAS, democracy is also promoted by the Rio Group, the Esquipulas Group, the Andean Group, the Caribbean Common Market (CARICOM), the Southern Cone Common Market (MERCOSUR), and the OAS/ Summit Working Group on Democracy and Human Rights. The recent creation of the South American Community of Nations and the Ibero-American Summits and Secretariat adds additional complexity to regional pro-democracy multilateralism.

In this diffuse environment, the Rio Group has emerged alongside the OAS as a particularly important pro-democracy agent. Established in 1986 from the merging of the Contadora Group (Venezuela, Mexico, Panama, and Colombia) and its support group (Argentina, Brazil, Peru, and Uruguay), the membership of the Rio Group contains the majority of Latin American countries. Much of the catalyst for its origin stemmed from the widespread perception that the OAS was a U.S.-dominated body, possessing little in the way of autonomous capacity on issues such as the Central American crisis during the 1980s. The defining trait of the Rio Group has remained its presence as a forum for dialogue among Latin American countries without U.S. participation and interference. In a manner similar to the OAS's, the Rio Group has set democracy as a criterion of participation, with members facing suspension for any interruption in democratic rule—as seen in the cases of Panama in 1989 and Peru in 1992. In accordance with its anti-hegemonic origins, the Rio Group opposes the use of military force to restore overthrown governments and/or unilateral interventions. Its preferred option—as alluded to in the cases of both Nicaragua and Paraguay—has been persuasion, through political dialogue and negotiation, not coercion.[28]

Another indication of the extent of institutional diffusion in the inter-American system has been the marked sub-regionalization of pro-democracy activity in the hemisphere. Pre-dating the Santiago Commitment and the Washington Protocol, the Andean Group in May 1991 reached agreement that its members would suspend diplomatic relations in immediate fashion with any government coming to power illegally.[29] In the aftermath of the Paraguayan democratic crisis of April 1996, MERCOSUR members adopted an analogous "democracy clause" called the Ushuaia Protocol. More concretely, MERCOSUR members (with Brazil in the lead) were instrumental in helping to bring about a quick resolution to Paraguay's political crisis in 1996 and March 1999.[30] Taking on a similar form of collective responsibility,

CARICOM played a pivotal role in alleviating post-electoral tension in Guyana in 1998.

The inter-American system itself has been extended in recent years. To the three main pillars of this system in the postwar period: the OAS, the Inter-American Treaty of Reciprocal Assistance (Rio Treaty), and the Inter-American Development Bank,[31] there has been added a fourth: the summit process begun in Miami in 1994. While in principle free to develop its own agenda, in practice the OAS has increasingly begun to take its cues from these well-publicized meetings of heads of state of the Americas held every 3–4 years. The relationship between the OAS and the summits, therefore, has become an ambiguous one. With respect to the preparation and implementation processes of the summit, the OAS serves as an informal secretariat. But in its capacity as a regional organization the OAS coexists with a separate summit-oriented ministerial level organism—the Summit Implementation Review Group (SIRG).

In overall terms, this diffuse condition means that the refinement and operation of the inter-American democratic solidarity doctrine increasingly occurs at multiple levels and in varied forums of the hemisphere. If a democratic division of labor is emerging, it is evolving in an ad hoc and awkward fashion. As heads-of-state meetings, the summits of the Americas have moved to the pinnacle of policymaking for issues related to democracy in the region. However, because these events occur only periodically and address a wide range of policy priorities, extending from education and the environment, to security and hemispheric free trade, their utility is diluted. Moreover, the Summits have generated literally hundreds of new mandates for which the OAS and the Inter-American System continue to have inadequate numbers of personnel and financial resources.

The effectiveness of the OAS to deal with a widened agenda relating to the defense and consolidation of democracy must also be questioned. The most serious challenge to the OAS's credibility concerns the issue of rapid response to democratic crises. The OAS has the potential to play a vital function through its newly formed Secretariat for Political Affairs in terms of the prevention of coups d'état and the mobilization of projects designed to promote democratic consolidation. It can also perform a significant coordinating role in times of crisis. As the first Paraguayan crisis of 1996 revealed, though, the OAS has sometimes been left on the sidelines in times of crisis. By the time the OAS Permanent Council had convened as per Resolution 1080 and gathered reliable information about the events on the ground, the Paraguayan crisis had abated.[32] Both in 1996 and 1999, it was Paraguay's MERCOSUR partners together with the United States that filled the gap, providing the more immediate diplomatic response that proved vital in resolving these Paraguayan crises.

The deficiencies of the OAS have been compounded by specific problems attached to its institutional culture. The OAS tradition of consensual decision-making within a club-like atmosphere is particularly salient here. On routine matters, involving little or no controversy, the OAS works well. On higher-profile issues where there are profound differences of opinion, as on the question of how to resolve a crisis, the process is prone to some considerable stalling if not immobilization. This deficiency came to the fore most notably in the case of Haiti in 1994. Subsequent to the overthrow of President Aristide in September 1991, Secretary-General Baena Soares immediately invoked Resolution 1080 and a meeting of the Permanent Council of the OAS was held. Yet, if there was a consensus that the coup d'état should be condemned, a sharp split formed over the issue of coercive intervention. Accepted on principle was a menu of sanctions that included the freezing of assets in international banks; the suspension of credit, international assistance, and commercial flights; and an imposition of trade embargo, with exceptions being made on humanitarian grounds. But in terms of an intervention force, the OAS was able to send only a small grouping (18 members) of a civilian mission known as OAS-DEMOC. The mission established itself in Haiti in September of 1992. However, its functions were quickly subordinated to the role of the UN as requested by Secretary General Soares. Eventually, after other means failed, in July 1994 the UN Security Council passed a resolution allowing the de facto regime to be removed by "all means necessary," a step that led inevitably to the U.S. military intervention in September 1994.[33]

Underscoring all of these organizational defects has been the relative scarcity of resources. The OAS remains in a relatively weak financial position. Frozen in the mid-1990s, the OAS total budget remained until 2006 a modest $78 million, a figure less than the annual operating budget of a typical mid-sized U.S. university. Its operations and programming are further hurt by the fact that a significant number of its members continue to be in arrears on their annual contributions, owing almost $107 million in unpaid dues as of mid-February 1999. During the June 2000 OAS General Assembly, held in Windsor, Ontario, Canada, it was reported that the United States owed $35.7m, while Brazil was $23.8m in arrears and Argentina $5.3m.[34] Although an important announcement was made at the Windsor meeting for the establishment of a new Democracy Fund target endangered democracies, no commitment was made to strengthen the budget of the UPD.[35]

The operations of the UPD/DPD have been negatively affected by this shortfall. It must fund an ambitious array of hemisphere-wide, democracy-enhancing activities, from democratic institution-building, elections monitoring, and technical assistance to demining in Central America.[36] Its election observation missions, a cornerstone of its operations, are funded precariously by voluntary contributions at the national level instead of a permanent fund within the OAS.[37]

To make this commitment–resource gap more acute, the inter-American democracy mandate contains the danger of overstretch. In the areas of democracy, justice, and human rights, the Santiago Summit identified a number of new initiatives. The creation of a hemispheric center for justice studies and the position of a Special Rapporteur for Freedom of Expression add to the organizational burden placed on the OAS. The membership has also agreed to fund educational programs for democracy in their respective countries. In the area of election monitoring, the OAS is faced with a situation where a monitoring role is required in a growing number of countries. The OAS has organized more than 90 electoral missions throughout the region.[38]

Weak funding at the inter-American level is matched by poor resource allocations on a national basis. At odds with the structural power it possesses, the United States has been erratic in its performance as a contributor to the democratic solidarity agenda. Flying in the face of the declaratory policy from the 1994 Miami Summit, with its stated pledge to "preserve and strengthen the community of democracies in the Americas,"[39] the United States subsequently cut back aid to the Americas. From 1992 to 1995, U.S. Official Development Assistance to Latin America shrank to almost half its former level. In large part this shift reflects a dominant situational factor: the relationship of the budgetary process to the Republican-controlled Congress. However, this condition also reflects the trend toward linking foreign policy issues with U.S. aid, which is being increasingly tied to specific programs to combat narcotics trafficking. Annual funding for the promotion of democracy hovers around US$16 million.[40] Such resources appear to be particularly derisory when compared to other high-profile items, above all the budget of US$1.3 billion that the United States allocates for the Plan Colombia, the initiative that fights drug trafficking in that single country.

Nor has it been easy for most other countries in the region to fill the void left by the lack of top-down leadership. In some cases, an inability to raise the level of financial commitment goes hand in hand with the intrusion of internal economic crises and/or competing priorities. This capability problem is particularly associated with the intermediate or middle states in the region. Brazil provides one illustration of this trend. Propelled by its own internal democratic transition, Brazil raised its level of activism on the external democracy front. Brazil, for example, took on the role as coordinator (with Canada) of the OAS Working Group on Democracy and Human Rights. In the aftermath of the financial crisis of January 1999, however, Brazil's ability to stay the course in privileging the democracy agenda became increasingly contested.

In other cases, this commitment–capability gap reflects the traditional limitations of size and strength. These sorts of conditions curb the activities particularly of Chile and Argentina, arguably the two countries that possess the greatest incentives for taking part in democracy promotion programs as they have had their own experiences of transition from repressive to democratic regimes. Up to the 1990s, Chile's foreign policy reflected its modest resources, although this constraint was lifted as the economy flourished. Despite an activist and prestige-oriented psychology, Argentina's level of external involvement has been held back by budgetary limits as well. Hit hard by the economic/debt crisis since December 2001, Argentina remains sensitive to potential resource constraints posed by external vulnerability and the relatively small size and fragile condition of its economy.

It would be misleading to suggest that the expression of leadership for inter-American democracy rests exclusively on capabilities. When trying to locate potential sources of initiative and innovation, the question of will must also be taken into account. The sources of leadership, from this perspective, are both systemic and domestic. While systemic strain may prompt policy initiatives, these responses are shaped and conditioned by domestic factors. With issues such as democracy in ascendancy, there are higher expectations for involvement in both "domestic" issues having international ramifications and those "international" issues that spill over into the national area. Nonetheless, this heightened form of internal pressure also introduces a strong element of constraint on policy innovation and reform.

The ambiguity of the U.S. position to the democracy agenda reflects this combination of systemic and domestic constraints. As mentioned in the previous chapter, the relationship between the United States and the Americas improved considerably immediately after the end of the Cold War. Still, despite this opportunity, the United States has not seized the opportunity to head up the construction of an authentic Latin American democratic community.[41] On the contrary, according to Jorge Domínguez, Latin America has become "marginalized" in the post–Cold War era.[42] Internationally, the United States has focused its attention elsewhere, through economic crises in Asia and Russia, to the conflicts in the former Yugoslavia, through to September 11, Afghanistan, and the Iraq War. To the extent that the region has figured significantly in U.S. policy circles, it is mainly to react to problems within the Americas such as drug-trafficking, with potentially serious repercussions for the U.S. economy and society. Both the Clinton and the George W. Bush administrations have clearly lacked a longer-term, forward-looking, post–Cold War vision for the hemisphere,[43] in which the consolidation of democratic solidarity would become the present day equivalent to the Kennedy administration's Alliance for Progress.

The ambiguity on the part of the United States has opened up greater opportunities for intermediate—or middle—states to use their enhanced space of maneuver in the post–Cold War era to widen their repertoire of activity.[44] Given their resource limitations, these states have not moved to share structural power with the United States. Instead, the potential for leadership for this cluster of countries has been based on nonstructural forms of influence associated with the energetic use of their diplomatic talents. Notwithstanding some fundamental similarities in the pattern of behavior, the differences in operating procedures found among this category of countries are striking. The way in which systemic and domestic factors limit—as well as stimulate—initiative-taking behavior varies considerably among them.

The importance of entrepreneurial flair and technical competence is found in the case of Canada's diplomatic approach toward the Americas. Despite the short trajectory of its experience in the OAS, dating back only to 1990, Canadian activism has gained some widespread respect through Latin America and the Caribbean. By adding a new voice and set of diplomatic competencies, Canada helped revitalize the OAS after its relative decline during the 1980s.[45] Its autonomous stance toward Cuba has mitigated any concern in Latin America that Canada would be a passive follower of the United States. Canada's role in fostering favorable conditions for the development of representative democracy in the region has focused on the creation and funding of the UPD, partic-ipation in peacekeeping activities in Central America and Haiti, demining activities, and advocacy for a hemispheric multilateral approach to the problem of the drug trade.[46]

In terms of the distribution of labor, Canada has been particularly well suited to take the lead in strengthening the inter-American democratic solidarity paradigm. With its permanent representation at the OAS enjoying the respect of both the Latin American and U.S. delegations, Canada is well positioned to serve as a bridge or linchpin within the hemisphere. As a latecomer to the OAS, Canada has not figured prominently in the historical debate over the predominance of the two contending visions (one a U.S.-based vision, the other a Latin American–based) about the future of the hemisphere. As is apparent in the cases at the core of this book, Canada has also the ability to devote diplomatic skills and energy at both the ministerial/political and bureaucratic levels on an issue-specific basis.

This positive assessment of Canada's diplomacy should not be taken to suggest the absence of any serious constraints on this approach. Canada's interest in promoting democracy in the hemisphere is diluted by competing priorities in Canada's foreign policy. Geographically, the Americas continue to be but one region among several that are competing for attention and resources within the framework of Canada's perceived role as an activist, middle power and the realities of its North American location. Canada's membership in a wide number of other organizations (NATO, the Commonwealth, the francophone summit, APEC) also detracts from Canada's focus on the Americas. The maintenance of this international activism has been further put into question also—by the tendency post–September 11—by an inward focus on the main game of Canada's foreign policy, that is, the United States in general and the Canada–U.S. border more specifically.[47]

Argentina and Chile—notwithstanding their capability limitations noted above—have both also continued to be active in the international promotion of democracy-building.[48] This effort points to another variation of the inverse relationship between structural power and activism in favor of democracy.[49] That is to say, in traditional terms, it has been the regional powers of Brazil and Mexico that have been the most non-interventionist. Conversely, countries with lesser capabilities have demonstrated the greatest sense of will in this area. Notwithstanding its economic constraints, Argentina has demonstrated a strong commitment to an external as well as an internal democracy agenda. At one level Argentina has played a significant role in the formulation of the Cartagena and Washington Protocols. At another level Argentina has made an impressive contribution to peacekeeping, peace-building, and humanitarian assistance, including active participation in the OAS and UN initiatives to restore President Aristide after the 1991 coup in Haiti and the promotion of the "White Helmets" assistance corps.[50]

Chile has also maximized its potential in terms of agenda setting, compensating will (and skill) for resources. This diplomatic ability was evidenced by its success in promoting the passage of the Santiago Commitment and Resolution 1080 during the OAS General Assembly held in Chile in 1991. In the lead-up to the 1998 summit of the Americas, Chile's work along these lines was helped by its status as a member of the SIRG troika. Buttressed by its existing links with MERCOSUR and the Andean Group, this role allowed Chile to play a valuable function as a mediator or interlocutor between North America and its Latin American neighbors.

To suggest that Argentina and Chile have become catalysts and facilitators on an issue-specific basis is not to deny the constraints preventing them from fulfilling these roles. The difference between these countries and other larger powers is that these constraints appear to be as much situational as structural. The limitations imposed on Argentina's initiative-oriented diplomacy in the Americas by resource constraints are serious. But so are the impediments placed on these activities by the legacy of the Menem government's foreign policy strategy. By tilting so severely toward a pro-U.S. alignment and demanding that it be elevated to a special status as a non-NATO ally, Argentina reduced its coalition-building capabilities within a region in which suspicions of U.S. hegemony still linger. Indeed the magnitude of the backlash against these overtures is evident in some of the initiatives of the Kirchner government, most notably the call for the replacement of the Washington consensus with a Buenos Aires consensus, and Argentina's participation in the G20+ of trading states in the context of the Doha Round within the WTO.

While sympathetic to multilateralism and the strengthening of organizations such as the OAS, the Alywin and Frei—as well as the Lagos—governments in Chile have adopted a low-key style of diplomacy.[51] As suggested above, the constraints on a more robust style are largely economic in nature. It also must be mentioned that the influence of a strong anticommunist right wing faction in the country—even in the post-Pinochet era—has also delimited Chile's stance on some selective issues, such as Cuban democratization.

Venezuela extends the complexity of this discussion in a different direction, as it provides the most vivid case of a traditionally strong pro-democracy country in the region constrained by the weight of domestic political circumstances. Venezuela was a prominent promoter of Resolution 1080 and under the leadership of President Rómulo Betancourt, a key proponent of the adoption of the so-called Betancourt Doctrine within the Andean Group and by the inter-American system during the early 1990s. Recent internal developments, however, have cut into its activist profile. A prolonged economic crisis during the 1980s and 1990s was a source of constant distraction for government officials that also severely constrained funding of diplomatic activism. Politically, Venezuela's international credibility has fluctuated with the style and fortunes of its leaders. President Carlos Andrés Pérez emerged as one of the region's champions of democratic solidarity, as witnessed by his declaratory response to the Haiti coup: if successful, this action would "not only break the constitutional order, but might foster the illusion in other countries that it is possible to step back in history."[52] Disappointingly, though, this era ended when Pérez's own personal credibility was punctured in 1993 by his impeachment for corrupt practices.

Venezuela's credentials as a model of democracy for the region were further damaged by two very different attempted coups d'état. With one of the former coup conspirators, Hugo Chávez, having legitimately won the election based on a transformative domestic agenda, it is unlikely that Venezuela will resume the pro-democracy foreign policy platform of the former Pérez government. On the contrary, as demonstrated by a number of illustrations central to this book, the Chávez regime moved from support to resistance on the democratic solidarity doctrine. Rejecting dogmatically the claims of "representative democracy," Chávez has personally championed an alternative notion of "participatory democracy" in his Bolivarian Revolution as well as respect for countries' sovereign rights.

As witnessed by the Venezuelan case, the inconsistency of leadership performance within as well as between countries highlights the linkage between individual and national leadership. As in the development of other institutional regimes,[53] individual leaders clearly make a difference in either pushing or holding back the movement toward an agenda of democratic solidarity in the Americas. Yet, there are pitfalls as well as advantages in relying too heavily on this particular expression of leadership as a guide to action. As witnessed by the Venezuelan case, individual leadership can take on an ephemeral character. As quickly as the style of leadership expressed by individual politicians becomes associated with an institutional culture, personalities change and the form of national leadership is substantially altered.

Brazil features a mix of leadership potential and constraints. Facilitated by President Cardoso's strong personal interest taken in human rights, democracy, and justice issues, Brazil in some ways has been able to build on its potential to be a key actor in the strengthening of the region's democratic solidarity doctrine. Brazil's willingness to take on the role of co-coordinator of the OAS Working Group on Democracy and Human Rights is indicative of this trend. In a more geographically restrictive fashion, so was the initiative by the Brazilian foreign minister Luiz Felipe Lampreia to hold a Latin American conference on democracy in

September 2000 in Brasilia. However, the limitations placed on the extension of this national (and individual) leadership role remain enormous. Furthermore, the current economic problems reveal just the tip of this condition. In the late 1990s, the country was preoccupied with the politics of constitutional reform, especially in terms of pension reform and state downsizing.[54] Brazil's tilt toward activism in the region also exposes the contradictions between external and domestic behavior. Brazil's ability to be a role model in the Americas is truncated by a mixed record on the domestic front in terms of democracy and justice. While democratization has occurred at the formal level of Brazil's political institutions, at the societal level, human rights abuses, judicial corruption and inequality, and violence are endemic.[55]

These contradictions have not gone away with the election of President Luiz Inacio Lula da Silva. Given his status as long-time opposition leader, the election of Lula was a positive expression of democracy in the largest country in South America. Moreover, his democratic credibility appeared to be of the highest order, a rank that was confirmed by his policy push on Brazil's social agenda. Yet, as reflected most dramatically by recent corruption allegations as well as the initiatives taken by his government on press censorship, there have arisen as well some notes of concern.

On top of all of these problems, Brazil remains resistant to any alterations to the established notions of sovereignty and non-intervention. The assumption of any sustained leadership within the hemisphere on the democracy agenda is constrained by Brazil's reluctance to bend these principles. In declaratory terms, Brazil is wary of the elaboration of a convention of collective intervention in the region for fear of setting a precedent for action in other arenas: such as an international convention in defense of the environment within its own borders.[56] In operational terms, Brazil has traditionally been a strong resister of collective action by the OAS to defend democracy. Sensitive to the perception of its immediate neighbors about a hegemonic design, Brazil has been reluctant to forge an assertive leadership role for itself, preferring to work in pursuit of diplomacy—not power leverage. At the same time, much of the focus of Brazilian actions has become increasingly channeled through the conduit of MERCOSUR. That this process of subregionalization extends to the democracy agenda was evident during the Paraguayan crises of 1996 and 1999 in Brazil's mediation effort; a diplomatic effort in which Brazil consulted closely with its MERCOSUR partners.

Resistance to the pursuit of an ambitious democracy agenda has been even more exaggerated in the case of Mexico. With its strong ingrained defense of the principles of sovereignty and self-determination, Mexico has possessed far less immediate potential for leadership by way of a contribution toward the collective promotion of democracy. Mexico was the only country to oppose the Washington Protocol and remains a vociferous critic of collective action to restore democracy. Through the long period of PRI domination, Mexico was profoundly suspicious of the underlying motives behind collective interventions, attributing them mainly to the residual hegemonic interest of the United States. Furthermore, Mexico is highly skeptical of the potential of democracy being inculcated or imposed from outside and is convinced that regime change must be a sovereign act stemming from an outgrowth of domestic social forces. In conceptual terms, Mexico has been a strong proponent of the Estrada Doctrine: respect for political pluralism and the automatic recognition of de facto governments regardless of their regime type or ideological orientation.

Having said that, there is some indication that Mexico has been softening its resistance as a consequence of its growing interdependence and rapprochement with the United States through its partnership in the North American Free Trade Agreement (NAFTA) and its multiple informal economic, social, and cultural ties.[57] During the Panama crisis in 1989, for instance, Mexico refrained from criticizing the U.S. intervention to remove Noriega. Indeed, Mexico spoke out against Noriega's illegal assumption of power.[58] In a similar uncharacteristic manner, Mexico denounced the *autogolpe* in Guatemala in 1993.[59] In 1994, the Salinas government, for the first time in Mexican history, permitted the presence of foreign election observers.[60] In 1998, Mexico accepted the legal jurisdiction of the Inter-American Court of Human Rights. In April 2002, President Vicente Fox was one of the first and most vocal leaders to condemn the coup against Hugo Chávez in Venezuela.

These counterexamples, however, should not be given exaggerated credence as indicators of a major shift in Mexican foreign policy prior to the victory of President Fox in 2000. Mexico's actions vis-à-vis Panama and Guatemala, for instance, must be understood from the perspective of potential spillover effects that would drag Mexico against its will more deeply into Central American conflicts. Mexico had been the recipient, for example, of thousands of Central American refugees during the 1980s. Moreover, the negotiation of NAFTA during the 1990s had the unanticipated consequence of international media attention getting focussed on Mexico's human rights and democracy shortcomings at a time when the Mexican government was concerned with international investor confidence.[61]

It needs to be added here as well that the U.S. response to the 1994 election did not signal a complete shift in approach to democracy. Even when the United States moved indirectly to support Mexican democracy, these actions were motivated by a desire for order not democracy. As described by M. Delal Baer, the United States "stepped in to stabilize what it perceived to be dangerous post-electoral scenarios by supporting election observations via the channeling of financial resources and moral support through the National Endowment for Democracy (NED) and the U.S. Agency for International Development (USAID). . . . Official support for NGO activism was a thinly veiled substitute for direct U.S. government involvement."[62]

The tenor of these longer-term actions by Mexico, therefore, should be viewed as confidence-building measures alongside a commitment to democracy and human rights. As for the specific case of Mexico's recognition of the jurisdiction of the Inter-American Court of Human Rights, this is a favorable development for human rights and democracy in Mexico. But this action did not necessarily commit the country to accept other aspects of the inter-American system's democracy paradigm. Mexico remains a formidable opponent of outside interference through the OAS.

From this account the Fox/Castañeda agenda cannot be considered entirely a decisive break from the past. Structural forces felt from the early 1990s were building momentum long before the July 2, 2000 election. This was evident in various events, including the landmark decision—after a clean mid-term election in 1997—taken by the government of Ernesto Zedillo to accept the Democratic Clause in the context of their negotiations with the European Union. What the Fox/Castañeda coalition did immediately after the election was to provide a powerful sense of personal agency to the democratic component of this "new" foreign policy. From the time it came into office, the Fox/Castañeda coalition reconfigured its relationship with institutions devoted to the promotion of democracy as well as human rights and to ensure that rules of the game are locked in with respect to domestic politics. As the Mexican secretary of foreign affairs stated at the beginning of 2002: "This commitment implies, of course, that we open ourselves to external scrutiny. In contrast to the past, today we are convinced that . . . opening ourselves to the rest of the world will contribute decisively to strengthening democratic change in Mexico, making it irreversible."[63]

Overcoming Structural Constraints

As the Americas adjusted to the post–Cold War era, it appeared that a good deal of momentum was building up on the democracy agenda. Democracy remains squarely on the policy map, as witnessed by the profusion of new commitments at the Santiago Summit of the Americas on education for democracy, a Special Rapporteur for Freedom of Expression, and international exchanges on election campaign financing. However, this issue had not yet assumed a central position on the political/policy agenda as it had to deal with a host of competing demands and priorities: education, negotiations for the free trade area of the Americas, corruption, drug-trafficking, and the environment. This challenge to the ongoing prioritization of the external promotion of democracy is made more serious by the incomplete nature of the democracy agenda. The pandemonium in Paraguay in March 1999, and again in May 2000, the ongoing travails in Haiti, the aborted coup attempt in Ecuador in January 2000, and the precarious nature of the democratic condition in the two central cases for this book—Peru and Venezuela—sent out an alert that the democratic condition remains a fragile and often volatile phenomenon in many parts of the region. A growing number of scholars highlight also the authoritarian, delegative, or hybrid nature of contemporary Latin American representative democracies, not to mention their often worrisome human rights or judicial shortcomings.[64] In short, the tests before the democracy project remain formidable.[65]

This chapter identifies two key ingredients in this process. On the one hand, it argues that the democracy solidarity paradigm that emerged during the early 1990s still needed to be considerably refined in order to achieve operational effectiveness. Its collective action repertoire must be defined more explicitly, especially in regard to the use of force to defend democracy. On the other hand, it highlights the strong constraints imposed on the collective defense and consolidation of democracy. In part the presence of these constraints is a reflection of the absence of a strong, coherent form of leadership in the hemisphere. Pro-democracy activism from the countries of the region is hindered not only by the lack of an extant division of labor but also by a scarcity of resources and an imposing set of systemic and domestic constraints. Surmounting these problems will not be easy.

One sign of these problems, as mentioned above, is the continued lack of agreement on what the concept of democracy constitutes in the region of the Americas. One fundamental criticism of the OAS that remains is that the linkage of democracy with the formal process of representation in its institutional approach subordinates justice to the preservation of the status quo. Indeed, it may be argued that the January 2000 crisis in Ecuador provides some support for this critique, in that the OAS response concentrated on the formal procedure applied to regime transition (the legitimacy of the transfer of power from President Jamil Mahuad to Vice President Gustavo Noboa) as opposed to a response targeting the underlying concerns that provoked the crisis among the large indigenous population. To its credit, the UPD and now the broader Secretariat for Political Affairs at the OAS have tried to address some aspects of this larger problem by moving to a more all-encompassing approach toward citizenship. The idea here is to promote effective political cultural change, beyond a narrow interpretation of democracy through elections. Substantive questions remain, however, about what sort of constitutional order is envisioned.

Another indication that remains is the constraint of sovereignty. Tom Farer[66] and Fernando Tesón[67] have spoken of the "shrinking of sovereignty's prerogatives." Indeed the title of Farer's edited volume on the topic is *Beyond Sovereignty*. Yet in the Americas sensitivity to external intrusions on sovereignty remains intense. Paradoxically, pro-democracy activity in the region might have the perverse effect of solidifying the sovereign authority of certain governments to undermine democracy in their own bounded spheres of authority. Sovereignty practices related to intervention have certainly changed, but they have still not coalesced into a clear new meaning for sovereignty in the Americas. The reluctance to use armed force and the difficulty in addressing non-coup scenarios of authoritarian regression by incumbent elected leaders suggest that sovereignty is very much alive in the region. If these barriers to sovereignty are to be overcome the cutting edge for change must begin with specific cases. Moreover, there is a great deal of need for subtlety and flexibility and a curtailment of the traditional methods of unilateral intervention and the use of hard power. The signposts for the nexus between multilateralism and democratization in the Americas highlight instead a preference for soft, persuasive forms of intervention.[68] This repertoire, as developed by the OAS and a combination of state/societal actors in the 2000 Peru case, is evocative of how far this form of networked multilateralism could be stretched.

CHAPTER THREE

Defending Democracy? The OAS and Peru in the 1990s

Peru's ongoing travails with democracy provide rich case study material for an exploration of the complex inter-action of domestic and international factors in the multilateralism–democratization nexus. During the 1990s, Peru had the distinction of becoming one of the first test cases for putting the OAS's fledgling pro-democracy activism into practice. After Haiti in 1991, the Peruvian *autogolpe* (self-coup) of April 1992 represented only the second application of the recently forged Resolution 1080 crisis response mechanism. Peru was also an important training ground for the elections monitoring missions organized by the OAS's newly created Unit for the Promotion of Democracy. During the 1990s, OAS multilateralism in defense of democracy emerged as an external means to influence political change in a sovereign member state of the inter-American system, alongside more traditional bilateral relationships, most notably the U.S.–Peruvian relationship. OAS multilateralism itself underwent interesting changes toward greater complexity and networking as rising transnational civil society advocacy for democracy and human rights intertwined with the actions of more traditional state actors.

Peru's experience during the Fujimori years (1990–2000) represented both the entrenched obstacles and the glimmers of hope in OAS multilateralism in action. In hindsight we can see that the country was a living laboratory for studying the problems entailed in mounting collective defenses of democracy. At times, OAS democracy norms and principles appeared almost rhetorical and its tools ineffective. Then again, at odds with its negative organizational image, the OAS launched the crucial

Stein electoral observation mission and negotiated Resolution 1753 to respond to Fujimori's electoral fraud, from which a path-breaking High-Level Mission emerged to play an important supportive role in restoring democracy. Over a course of ten years, we see a clear evolution in the multilateralism-democracy nexus albeit still with some sizeable gaps in the OAS's collective defense of democracy paradigm. Ultimately, the insights garnered from the OAS's experience confronting the 1992 *auto-golpe*, monitoring elections in 1995 and 2000, and responding to the 2000 political crisis in Peru were the inspiration behind the creation of the Inter-American Democratic Charter in 2001, the subject of chapter five.

In this chapter and the following one, we examine OAS efforts to defend democracy in Peru during the 1990s. Chapter three covers the period under which efforts to intervene collectively in Peru occurred largely under the sway of club multilateralism. This was a time when Fujimori was able to resist quite successfully weak efforts to defend democracy and even to strengthen his position both domestically and internationally. We begin by going back to the democratic transition period of 1977–1980, a period in which the relative insignificance of foreign actors contrasted with their subsequent growing involvement in the 1990s in efforts to halt authoritarian regression. The chapter then turns to an analysis of the events surrounding the 1992 *autogolpe* and its aftermath, where Fujimori was able to overcome domestic and international resistance and emerge stronger than ever. It concludes with a look at what proved to be an important turning point in terms of OAS multilateralism: the controversial 2000 presidential elections. In the next chapter, we examine the innovative response by the OAS to the challenge of authoritarian backsliding by Fujimori: the OAS High-Level Mission and the *Mesa de Diálogo* (Dialogue Table). It was only then that we see a clear shift in the direction of networked multilateralism.

Peru's Democratic Transition, 1977–1980

The standard interpretation of Peru's democratic transition during 1977–1980 is one in which the divided and discredited Peruvian military dictatorship that had ruled the country since 1968 and failed in its effort to implement a top-down revolution extricated itself from power in the midst of a growing economic crisis and a groundswell of popular resistance against the regime.[1] Following the largest general strike in the country's history on July 19, 1977, General Morales Bermúdez announced a transition to democracy in which the elected Constituent

Assembly subsequently rewrote Peru's constitution in order to lay the foundations for a return to elected, civilian rule. During the roughly three-year-long process, the military undertook a controlled transition in which it forged an informal alliance of mutual convenience with the right-wing Popular Christian Party (PPC) and the center-left American Popular Revolutionary Alliance (APRA) against a plethora of leftist parties, unions, and popular organizations. In this reading of Peru's regime change, the key explanatory factors are clearly domestic.[2]

Yet while the main readings on this period focus on the internal dimensions of regime change, they also make occasional references to the role of external factors. To begin with, external economic ties had some bearing on the course of events. During the early 1970s, the Revolutionary Government of the Armed Forces (RGAF) turned to foreign loans to finance its ambitious revolutionary programs. As a result, from 1968 to 1980 Peru's foreign debt rose from $800 million to $8 billion.[3] Acute balance of payment problems contributed to the demise of General Juan Velasco Alvarado and his revolutionary agenda and his ousting by the more conservative General Morales Bermúdez. The question of how to address Peru's deteriorating economic situation, including how to meet the country's obligations to its international creditors, placed added strain on existing divisions among the country's military leaders and helped lead to an eventual rupture within the military's upper ranks. Moreover, the government's failure to reach agreement with the International Monetary Fund for stabilization assistance—from the onset of its balance of payment problems in the mid-1970s until May 1978—only exacerbated Peru's economic crisis, thereby further eroding the government's legitimacy domestically. Ultimately, where foreign loans acquired to finance development in Peru might have delayed the day of reckoning of the RGAF, they eventually helped undermine the regime.

Examining U.S. alienation during much of the regime adds another dimension to a more accurate picture of Peru's democratic transition. The military government's nationalization of U.S.-owned assets in Peru, such as the International Petroleum Company, its anti-imperialist rhetoric in the non-aligned movement, and its purchase of Soviet arms strained relations with Washington. While the United States did not actively seek to undermine the RGAF, when Peru encountered problems with its external debt servicing, it could not count on sympathy from the U.S. government or U.S. banks in its negotiations with the IMF. Following the U.S. cue and equally concerned with Peru's resistance to compensate appropriated foreign firms, World Bank and Inter-American Development Bank loan disbursements decreased during the Velasco years. Additionally, unlike brutal pro-American military counterparts in Argentina or Chile, Peru's military regime came under much closer scrutiny for its human rights record.[4]

When these various international and domestic dimensions are juxtaposed, the Peruvian transition experience comes out in a different light. From the previous description, we can discern at least two significant internal-external inter-actions that influenced regime change. First, rising popular mobilization against the dictatorship that was inadvertently triggered by the military's own efforts to organize the poor during the Velasco years coincided with growing pressures from Peru's external creditors and the IMF to meet its obligations and restructure its economy.[5] Add in the lack of U.S. support and both the regime's growing domestic and international isolation become apparent. Combined, these various developments contributed to a rupture among the ruling military officers, a decisive shift to the right by the Morales government in its economic policies, and the regime fatigue that underpinned the eventual decision to retreat from power.[6] This type of internal–external inter-action is clearly more *indirect* in the sense of not entailing the direct creation of transnational linkages or networks advocating change or significant interfaces among domestic and foreign agents. Instead, the combined weight of domestic and international developments fostered a more general movement toward regime change.

Second, the relations between U.S. embassy diplomats in Lima with Peruvian officials, once the transition process commenced, represent another, more *direct* form of inter-action. During the Carter administration, positive developments in Peru were rewarded with additional development assistance from the U.S. Agency for International Development (USAID). When amidst the transition process rising social unrest in Peru raised fears of a Southern Cone–style coup, embassy officials were instructed to dissuade any would-be military coup conspirators.[7] U.S. officials helped both to propel the transition process forward as well as to prevent any potential backsliding or counter-coup.

It is worth noting that the multilateralism–democratization nexus at the time of Peru's democratic transition was practically nonexistent. For the most part, Peru was off the OAS radar. On a positive note, Peru did ratify the American Convention of Human Rights in July 1978, a move undoubtedly in step with its political opening at the time. Nonetheless, as mentioned previously, the first sign of a substantial move within the OAS toward some form of pro-democracy doctrine came in 1979 with the passage of a resolution condemning the human rights record of the Somoza regime in Nicaragua.[8]

This more integrated analysis reveals that foreign-domestic inter-actions were more significant in a general sense, rather than in influencing the specific outcomes of Peru's transition process. That is to say, domestic forces were clearly of more importance than international ones in actually determining the legacy of the transition process. For instance, domestic factors, such as the military's control of the process, the elite domination of the process by the constellation of the military, APRA, and the PPC, and the Constituent Assembly's collective memory of executive-legislative gridlock during the failed Belaúnde presidency (1963–1968) are key in explaining the creation of a constitution that increased executive powers and the retention of important military prerogatives and privileges following the restoration of civilian rule in 1980. Here then, the path dependent models of democratization that look exclusively at domestic variables would seem to have their ammunition.[9] As we shall see, the democratic transition of 1977–1980 stands in striking contrast to the Fujimori presidency, when the OAS and other international actors became more intertwined in Peruvian political life.

The 1992 *Autogolpe* and Authoritarian Backsliding During the 1990s

The presidency of Alberto Fujimori magnified contradictions within the nexus between multilateralism and democracy. Originally a political outsider prior to his election in 1990, Fujimori became one of the definitive insiders both in Peruvian politics and in the Americas. His name became identified with both praise and controversy. On the one hand, he received international recognition for successfully fighting against Shining Path terrorism as well as for restoring economic stability and growth to Peru. On the other hand, he became the target of human rights critics and the international media for his repressive methods against the insurgency and eventually for undermining democracy. In doing so, he personified the flaws of the privileging of executive sovereignty within the OAS's club multilateralism.

On April 5, 1992, President Fujimori dissolved Congress, shut down the courts, suspended the constitution, and assumed special emergency powers. A variety of reasons have been cited for this *autogolpe*. These include congressional and judicial obstruction of the Fujimori government's economic and security agenda against a backdrop of economic crisis and worsening Shining Path terrorism, the recovery in popularity of archival Alan García and APRA, Fujimori's own authoritarian personality and his determination to rewrite the constitution in order to enable himself to be reelected for a second term, and elements within the military that had grown increasingly disgruntled after the ineptitude and mismanagement of two consecutive civilian administrations under Belaúnde and García.[10]

Irrespective of the true causes, Fujimori's break with democracy was hugely popular among the wider population, the military, and the business class.[11] Fujimori's actions resonated among a population whose faith in democratic institutions had eroded during twelve years of economic crisis, violence, and terrorism wherein elected officials and judges were perceived to have used their offices for personal enrichment rather than promoting the interests of the Peruvian citizenry.

However, whilst popular at home, Fujimori's actions evoked strong, critical reactions across the international community, including foreign governments, the OAS, international financial institutions, and foreign civil society organizations. At least five types of domestic-international inter-action were triggered by the self-coup. First of all, bilateral measures factored significantly among international efforts to confront the Fujimori government. The United States, for example, roundly condemned the coup and immediately suspended all military and non-humanitarian economic assistance to Peru, the latter form of aid totaling some $160 million in 1992.[12] Secretary of State James Baker stressed that the act of destroying democracy in order to save it was not justified.[13] The assistant secretary of State for Inter-American Affairs, Bernard Aronson, was deeply concerned about the potential spillover effect of Fujimori's self-coup in other countries if it was tolerated, especially in light of the recent coup in Haiti and the coup attempts in Venezuela.[14] Indeed, having just arrived on an official visit to Peru on the eve of the self-coup, Aronson was infuriated by having been caught by surprise by the events of April 5.[15]

Many of Peru's Latin American neighbors also sent strong messages. Almost all Latin American governments denounced the *autogolpe*. Venezuela and Panama suspended diplomatic relations with Peru. Argentina recalled its ambassador while Chile suspended talks over Peruvian access to the port of Arica. Ecuador cancelled an official state visit scheduled for the middle of 1992. In some of these instances, such as Chile and Ecuador, these criticisms were interwoven with bilateral relations under some tension. In other cases such as Venezuela, the champion of the Betancourt Doctrine, as well as Argentina, Fujimori's *autogolpe* was seen as a violation of their principled foreign policy.

Fujimori's actions revealed a rift between the aforementioned champions of democracy and still other states that staunchly defended the sovereignty rights entrenched in the OAS Charter. Countries such as Bolivia, Brazil, and Mexico were more tolerant of Fujimori's actions.[16] Among OECD countries, Germany and Spain were particularly vocal in their criticism of the Fujimori government. The European Union, of which they were members, announced that it would not negotiate any new programs or technical exchanges with Peru. Japan, Peru's second most important bilateral source of official development assistance, next to the United States, took a more cautious approach. It did not cut off its aid immediately or impose sanctions, opting instead to adopt a wait-and-see position and conditioning its own aid disbursement to that of the Inter-American Development Bank.[17]

Second, various regional governance organizations also responded critically. The Rio Group (Permanent Mechanism for Latin American Consultation and Political Concertation), a regional grouping formed in 1989 to provide a forum for Latin American countries without a U.S. presence, suspended Peru's membership.[18] The OAS, the region's principal multilateral governance institution since 1948, utilized a new mechanism that had been previously invoked only once: in the case of the military coup against President Jean-Bertrand Aristide in Haiti—Resolution 1080.[19] Forged the previous year during its General Assembly in Santiago, Chile, the resolution gave the OAS a mechanism for automatic multilateral response to interruptions in democracy among member countries plus the authorization for its foreign ministers to adopt any measures deemed appropriate.

In a rapidly convened session, the OAS Permanent Council passed Resolution 579 in which it determined that Fujimori's actions did in fact constitute an interruption of the democratic order, "deplored" the events taking place, and accordingly invoked 1080 to call an emergency meeting of member country foreign ministers.[20] The foreign ministers' deliberations resulted in three high-level OAS fact-finding missions to Peru involving the secretary-general and the foreign minister of Uruguay and the decision to press the Fujimori government to restore democracy. A second ad hoc meeting of OAS foreign ministers was held in Nassau, Bahamas, six weeks after the coup. At that meeting on May 18, Fujimori announced that his government would hold elections in November 1992 for a Democratic Constitutional Congress (CCD) that would rewrite the Peruvian constitution as well as serve as the country's legislature until the next presidential elections in 1995. The OAS subsequently sent an observation mission to the Constitutional Congress elections.

A third form of inter-action involved international financial institutions (IFIs). The IFIs sent conflicting signals to Peru. On the one hand, the Inter-American Development Bank suspended new loans and the disbursement of existing loans to Peru. Carlos Boloña, Peru's minister of the economy, received a hostile reception by most IFIs and by Washington.[21] The plans to constitute a 12-country IMF support group for Peru was dropped under intense pressure from several of its members, including the United States, Germany, and Spain. On the other hand, the World Bank proceeded with a planned loan for Peru.[22]

Fourth, combined with the general deterioration of the human rights situation in the midst of the civil war between the government and Shining Path, the *autogolpe* was an important catalyst for linking the actions of civil society organizations in Peru with those of their counterparts abroad. In a manifestation of what Keck and Sikkink have called "the boomerang effect,"[23] Peruvian human rights activists who encountered hostility and repression from Fujimori authorities toward their grievances turned abroad to cultivate international support and protection for their struggle. Human rights organizations such as the Washington Office on Latin America, Americas Watch, and Amnesty International channeled support to the Peruvian umbrella organization National Human Rights (CNDDHH) in its struggles to defend human rights and democracy in the extremely difficult context of a state of emergency.[24] These links were used to ferry information about human rights abuses from Peru to government and public audiences in the United States.[25] The links were not only with foreign civil society organizations; the CNDDHH communicated regularly with foreign diplomats in Lima and frequently sent delegates to the United Nations and OAS. In 1994, the coordinator had the symbolic distinction of receiving the first high-level Clinton administration delegation to visit Peru even before meeting with the Fujimori government.[26] In contrast to their relative absence during 1977–1980 period, coordinated, cross-border civil society actions began to take on significance around the time of the *autogolpe* in 1992.

Finally, the *autogolpe* episode illustrates not only domestic-international links but also the importance of the inter-action between and among external actors. In setting the OAS's course of action, debates raged among countries such as the United States who were in favor of a strong response to the Peruvian crisis and those such as Mexico or Brazil that favored restraint or defended the sovereign rights of self-determination and non-intervention. The OAS's position was inconsistent. For example, while the Inter-American Commission on Human Rights issued a special report that was strongly critical of the Fujimori government, the OAS's special envoy to Peru, Uruguay's foreign minister, Héctor Gros Espiell, publicly criticized the commission's report for telling half-truths and failing to document human rights abuses committed by insurgents, reporting in a way that seemingly justified Fujimori's self-coup. In turn, Americas Watch criticized Gros Espiell for making little effort to foster dialogue between Fujimori and the democratic opposition to the self-coup despite claims by Gros Espiell to the contrary.[27] Efforts to achieve consensus on an OAS course of action were also complicated by the diplomatic skill of Peru's permanent representative, Luis Marchand.[28] As hinted above, in other forums such as the IMF and its support group for Peru, similar confrontations over institutional response occurred between the United States, Germany, and Spain on one side and Japan on the other. State–civil society relations in foreign countries also took on growing significance, as in the case of the lobbying efforts of American non-governmental organizations vis-à-vis the U.S. government, such as those of the Washington Office on Latin America and Americas Watch.

In virtually all the aforementioned cases, we see the very *direct* nature of interactions between domestic and foreign actors: between the actions of the Peruvian government and the reactions of the international community, in the coordinated efforts of emerging transnational civil society networks, and in the often heated diplomatic exchanges within international organizations. The directness of inter-actions following the *autogolpe* stands in contradistinction to the more indirect relations among internal and external developments that influenced the Peruvian transition from authoritarian rule from 1977–1980.

Given the immense popularity of Fujimori's measures, exogenous actions largely explain his decision to restore some form of democracy in the country. Opposition within Peru to the coup was restricted to a narrow stratum of politicians, intellectuals, journalists, and human rights activists. In other words, Fujimori was opposed by many within the country's intelligentsia, a relatively small group in terms of population. Politicians for their part were widely despised among the wider population. Indeed, in his own particular brand of neo-populism, Fujimori scored a lot of political capital among Peruvians by public attacks on the alleged corruption and immorality of the "political class": elected officials, established political parties, judges, and trade unions.[29]

The combined weight of international pressures thus accounts largely for Fujimori's announcement before the OAS to hold elections for a Democratic Constitutional Congress that would rewrite the constitution and serve as the country's legislature until the next national elections in

1995. Fujimori's decision raises the question as to what type of leverage was exercised by international actors to compel Fujimori to back down, given the popularity of the self-coup. In this case, Fujimori's loss of international legitimacy in terms of world opinion was not an effective form of leverage. Rather, it was Peru's economic recovery and international reintegration following García's disastrous presidency that were threatened by the removal of economic assistance from the United States, Japan, the IMF, the IDB, and the European Union, which induced Fujimori to back down.[30] The loss of external economic support would also have undoubtedly put Fujimori's support among business elites in jeopardy and the negative effects on economic recovery would have eventually eroded his popular support.[31]

While the responses of the international community obliged Fujimori to restore some semblance of democracy, they failed to restore the "democratic status quo ante." In fact, from start to finish Fujimori's forces controlled the entire process of rewriting the constitution and restoring Congress. From declaring the coup on April 5 to issuing the election decree for the CCD on August 20 to holding elections for CCD delegates on November 22 to crafting the new constitution, Fujimori and allies manipulated the entire process for their own ends. Indeed, Peru's established political parties boycotted the elections in protest. The Fujimori government's electoral engineering met with little serious external resistance from the United States, OAS, or other parties. In fact, by sending election monitoring teams to observe the November vote, the OAS and the United States inadvertently gave their seal of approval to an electoral process that on the outside appeared fair and transparent but had been designed to exclude Peru's mainstream political parties. The Fujimori government emerged more powerful and consolidated than prior to the coup. It purged the courts of judges sympathetic to the opposition. Through the elections for the Democratic Constitutional Congress, it won control of the legislature and in the process severely weakened mainstream political parties. Finally, the new constitution permitted presidential reelection, strengthened executive powers, introduced the death penalty, and removed previous constitutional commitments to free elementary education, job security, and labor rights.

In sum, while domestic-international inter-actions altered the course of events following the self-coup, internal forces were still strong enough to steer the direction of political change in an advantageous direction. In the end, the inter-actions lacked a *sustained* impact. Again, inter-action leverage analysis is insightful. A number of factors weakened external leverage over Fujimori's actions. Though quite strong, international reactions to the *autogolpe* could have been even stronger had it not been for the aforementioned divisions among various external agents. There was also some reluctance to make international responses that were extreme because of the popularity and therefore popular sovereignty behind Fujimori's measures. The self-coup situation lacked the combined weight of international and domestic resistance pushing in the same direction. Finally, from an international diplomacy standpoint, though member states in the OAS were prepared to apply pressure on Fujimori to a point, sustained action was impeded by a reluctance to interfere in activities such as the rewriting of the constitution, that were clearly the dominion of the Peruvians themselves.

In terms of their impact, the self-coup also revealed that the arrows of influence in internal–external inter-actions point both ways. That is, in Gourevitch's sense of the "second-image reversed," not only did international actors affect the political process in Peru but also vice versa.[32] This two-way effect is most clearly evident in the case of changes in U.S. foreign policy toward Peru. Largely as a result of the coup, the United States made democracy and human rights central to its relations with Peru. Moreover, until 1992, U.S. democracy assistance had been channeled primarily to Peruvian state institutions. Throughout the rest of the decade, that aid was redirected mainly to Peruvian civil society organizations, many of which were opposed to the Fujimori government. In order to avoid accusations of foreign intervention in Peru's affairs, U.S. democracy assistance was also delivered indirectly through American NGOs to their Peruvian partner organizations.[33] Additionally, whether looking at the United States, the OAS, the EU, or the IFIs, the *autogolpe* reinforced a growing international trend toward political conditionality. Specifically, foreign economic assistance was increasingly linked to a country's democracy and human rights performance.[34]

The OAS's efficacy in defending democracy was also suspect in 1995. During Peru's national elections that year, the OAS electoral monitoring mission, officially invited by the Fujimori government, failed to account for the conspicuous disappearance of some 600,000 ballots. Furthermore, its final report appeared only several months after the elections were over, long after its findings could have had any significant impact on revealing shady processes and addressing the problems.[35] The 1995 legislative elections, which gave a majority to Fujimori's *Cambio 90/Nueva Mayoría*, were also highly suspect, with some 40 percent of the ballots being annulled. Although an OAS observation mission had been on hand, it failed first to register and then to question the invalid ballots issue.[36]

Having managed to get away with a self-coup, the rewriting of the constitution, and manipulating elections, Fujimori and his sinister security chief, Vladimiro Montesinos, undoubtedly calculated that their next equally daring move, to run for an unconstitutional third term of office, could successfully weather any opposition from the inter-American system. In fact, international resistance to Fujimori's reelection efforts, apart from the protest staged by a group of international human rights organizations working in solidarity with their Peruvian counterparts, was minimal. In August 1996, the Peruvian Congress passed the Authentic Interpretation Law that provided a questionable interpretation of the constitution in favor of Fujimori's right to run again for president. In 1997, no international action was taken when Fujimori dismissed three constitutional tribunal judges who had ruled his reelection bid unconstitutional according to the very same constitution that had been rewritten by his supporters.

The unconstitutional reelection project was only the tip of the iceberg in terms of the Fujimori government's authoritarian redesign of Peru's political system. The separation of powers was effectively undermined by the creation of executive commissions answerable directly to the president, this was done in order to replace judges that had been dismissed during the 1992 self-coup. In what came to be dubbed an "infotatorship," Montesinos brought most of the Peruvian media under government control through bribery, blackmail, or coercion.[37] In July 1999, the Peruvian government formally withdrew Peru from the jurisdiction of the Inter-American Court of Human Rights in protest against a series of rulings that were critical of the country's continued use of secret and faceless military courts,[38] instead of civilian ones, in its alleged campaign against terrorism. Thus, when the OAS finally began to adopt measures to defend democracy in Peru during 2000, the country had long since descended into de facto authoritarian rule.[39]

Bending Club Multilateralism? The Stein Mission

During the spring of 2000, Fujimori's efforts to win an unprecedented third presidential term triggered a major political crisis.[40] After the first-round of elections on April 9 failed to produce a winner with more than 50 percent of the vote, the Fujimori government resorted to electoral irregularities in order to ensure his victory in the May 28 second-round election, prompting widespread indignation and resistance both within Peru and externally.

There were at least three important clusters of domestic-international inter-actions in the evolution of the crisis: the Stein mission and other forms of international monitoring during the first and second round of presidential elections; the crafting of Resolution 1753 at the OAS General Assembly in Windsor, Canada; and the insertion of an OAS High-Level Mission into Peruvian political life. Throughout these clusters, the combined weight of international pressure and domestic opposition both de-legitimized the Fujimori regime and constrained its scope for independent action. The latter clusters, which animated important instances of networked multilateralism, are explored in the next chapter. However, the Stein mission and international election observations merit treatment here as antecedents of significant transnational coalition building among state, inter-governmental, and non-state actors in the defense of democracy. Though not quite a developed form of networked multilateralism, the Stein mission as we shall see, had the effect at least of bending more traditional practices of club multilateralism.

The narrative of domestic-international, indeed transnational, electoral inter-actions begins well before the actual 2000 elections. In the context of the 1995 elections, the National Democratic Institute (NDI) helped found and strengthen Peru's most important pro-democracy civic organization, *Transparencia*. This included assisting *Transparencia* in the training of 9,000 volunteer observers as well as building its technical capacity for quick counts and media analysis.[41] In 2000, *Transparencia*'s quick count was the most widely accepted in Peru for its accuracy and reliability. It was pivotal in preventing sinister forces within the Peruvian government from manipulating the vote count to ensure a decisive first round victory for Fujimori.

The *Transparencia*-NDI network established during the mid-1990s ultimately served as the basis of an even larger informal transnational coalition of electoral observation organizations working in close unison to prevent electoral fraud in Peru in 2000. The enlarged network included the Office of the Peruvian Ombudsman (*Defensoría del Pueblo*), the Peace Council (*Consejo por la Paz*), opposition party observers, and electoral monitoring missions from the OAS and the European Union.

Ironically, the very same international observation organizations that would prove Fujimori's nemesis were originally extended an official invitation by his government to monitor the 2000 elections. The NDI-Carter Center mission and the OAS Electoral Observation Mission (MOE), from their arrival in November 1999 and March 2000 respectively, were a thorn in the side of Fujimori. Their numerous, regular preelectoral mission reports consistently criticized the Fujimori government for a political climate and electoral conditions that were far from free and fair. Significantly, these missions were deliberately outspoken and high profile, drawing domestic and international media attention to Peru's electoral transgressions.

In the case of the OAS-MOE led by former Guatemalan foreign minister Eduardo Stein, it adopted an "*active* observation stance" that was unprecedented for UPD electoral missions.[42] In short sequence, however, we see the OAS adopting an equally critical position during its observation mission to the May 21, 2000 legislative elections in Haiti.[43] Together, these two monitoring missions suggest a new willingness on the part of the OAS, certainly of its secretary-general, to expand an external validation power of the organization, even with the knowledge that this new approach would invariably trigger controversy among member states. In conjunction with their Peruvian partner organizations, the Stein mission as well as other international monitoring groups helped dramatically erode voter confidence in the elections and, by extension, the very credibility of the Fujimori government.

In the immediate aftermath of the first round of the April 9 elections, this loose transnational network effectively prevented Fujimori and his associates from padding his share of votes to ensure a decisive first round victory. Peru's government-controlled National Office of Electoral Processes (ONPE) suspiciously took four days to officially announce the results, evoking strong public criticism from Stein. The delays prompted Stein to comment in a press conference that "something very sinister is happening." Mysteriously, the ONPE closed its computing centers on the morning of Monday, April 9, offering the explanation that its staff had worked until 3 am the night before and needed rest. Stein demanded to know what the ONPE was doing until so late at night when according to the ONPE on Monday morning most processing centers had still not received the official vote counts (*actas*) from the voting centers.[44] Stein's OAS mission, NDI/Carter team, and the Europeans insisted that *Transparencia*'s quick count, which calculated that Fujimori had earned 48.73 percent of the vote, signaled that a run-off election must be held.

During the painstaking waiting period for the ONPE's official tally, Secretary of State Madeleine K. Albright, White House spokesperson Joe Lockhart, officials from the U.S. House of Representatives and the European Union added their voices to the legion of those calling for a second round of elections between Fujimori and runner-up presidential candidate Alejandro Toledo.[45] In Lima, external pressures coincided with mass demonstrations led by Toledo and other losing presidential candidates. Undoubtedly as a result of intense and inescapable domestic and international pressure, the ONPE finally conceded on April 12 that Fujimori had not succeeded in garnering the necessary 50 percent plus one of the votes and that a second round of elections was therefore necessary.

The Fujimori government again felt concerted transnational pressure prior to the run-off election on May 28. Virtually all independent election observers both domestic and foreign, as well as Toledo with observers from his party *Perú Posible*, demanded that the ONPE and the Peruvian government adopt reforms to ensure the fairness and transparency of the run-off election. However, the date set for the election by the National Electoral Tribunal (*Jurado Nacional Electoral*), May 28, provided insufficient time for opposition and observer concerns to be addressed satisfactorily by the ONPE. Eduardo Stein, the observer missions, their Peruvian partners, and the Toledo team, led a movement with U.S. government support to postpone the elections, a movement that was ultimately unsuccessful. On May 18, Toledo officially withdrew in protest from the elections. Making good on their own threats to withdraw if reforms were not implemented, on May 25 the OAS-MOE, the NDI-Carter and European Union missions, *Transparencia*, and the National Ombudsman's Office announced the termination of their monitoring activities.

Capturing their collectively held sentiments, the Stein mission issued a bulletin for wide release in which it stated that "according to international standards, the Peruvian electoral process is far from being considered free and fair."[46] While the efforts of Stein and the transnational observation network failed to delay the election, Fujimori's democratic credentials were severely damaged both at home and abroad.

Fujimori's uncontested electoral victory sparked mass demonstrations in Lima and across the country, most notably in the Plaza San Martín and in the high profile July 28 March of the *Cuatro Suyos*. It also triggered a flurry of diplomatic activity, first in Washington, DC, and then at the OAS General Assembly in Windsor.[47] Interestingly, not only were the main actors multinational but—thanks to the diplomatic struggles in Washington, DC, and Windsor—so too was the terrain of conflict. Beginning at Windsor, the fate of Peru no longer solely relied on what happened within that country's borders. The Fujimori government found itself battling on two fronts: at home in Peru against domestic opposition and abroad in Washington, at the OAS Permanent Council, and then the General Assembly.

As we shall see in the next chapter, in response to the discredited May 28 runoff, the OAS convened a special session of its Permanent Council on May 31. The Stein mission served as the basis for discussions on what course of action the OAS should take.[48] Stein stirred controversy on whether he had overstepped the mission's mandate in his actions. On the one side, the defenders of absolute sovereignty in the Permanent Council charged that Stein had interfered in the internal affairs of a member state. On the other side, Stein could claim that he was simply following the UPD election observation manual to the letter. Moreover, it appears that Stein was receiving at least some positive signals from Secretary-General Gaviria in pursuing his "*active* observation stance." In retrospect, the Stein mission signaled that the OAS had opened up a more critical line of pro-democracy activism that belied conventional perceptions of OAS inertia and ineffectiveness.

Defending Democracy in Peru: Progress or Setbacks?

During the 1990s, the OAS began to test some of its new diplomatic tools for defending and promoting democracy. Peru was certainly not the only site for OAS pro-democracy intervention but it does reveal clearly the challenges presented by the ongoing tension between the more established club-style multilateralism and nascent forms of networked multilateralism. In declaratory terms, the OAS put forward a strong voice for the promotion of democracy. As Peru illustrates, however, in operational terms efforts to mount responses to the 1992 *autogolpe* and to the undermining of democracy by Fujimori over the course of the decade had to run through the filter of existing OAS multilateral practices often inimical to decisive action.

The Peru experience underscored two critical shortcomings in the OAS democratic solidarity paradigm. First, though the OAS invoked Resolution 1080 rapidly in the coup context of April 1992, it appears to have been largely ineffective in the face of the numerous forms of authoritarian backsliding that occurred in the country. Peru pioneered the self-coup as the most blatant form of anti-democratic regression but the rest of the decade represented a slower but systematic erosion of democracy by an elected incumbent government, during which the OAS effectively stood by and watched helplessly without the authority, determination, or tools to intervene effectively.

Secondly, the official manipulation of elections in 1992 and 1995 put the credibility of the OAS's external validation of election processes in doubt. Indeed, the OAS's electoral observation shortcomings helped legitimize a democratically suspect Fujimori government. Fortunately, in the April and May 2000 presidential elections, the Stein mission proved that the OAS had the ability to de-legitimize the government of a member state for electoral fraud too. In doing so, Stein seriously challenged one of the fundamental tenets of club multilateralism, that is to say, executive sovereignty. As we see in the next chapter, only some timely, dramatic diplomatic innovations together with combined pressure from without and within, what we call networked multilateralism, could defend democracy decisively.

CHAPTER FOUR

Networked Multilateralism in Action: The OAS and the 2000 Crisis in Peru

The active involvement of the OAS in the successful resolution of the 2000 political crisis in Peru highlights its evolution from club to networked multilateralism. In spite of the signs of progress toward a democratic solidarity paradigm, up to the Peru crisis it was the organizational limitations of the OAS, rather than its strengths, that continued to dominate attention. Mirroring the contested nature of foreign policy principles found more generally in the region, tension has remained extant between the advocates of pro-democracy collective interventions and defenders of the foundations concerning non-intervention.[1] Therefore, in operational terms, OAS actions to defend and strengthen democracy remained reactive and incomplete. The walls of state sovereignty remained tough to penetrate.

These institutional deficiencies cast a long and imposing shadow over the intervention of the OAS in the 2000 Peru crisis caused by President Alberto Fujimori's efforts to win an unprecedented third term of office. While the Peruvian crisis offered an excellent opportunity to extend democratic values through regional governance institutions, a number of serious constraints had to be overcome. From an historical perspective, the OAS had to struggle with the stigma associated with past failure (mentioned in the previous chapter). Renewed political crisis in Peru during 2000 presented the OAS with a form of moral hazard: another weak or ineffective collective intervention akin to the 1992 debacle might undermine its credibility and encourage future anti-democrats in the region.

From a situational perspective, the OAS had to make an assessment of a crisis whose nature fell in between well-defined categories of action.

Unlike the other cases in which the OAS had intervened under Resolution 1080, Peru did not witness an explicit interruption of democracy, nor did the regime suffer an ultimate loss of authority. As noted, the May 28, 2000 presidential elections failed to meet what Dr. Eduardo Stein, the head of the OAS electoral observation mission to Peru, termed "the minimal international standards of a free and fair election."[2] Yet, even this language of condemnation was highly nuanced. While Stein and the OAS observation team found the elections to be full of irregularities they did not come out and say they were explicitly fraudulent. Indeed a good deal of its criticism centered on technical questions relating to a problematic election software program or much wider issues pertaining to Fujimori's abuse of the news media and state resources in order to ensure his re-election.

From a collective action perspective, the OAS had to try to put a consensus together on measures that were highly contentious. The champions of the democratic solidarity paradigm demonstrated a robustness that was at odds with the norms of behavior within the hemispheric community. These actors were also highly innovative in the embrace of networked multilateralism. Even if ascendant, however, these forces of change were far from dominant. The hold of the older habits of club multilateralism remained strong in its resistance to explicit forms of intervention. In conceptual terms, there was no universally accepted definition of democracy in the inter-American system. Even within the relatively narrow confines of representative democracy, based on free and fair elections, there was no consensus as to what was an acceptable model.

These obstacles in tandem meant that any bid to launch an initiative targeting the 2000 Peru crisis constituted an enormous test of organizational will and capacity. The initiative would have to be action-oriented enough to gain the confidence—if not the active participation—of those who perceived the OAS as a talk-but-no-action type of organization. It would have to make clear what objectives could (and could not) be achieved based on a clear assessment of problems and potential outcomes. Moreover, getting any initiative off the ground would entail cutting through or circumventing the established mechanisms contained within the institutional makeup of the OAS. Any form of engagement that mattered would entail both compromise and controversy.

Under these circumstances, the fact that the OAS put together an initiative that made a difference in the 2000 Peru crisis is highly impressive. Although facing enormous constraints along the way, the OAS put together a highly effective and sustained mission to Peru. The OAS intervened in this crisis of democracy not via its standard repertoire of activities but rather in a highly flexible and persistent manner. Detours were made to circumvent institutional blockages and political impasses. The initiative blurred the lines between the internal affairs of a sovereign state and multilateral involvement. Although in principle sensitive to the doctrine of non-intervention, the initiative resulted in significant mission creep that contained a high degree of intrusiveness in the domestic affairs of a member state of the inter-American system. Diplomacy mixed with policymaking. Over the course of August to November 2000, the OAS mission became thoroughly lodged in Peruvian political life and within the hard shell of state sovereignty, enmeshed and intertwined with the hitherto polarized forces of the country's government, elected opposition, and civil society within a dysfunctional political-institutional environment.

For all of this apparent success, nevertheless, the achievements of this OAS initiative should not be over-blown. The Peru initiative as an expression of networked multilateralism remains highly case specific, not only in terms of the constellation of pro-democracy forces that served as its trigger but also the personalities and shocks related to the episode. Ad hocism, not grand strategy, created and reshaped its design. At the same time, the potential of the Peru initiative to serve as a model for future pro-democracy activity should not be underestimated. If a "Peruvian model" exists, what it illustrates is the blend of seemingly contradictory ingredients that facilitate (albeit not ensure) success for networked multilateral diplomatic interventions. Consistency of purpose needs to be offset by tactical improvisation. Risk taking on the part of key individuals must blend with a team approach. Rapid response is vital but so is painstaking technical work. The role of the helpful fixer at the inter-state level must mix with an emphasis on getting deeply polarized forces to buy into the process at the intra-state level. The equity of a high degree of inclusiveness in terms of participation needs to be balanced by the efficiency of working with small numbers.

The Catalytic Stage

In chronological/functional terms, the OAS initiative on Peru encompasses three distinct phases: catalytic, mission creep, and consolidation. The first stage corresponded to the initial response of the OAS to reports of electoral irregularities during May and June 2000. It began with the pull-out of the OAS electoral observation mission led by Dr. Stein and culminated in the passing of Resolution 1753 at the OAS General Assembly in Windsor. Pressure built up both within the inter-American system and among a wide constellation of Peruvian domestic forces for immediate action to punish the Fujimori government.

However, before any initiatives on Peru could be mobilized, the coalition within the OAS in favor of collective action had to contend with entrenched opposition to an interventionist approach. The main source of externally directed opposition centered on a concern with sovereignty and non-intervention. Consistent with their traditional set of concerns, this attitude was most evident in the resistance from Brazil and Mexico. Both countries sent out clear signals through the pre-mission phase that the Peruvian situation did not justify the application of Resolution 1080. Mexico remained adamant that, considering the merits of the case, invoking 1080 in the Peruvian crisis was inappropriate. Underscored by the public statements of its OAS ambassador, Claude Heller, Mexico's stance was that 1080 could only be triggered in the aftermath of a coup d'état, a situation clearly not present in Peru. In classic club form, Mexico further argued that strict delimitations of parameters for external intervention were necessary. Whatever the situation, the conduct of elections remained an exclusively domestic matter. In the words of Heller, the OAS "at no time should be a substitute for the functions which correspond to state institutions."[3] Moreover, Mexico insisted that if any OAS intervention were launched it would require a formal invitation from the Peruvian government.

Brazil expressed its support for the status quo both in words and action. Brazil's president, Fernando Henrique Cardoso, the then senior democratically elected leader in South America, echoed Mexico's stance that "the people of Peru took the decision."[4] Instrumentally, Brazil lent its considerable weight to the campaign to shelve the 1080 scenario. Symbolically, Brazil went out of its way to buttress the legitimacy of the Fujimori government. Indeed Brazil ended up as one of the only three countries officially represented at Fujimori's inauguration.

The entrenched doctrine of some members of the OAS club was compounded by the opportunism of others. Various members of the inter-American system dug in their heels on 1080 out of fear that they might become the next targets of intervention. The Chávez government stands out as the most explicit representative of this category of countries, with the foreign minister of Venezuela, José Vicente Rangel, voicing "deep concerns" that "a precedent [would be] established through the OAS involvement in Peru's affairs."[5] This negative sense of solidarity permeated through the ranks of the resisters. Brazil remained acutely apprehensive that a Peru initiative might establish a precedent for future collective interventions into its own domestic affairs, namely the human rights and environmental domains. Mexico faced the prospect of international criticism in its own forthcoming July 2, 2000 general election. The OAS's determination to solve the crisis in Peru therefore was perceived by some member states as holding considerable potential for a contagion effect in other parts of the Americas.

Still other countries simply went along with what they considered to be a fait accompli. Fully aware of the differences between the ambiguous conditions underscoring the Peru case and an explicit military coup, Chile became the most obvious example of a country adopting this position. In doing so, it attempted to direct attention away from the immediate crisis toward building democratic foundations that would work in the long-term. While acknowledging the need for the strengthening of "democratic and electoral systems" in the hemisphere, the Chilean foreign minister made it clear that he was operating on the premise that the Fujimori government "is a reality."[6]

The Fujimori government exploited all of these mixed motivations. In synch with the beliefs of the core resisters, the principle of sovereignty was evoked to explain and justify its actions during the entire electoral process. The Peruvian ambassador to the OAS, Beatriz Ramaciotti, declared that the "political" role of Dr. Stein and the OAS observation team constituted interference in the internal affairs of her country.[7] Fernando de Trazegnies, Peru's foreign minister, held this hard-line up to and through the time of the Windsor General Assembly meeting in early June. Arguing that other countries had no right to pass judgment on the election, de Trazegnies said it was not possible "to declare the Peruvian elections void from abroad. We are an independent country."[8]

The Peruvian government made an even more basic appeal to the pragmatists. Casting aside principle, the argument was made that the demise of the Fujimori government would mean chaos. Economically, the choice was painted as one between the stability achieved during the 1990s and a return to disastrous populist policies of the type implemented during Alan García's presidency. Politically, a number of worst-case scenarios were laid out including military coups, mutiny, and civil war.

This set of resistant forces provided a formidable barrier to organizing any bold OAS initiative. Overcoming these obstacles put a heavy reliance on diplomatic skill as opposed to pure muscle power. With the long-standing culture of consensus within the OAS still firmly in place, collective action proponents needed to accommodate the resisters rather than directly challenge and overpower them. Any mission that was based on idealistic precepts remained a nonstarter. Lastly, OAS mission advocates needed to get Peru on board if they had any hopes of achieving the consensus they required.

Here it is important to mention the actors that pushed for an OAS multilateral initiative. The United States responded to the crisis by becoming a key engineer for change. Moving out front, the United States attempted to build a pro-democracy coalition to punish the Fujimori government for its behavior surrounding the May 28 run-off election. At a special session of the OAS Permanent Council, called to discuss the Peru situation on May 31, 2000, the U.S. permanent representative to the OAS, Luis Lauredo, pushed for collective action based on the 1080 model to be taken against Peru. Lauredo's main point was that Peruvian authorities had gone ahead with the second round in the presidential vote "without addressing the well-documented concerns" of international observers from the OAS and other external organizations or reputable Peruvian organizations such as *Transparencia*.[9]

Despite its position as the dominant actor in the hemisphere, the United States could not impose its will on others in this case. It possessed too much baggage from its own unilateralist forays in the past to act as an effective catalyst for collective action. Try as it might, the United States could rally little by way of support for this campaign. When put to the test, only Costa Rica was willing to back the move to invoke Resolution 1080 in the Peruvian case.

Although the ability of the OAS for action was severely constrained, any retreat toward a do-nothing stance was unacceptable. Letting the Fujimori government completely off the hook would seriously damage the reputation of the OAS in the run-up to the Windsor OAS General Assembly and a 2001 Summit of the Americas in which democracy was to be a major theme. Moreover, from an operational point of view the OAS possessed a number of strengths that allowed it to construct a tangible if not entirely coherent fall-back strategy to engage the crisis in Peru. Although at odds with its standard repertoire, the improvised result demonstrated its determination to act collectively in the defense of democracy.

One advantage possessed by the pro-intervention advocates in the OAS was the indirect association of the initiative with the United States. As clearly shown by its failure to implement Resolution 1080, the United States could not determine the course of action adopted by the OAS. But the prominent position of the United States in the ranks of the pro-democracy countries was vital to the bargaining process among foreign ministers at the Windsor OAS General Assembly. By raising the bar for action, space was created for a fall back option by which a mechanism could be established for an inter-American dialogue on Peru. U.S. officials moved publicly to suggest that this option was just as good a mechanism to deal with the crisis as Resolution 1080.

These second thoughts about its tough line on Peru reflected a wider dilemma for the United States. From a foreign policy perspective, this approach risked facing a concerted backlash from Latin American countries closing ranks against external interference. From a bureaucratic perspective, it exposed the divisions within the U.S. domestic policy community. The State Department remained adamant that some action needed to be taken while other key players in the intelligence/defense community took a far more ambivalent stance. Concerns about an overly ambitious pro-democracy agenda were balanced against a sense of appreciation of the Fujimori government for its effective support in the war against terrorism and drugs in Latin America.

This softening did not mean a complete retreat in that the United States demonstrated its continuing will to do something in response to the Peru crisis by sending a high-level delegation to Windsor. In attendance along with Lauredo were Thomas Pickering, the undersecretary of State, Arturo Valenzuela from the National Security Council (NSC), and Peter Romero, acting assistant secretary, Bureau of Western Hemispheric Affairs at the State Department. This display was in itself enough to provide the impetus for some sort of OAS initiative on Peru. On top of paying diplomatic attention the United States flexed its muscle. To the calls for Resolution 1080 were added more tangible threats of reductions or outright suspension of bilateral assistance.[10]

Another source of strength was the presence of other countries constituting a diverse but active pro-democracy lobby within the OAS. Most of these countries, such as Costa Rica, Guatemala, and some of the Caribbean island states such as Antigua and Barbuda, were too small to possess much diplomatic weight or capacity in their own right. On a selective basis, nonetheless, all of these countries could make a contribution to the process of a pre-mission mobilization. Costa Rica possessed the Oscar Arias reputational factor that set a standard of performance. The impressive ex–foreign minister from Guatemala, Dr. Stein, headed up the original OAS election observation team. Antigua, through the performance of its ambassador to the OAS, stood out as an articulate voice calling for the extension of democratic norms in the region.

A greater burden fell as expected on two middle powers, Argentina and Canada. Argentina's capacity for leadership on this issue was reduced by its domestic preoccupation with its political transition from the Menem to the de la Rúa presidency and its own mounting fiscal problems. Moreover, Argentina's foreign policy alignment with the United States in recent years did not endear it to its Latin American neighbors. Still, at least in declaratory terms, Argentina's expression of concern about the credibility of Fujimori's reelection was valuable in partially offsetting the forces of resistance. While rejecting any thought of sanctions, de la Rúa went on record that notice had to be taken of the wider implications of the voting irregularities: "What worries me most is what has gone on in this electoral process."[11]

Canada had a number of constraints on its role in promoting democracy in the hemisphere of the Americas. Canada as mentioned previously was a country that had traditionally kept the Americas off its mental map. Canada had joined the OAS only in 1990. More specifically, Canada had only a thin connection with Peru. Notwithstanding its expanding profile in the Peruvian mining sector, Canada's economic links were neither wide nor deep. Two-way trade between the two countries remained at only $400 million a year by 1998. Development assistance allowed Canada to forge important ties with Peruvian NGOs, but this link was still overshadowed by the contributions from the United States and Japan.

The dynamic behind Canada's heightened involvement in the Peru situation was mainly circumstantial. As the host of both the June 2000 OAS General Assembly in Windsor and the April 2001 Quebec City Summit of the Americas, Canada had a strong incentive to avoid another crisis of credibility for the OAS and the inter-American community. If not for the buildup of pressure contesting the results of the presidential election, Canada might have been content to maintain a more low-key role. With the call for action by both the pro-democracy camp inside the OAS and demonstrators outside on the streets of Windsor, Canada had little choice but to get involved as its organizational continuity and legitimacy was at stake.

Once engaged, however, Canada had an extensive range of attributes and skills to provide to the OAS.[12] In Lloyd Axworthy, Canada had both an activist and (in his capacity as chair of the OAS meeting) a well-positioned foreign minister. Its state officials had a well-deserved reputation for technical acumen and problem-solving ability. Most notably, Canada's ambassador to Peru at the time, Anthony Vincent, had played a significant role in trying to resolve the protracted 1996–1997 hostage crisis within the Japanese embassy in Lima.[13] As a key force behind the creation of the Unit for the Promotion of Democracy in the OAS, Canada had strong pro-democracy credentials. Its resistance to the Helms-Burton Act in 1996 earned it respect by demonstrating that it was capable of autonomous action vis-à-vis the United States.

A third source of strength was the OAS's own improved institutional capacity, particularly in reference to the secretariat. As noted, César Gaviria, the secretary-general of the OAS, did much to reform the practices of the organization.[14] Gaviria was more of a risk-taker than his predecessors. Rather than going along with the accepted ways of doing things, he was willing to test the limits of the possible for the OAS, specifically his own scope for action independent of the Permanent Council. The Peru case gave ample evidence of this trait, in that he allowed the UPD to move in a more politicized fashion with the OAS's electoral work becoming part of the public debate. Not only were Dr. Stein and his team prepared to be on the ground for a sustained period of time, three months, but Stein himself was given a large amount of autonomy. As previously mentioned, Stein could claim that his actions were in strict accordance with the guidelines set out in his UPD election mission manual.

Operating as a loose coalition, these activist forces had the appropriate mix of leverage, reputation, and organizational capacity to build some momentum toward achieving a result at Windsor. Although still kept within strict boundaries, space was created for some compromise acceptable to both sides of the contest. In the face of mounting domestic and international attention, the Peruvian government and its allies were prepared to demonstrate some flexibility in order to ease the pressure to strengthen its democratic institutions. What the resisters demanded, as a condition for a measure of accommodation in the details of the future architecture of Peruvian politics, was that the OAS unconditionally accept the Fujimori government as legitimate and allow it to stay in office for its five-year term.

Diplomatic leverage and skill on the part of a variety of actors in the inter-American community ensured that a deal would be struck which balanced collective action with a sense of consensus. Although careful not to wield its weight too crudely, the Clinton administration hinted openly during the Windsor OAS General Assembly that it was prepared to cut off some of its $128 million in military, antidrug, and humanitarian bilateral assistance to Peru as well as use its influence in the IMF and World Bank to do the same in the multilateral arena. Pickering made it clear at the conclusion of the meeting that his government's patience was running out with the Fujimori government's record of reform where "results have been less than promising."[15] Pickering warned that if the United States did not see more substantive changes it would resort to unilateral efforts to apply leverage.

Gaviria and the Canadians, working with a variety of other actors within the inter-American system, provided ingredients for a face-saving solution. Consistent with the embedded tenets of sovereignty and non-intervention, the 1080 solution was shelved. Alternatively, Resolution 1753 was introduced in which at the invitation of Peru, an OAS High-Level Mission to Peru consisting of Axworthy as chair of the General Assembly and Gaviria as secretary-general of the OAS was established. Developed out of protracted negotiation, the aims of the resolution carried a vague if open-ended air: "exploring, with the Government of Peru and other sectors of the political community, options and recommendations aimed at further strengthening democracy in that country." The resolution further instructed the mission to report to OAS foreign ministers "in order to allow for full consideration of its findings and recommendations and to initiate follow-up as appropriate."[16]

1080 allowed the OAS to intervene directly in the affairs of a member country, whereas 1753 operated only on a "voluntary" basis. Although pointing toward a firmer set of democratic institutions in the future, its mandate accepted to work within the confines of the May election results and the good offices of the Fujimori government. As revealed by the different spin put on the initiative by the foreign minister of Uruguay, Didier Operti, the key to the triggering of the OAS mission was its cooperative not intrusive quality: "We are not against Peru. We're responding to a request from a member for help."[17]

The representatives of the Fujimori government therefore were willing to bend but not break on their bottom line. Shifting from its absolute defense of the principles of sovereignty and non-intervention, the Fujimori government agreed to a measure of external scrutiny. What they worked hard to ensure were a number of concessions concerning the nature and parameters of the OAS mission. Instead of looking back at the events of the April/May election, the initiative would be exclusively forward looking. It also depended on a formal invitation by the Peruvian government, issued by foreign minister de Trazegnies on June 13, 2000. Foreign minister de Trazegnies summed up the new balance: "There was no fraud . . . but you are welcome [to] come and help us strengthen our democracy".[18] President Fujimori added in the same vein: "The objective of the OAS is to promote and consolidate representative democracy, respecting the principle of non-intervention."[19]

Because it did not reverse the results of the presidential election, Peruvian opposition parties and civil society with their international allies in attendance at Windsor criticized this compromise solution as a cosmetic gesture. These groups perceived the mission as a "sell out" that validated a fraudulent election. A June 6, 2000 press release from Peruvian human rights groups and Canadian churches was entitled: "Don't betray the Peruvian people."[20] Sofía Macher, the executive secretary of th Peruvian National Human Rights Coordinator (CNDDHH), reiterated this message in a number of public statements during the General Assembly meetings: "The ministers would be wrong if they think the most workable solution is to reach an agreement with Fujimori."[21]

What Resolution 1753 lacked in terms of disciplining the Peruvian government, however, it made up for in terms of a mission marked by subtlety and duration. Instead of having a map provided for by Resolution 1080, the OAS mission had to make it up as they went along. Although originally shaped to the contours of what was acceptable to the inter-American community as a whole, its mandate still allowed for a good deal of "mission creep," that is, the expansion of the OAS role in resolving Peru's political crisis beyond Gaviria's and Axworthy's initial consultative trip. One sign of its sense of commitment to the task came in the speed of delivery. Consistent with the notion of "just in time" diplomacy, the OAS mission was launched with little delay. Soon after the Windsor General Assembly, a pre-mission (made up of Peter Boehm, Canada's ambassador to the OAS and Fernando Jaramillo, Gaviria's chief of staff) was organized to go to Peru. By the end of June, Axworthy and Gaviria arrived in Lima to implement the OAS's High-Level Mission.

Mission Creep or Pushing the Limits

The second phase of the initiative contained a dramatic amount of mission creep. Pushing the limits, the OAS mission successfully extended and expanded its mandate. From the time the OAS mission arrived for its three-day visit, it revealed a willingness to insert itself directly (if unevenly) within multiple and highly sensitive areas of jurisdiction related to national policy and domestic politics. Although the question of new presidential elections continued to be avoided, this limitation was the only clear boundary on the mission. Following extensive consultation with Peruvian representatives from government, opposition, and civil society, Axworthy, Gaviria, and their advisers devised a list of 29 points for strengthening Peruvian democracy. The list was subdivided into five key areas for reform: judicial reform and strengthening the rule of law, freedom of expression and the press, electoral reform, congressional oversight and combating corruption, and civilian control over the intelligence service and military as well as the professionalization of the armed forces. The intention was that these 29 points would serve as the bases for a reform-oriented dialogue among Peru's political elites. Nonetheless, the OAS mission became convinced from the outset that while these measures were necessary they were not sufficient to lend credence to the exercise. Neither could the OAS mission be seen as the end rather than just the start of the process; as acknowledged by Axworthy, in one of the statements he provided to the media during the trip: "if we came in and did a quick hit and said [we've got freedom of the media etc.] and now we can go home well that would have been pretty cosmetic."[22]

To give authenticity to the mission, a number of ingredients had to be added to the mix. The process of reform needed to avoid the image of superficiality. Crucial to this goal was the inclusion of some form of schedule to ensure that results would be carried out. The emphasis here was on trying to work toward a set of detailed results within a set time frame, initially envisioned as two years. From the other side, the reform process was widened to encompass previous "no-go" areas. The initial meetings between Gaviria and Axworthy with President Fujimori sent a signal that the OAS mission was prepared to deal not only with the surface manifestations but also with the underlying causes of the democratic crisis in Peru. As encouraged by the opposition and civil society, this extension of the target of reform meant tackling the atmosphere of corruption and fear created by the relationship between the Fujimori government and the SIN intelligence apparatus run by Vladimiro Montesinos. As the OAS secretary-general noted in an interview during the mission: "[Peru] has to put a limit on what the intelligence services can do and put into better balance security and rights of individuals."[23]

Instead of acting as a detached one-off "fact finding" mission, as conducted in a number of crises in the past, the OAS mission also needed to become thoroughly embedded as a form of networked multilateralism in a process of negotiation within and between Peruvian state and society. This entrenched process of engagement took shape in part through a sense of institutionalization provided by the creation of a permanent OAS mission in Peru. The real claim to originality for this process, however, was made in the forum used to facilitate the actual negotiations. If there is one thing the OAS mission will be remembered for, it will be the creation of a Dialogue Roundtable or *Mesa de Diálogo* to allow a protracted and detailed conversation on the political future of Peru.

In its original form, the *mesa* was constituted with 18 members. On one side sat the OAS facilitator. Great pains were taken to underscore that the facilitator's role was completely impartial. That is, his sole function was to moderate and promote *mesa* dialogue and not to make any decisions. Decisions were the sole responsibility of Peruvians at the table. Around the second side sat four members representing the government. The third side was occupied by eight opposition party representatives. The fourth side was for four members from civil society and two special invitees. Discussion would always follow the same sequence: government representatives spoke first, followed by opposition parties and the civil society section. Decision-making at the *mesa* would be consensual, with votes reserved only for government and opposition party representatives. Although civil society members and special invitees had the right to speak at the *mesa*, they could not vote.

From an organizational perspective, one of the most interesting aspects about the *mesa* process was its pluralistic quality. The OAS supplied a small secretariat for the *mesa*. On the advice of Gaviria, the former foreign minister of the Dominican Republic, Dr. Eduardo Latorre, was appointed permanent secretary to the mission with chief responsibility for serving as "facilitator" of the *mesa*. Acutely sensitive to the possibility of accusations of foreign intervention being flung, Latorre shaped the low-key but effective style of this extended component of the OAS mission, allowing a dialogue to take place. Avoiding the temptation to rush or set expectations too high, Latorre got a very large (and antagonistic) cross-section of Peru's political elite to sit around the *mesa* and talk. While acknowledging significant differences among the participants, Latorre started with the task of establishing a timetable for the 29 points and then working toward these reforms on an item-by-item basis.

With respect to individual national contributions, the role of the United States remained deliberately understated. The idea that an American representative be at the table was quickly discarded. Instead a good deal of the work to launch (and to run) the OAS mission was taken on by Canada, as an extension of its chairmanship of the OAS General assembly. The Canadian ambassador to Peru, Graeme Clark, and his staff were instrumental in picking the venue for the *mesa* (the Hotel Real country club), in selecting the shape of the actual table (rectangle, not round), and in bringing together the constituent groups (government, opposition, and civil society). They also engaged in an extensive campaign of telephone diplomacy to ensure that the mutually hostile representatives of the increasingly embattled Fujimori government and key figures from the opposition and civil society would turn up at the first meeting of the *mesa* held on August 21, 2000. Sitting at Latorre's side at the *mesa*, Clark in effect became co-chair of the dialogue process.

The Fujimori government grudgingly accepted a position within the *mesa* process. What it withheld was the opportunity for the opposition to meet directly with government representatives. Rather than selecting ministers to sit at the *mesa* directly as members of the executive, the Fujimori government pursued an indirect form of representation. Ministers were appointed not as ministers per se but in their capacity as members of the so-called Presidential Commission for the Strengthening of Democratic Institutions (*Comisión Presidencial para el Fortalecimiento de las Instituciones Democráticas*). Such a formula, even with the later addition of a number of representatives from political parties within the government's congressional coalition, demonstrated the serious reservations that the Fujimori government had about the process.

The attitude of the opposition forces accentuated the problems. By looking into the future, with the expectation that the Fujimori government would rule Peru for another five-year term, the OAS was interpreted by all the opposition forces as propping up an illegitimate regime. This fixed attitude made it very difficult for them to engage seriously in the *mesa* process as it was put into operation. Although a variety of opposition representatives took part in the process, they did so with a combination of opportunism and suspicion. Not surprisingly, the coolest reception given to the *mesa* process within the opposition came from Alejandro Toledo and his *Perú Posible* political party. Deprived from winning the presidency, Toledo was in no mood to engage in a dialogue with the Fujimori government. Nor did he have much practical incentive to get involved. Before his boycott of the May 28 run-off election, Toledo was the dominant figure on the opposition side. Despite adverse conditions including being closed off from many of the media outlets, he had won 40 percent of the presidential vote in the first round. The other opposition candidates had in comparison polled only single digit support. Yet, the format of the *mesa* did not reward him for this performance. Given only one seat at the table, Toledo's political party was given parity with the representatives from seven other opposition political parties. Moreover, because of the government's indirect form of representation, Toledo did not even have the chance of confronting Fujimori man to man at the *mesa*.

Toledo did not want to isolate his party from the *mesa* completely but neither did he want to be seen to be buying into the OAS mission. The result was that he remained at the edge of the process, allowing other prominent members of *Perú Posible* to take the available seat, including the respected Congressman Luis Solari, without giving the *mesa* his own personal stamp of credibility. Toledo concentrated his own attention on trying to look presidential before international audiences and organizing massive pro-democracy rallies in the streets to protest the inauguration of Fujimori.

The question of extending the fabric of networked multilateralism via representation from civil society remained equally contentious. The OAS made a number of inspired choices in drawing up the list of special invitees to the *mesa*. One was the selection of the well-regarded National Ombudsman (*Defensor del Pueblo*), Dr. Jorge Santistevan de Noriega. Another was the choice of Monseñor Luis Bambarén, the president of the Peruvian Episcopal Conference, as the representative of the Roman Catholic Church in Peru. On a representative basis these picks certainly had their deficiencies. Santistevan represented with Sofía Macher, the executive-secretary of the National Human Rights Coordinator (CNDDHH), a highly visible and transnationalized human rights constituency. But it left other groups, including most of the indigenous population, without direct representation. Monseñor Bambarén, a Jesuit, was picked at the expense of other possibilities such as representatives of the conservative wing of the Roman Catholic Church (such as the Opus Dei) or the Protestant evangelical movement. Evaluated on the basis of their own merit as individuals, however, these two picks reinforced the credibility of the *mesa* process.

The other representatives of civil society were even more problematic. The choice of two representatives from the peak business and labor federations, the National Confederation of Private Enterprise Institutions (CONFIEB) and the General Confederation of Peruvian Workers (CGTP), introduced a top-down orientation to the process. Most significantly, the informal sector was not represented. The representation problem was accentuated by the refusal of *Transparencia*, the most respected pro-democracy NGO in the country, to take a seat at the *mesa*. The OAS high mission selected the controversial political personality, Francisco Diez Canseco, of the National Peace Council, to take *Transparencia*'s place. Together with the inclusion of Dr. Aurelio Loret de Mola from the *Somos Perú* Party (a vice president of Congress in 1992), Diez Canseco's presence gave considerable weight to selected individuals in the process.

Passing the Test of Consolidation

The third stage of the OAS's Peru initiative involved the consolidation of the *mesa*. Taking advantage of the expanding space available for its activities, the OAS mission became locked into the Peruvian political process. No longer having to justify its existence, the focus shifted to a more "routine" agenda. Although pressure tactics were still applied on a selective basis, the motor driving the OAS mission became increasingly the detailed work of the *mesa*.

During its initial meetings, it appeared as if the *mesa* began with a hopeless impasse between an intransigent government representation and the attendees from opposition parties and civil society. In fact, Fujimori and his security chief Montesinos attempted to divert attention away from the *mesa* on the date of its first meeting, August 21, 2000, by appearing on national television to announce that they had successfully dismantled an arms smuggling operation in Peru that had sold weapons to Colombian guerrillas. However, it would be misleading to suggest that the *mesa* remained completely immobilized. One sign of early progress came at the second meeting on August 25 when representation on the governmental side was opened up to include members from each of the three parties grouped in the Fujimori congressional coalition: (*Vamos Vecino, Nueva Mayoría*, and *Cambio 90*. This change broke the sense of disconnect between the negotiating process in the *mesa* and congressional politics. Another sign came with an agreement to divide the work of the *mesa* into smaller units through the establishment of four working groups. This move allowed both specialization and some degree of depoliticization to take place. Neither of these decisions though were indications of a major breakthrough.

It was only following a series of detonating events that ripped apart the landscape of Peruvian politics and society in late 2000 that the *mesa* became successful. The first of these shocks came on September 14 when the country witnessed a video broadcast on national television showing national security chief Vladimiro Montesinos bribing opposition congressman Alberto Kouri in exchange for joining Fujimori's congressional coalition, Peru 2000. This episode prompted Fujimori's announcement of new elections—eventually set for April 8, 2001 (he in effect renouncing power), the dismissal of Montesinos, and the deactivation of the National Security System (SIN). A second shock occurred toward the end of September when Montesinos sought asylum in Panama with support from the Peruvian government, Secretary-General Gaviria, and the U.S. government. This was followed by a third shock a month later when Montesinos returned suddenly to Peru on October 23, 2000 creating fear of an imminent coup d'état. The fourth shock came when Fujimori faxed his resignation to Congress on November 20, 2000 from Japan.

The *mesa* became increasingly prominent as a political forum with de facto political decision-making power as these shocks unfolded. In an institutional void caused by congressional deadlock, few other nonviolent choices existed. As events during September and October led increasingly to a showdown between Fujimori and Montesinos, the former began to display greater willingness to agree to political reforms in exchange for support from the OAS and the Peruvian political personas assembled at the *mesa*. For all of the suspicions harbored by the opposition, the *mesa* remained a useful fallback option and protective buffer against the threat of military disruption. Notwithstanding the lingering concerns about autonomy, it offered the crumbling government groupings a convenient escape route. However, the *mesa* was not just a receptacle. It also had a number of attributes that allowed it to take on a life of its own.

The events of late 2000 compelled the *mesa* to pass a number of further tests for its credibility. The most serious of these concerned the OAS's response to the issue of asylum for Montesinos. Worried about the possibility of a military coup, Gaviria, supported by the United States, took a narrow problem-solving stand on this question: viewing a soft-landing for Montesinos as an acceptable cost for breaking the imbroglio on democratic reform. Arturo Valenzuela, acting as the point person from the NSC, made a number of phone calls to the Panamanian government asking for asylum. On September 23, Gaviria himself wrote a letter to the Panamanian foreign minister, José Miguel Alemán, requesting that the government of Panama reconsider its initial reluctance to grant asylum for Montesinos.

This club-like pressure campaign elicited a fierce backlash from Peruvian civil society. Viewing the OAS as guilty of complicity in the escape by Montesinos from justice as well as of failing to consult with its Peruvian *mesa* partners—Sofía Macher from the CNDDHH together with José Risco of the National Workers Confederation walked away from the *mesa*. Also, the explanation that the OAS secretary-general was trying to assume a burden of responsibility that was in reality shared by a number of other countries (including some in the pro-democracy lobby) did not help appease this anger. Faced with a boycott from these two vocal champions of human rights in Peru, the *mesa* suspended operations for a short stretch of time. It was only after Axworthy went on public record to oppose the asylum plan that Macher and Risco were brought back to the table.

If this incident strained the internal coherence and commitment of the OAS, it pointed to the unanticipated advantages of maintaining a pluralistic form of leadership. Gaviria's stance represented the older club-oriented habits of the inter-American system. Wary of the mission creep found within the initiative, the resistant countries (most notably Brazil, Mexico, and Chile) could be reassured about the boundaries of intervention. Axworthy's position alternatively reassured Peruvian civil society about the level of networked multilateralism and self-scrutiny introduced into the mechanics of OAS decision-making.

A second and more protracted test came on the issue of whether there should be some connection between national reconciliation and amnesty. For many members of the opposition, any linkage of this type presented a deal-breaker. No leniency should be shown to those officials who had perpetrated abuses during the campaign against terrorism in the 1990s. Nor should any differentiation be made about degrees of guilt. Conversely, in the view of the representatives of the increasingly fragile Fujimori government, an amnesty law was the deal-maker. Unless the opposition agreed to this proposal, these forces threatened to completely stall the *mesa* process. Not only would further progress be stymied but a retaliatory form of backsliding would begin. Even those procedures previously agreed to at the *mesa* would be undone.

This deadlock was only broken on November 20 with the resignation of President Fujimori and the establishment of an interim government under Valentín Paniagua (a member of the *mesa* from the opposition Popular Action Party). This new government moved quickly to address issues relating to justice and human rights. A Commission of Pardons was established to review cases involving charges related to terrorist activity. A working group was established to consider setting up a Truth and Reconciliation Commission to address cases of forced disappearances, extrajudicial killings and torture since 1980—a proposal that was later acted on.

A Recipe for Success?

Much of the recipe for success came in the way the OAS balanced intrusiveness with sensitivity vis-à-vis the Peruvian domestic political culture. By moving inside the political system of one of its member states, the OAS mission opened itself to charges of meddling within the club. The extent of the intrusion attributed to the OAS mission, however, was lessened by its problem-solving approach. Facilitation through networked multilateralism did not mean mediation, never mind imposition. While nudging the government, opposition, and civil society forces forward in the struggle to seize opportunities for strengthening democracy, the OAS left the details to the Peruvians themselves.

A second ingredient in the *mesa*'s success involved the way that civil society was incorporated into the process. Civil society did not sit at the *mesa* as a complete equal; its representatives had a strong voice but no vote. Ultimately, it was the political class in Peru that made the decisions about democratic reforms. At the same time, however, the inclusion of civil society added a great deal of transparency and accountability to the process. This element made it difficult for face-saving deals to be implemented that reinforced the patterns of old not new multilateralism.

A third component of success in the OAS mission was the mixture of intensity and incrementalism. When quick decision-making became necessary, the OAS raised the bar. The result was sometimes a second best option, as in the case of the Windsor meeting. In other episodes, most notably on the asylum question, the actions of the OAS were deemed by many critics to be misjudged and ill-informed. If some of its actions were controversial, the OAS cannot be deemed to be irresolute. Throughout the Peru crisis, the OAS mission displayed remarkable determination. Working the corridors and phones, liaison efforts, and shuttle diplomacy were all used to push the process forward.

Moreover, the pluralism of leadership provided a great deal of flexibility to the project. Although the stamp of authority given by Gaviria and Axworthy was crucial to getting the initiative off the ground, substitutions were allowed. For example, the role of Canada's permanent representative to the OAS, Peter Boehm, was accentuated when Axworthy left politics in October 2000. Taking up from where the Canadian foreign minister had left, Boehm went with Gaviria and Gaviria's chief of staff, Fernando Jaramillo, on follow-up missions in September and October to ensure the stability of the *mesa* process. Meeting with Fujimori and the other key players, Boehm was elevated to the status of a key broker within the OAS effort to keep the democratic reforms on track.

In terms of the incremental side of the mission, pride of place goes to the quiet and patient style of the *mesa* process. By breaking the agenda of reform down into 29 points, a more workable approach was established. Instead of swallowing the OAS reform package as a whole, the Fujimori government digested select bits of the package over a period of time. A good illustration of this focused, step by step process came in the first few meetings of the *mesa*, when the government representatives themselves showed willingness to initiate action on the so-called Baruch Ivcher affair. Ivcher, of Israeli origin, was stripped of his nationality in 1997 in what was widely viewed as a pretext for taking over his television stations that had been critical of the government. Early on in the *mesa* process the announcement that Ivcher's nationality would be restored did not tackle the real crux of the issue (for it did not restore ownership of the television channels). But it did reveal that a process of bargaining had started. Specialized working groups consolidated this pattern of doing things. Although this mechanism did not deliver immediate results, it allowed discussion on an issue-specific basis. The working groups also did much to break up the polarized atmosphere of the *mesa* process. Instead of talking across the table at each other, members of the government, opposition, and civil society were divided up into smaller clusters wherein the atmosphere was more conducive for problem solving. In terms of resources, these working groups could bring in the expertise of technical advisors, such as the knowledgeable staff of *Transparencia* and a specialist from the Canadian embassy for planning electoral reforms. In terms of the incentive structure, the working groups were given a schedule to make recommendations to the *mesa* in their respective area.

Concluding the Initiative

On January 16, the *Mesa de Diálogo* was formally closed by Secretary-General Gaviria and Permanent Mission Head Dr. Latorre.[24] It managed to reach agreement on 16 of its agenda items for reform. Its concrete achievements in terms of strengthening democracy included: the deactivation of the SIN, reforms that ensured the independence of the Peruvian judiciary from governmental interference, the restoration of Baruch Ivcher's citizenship, and agreement on electoral reforms and the selection of new electoral authorities in order to guarantee transparent elections on April 8, 2001.

To point to the OAS mission to Peru as a success story of regional intervention and networked multilateralism is not to overlook its flaws. Without the guidance of an established design, or set mode of operation, the initiative relied on an improvised repertoire. This dynamic allowed innovation but also occasionally gave rise to awkwardness and enormous tensions.

In responding to the Peru crisis, the pro-intervention proponents in the OAS could test the limits but not entirely overcome the culture of caution, compromise, and consensus built into the inter-American system. While pushing on with its effort to strengthen Peruvian democracy, it found itself being pulled back by the accepted parameters of action. The original shape of the mission was conditioned by these cultural limitations. So was the decision of Gaviria and other actors to promote an exit strategy for Montesinos. The limitations of the *mesa* process are also obvious. Accountability and the inclusion of civil society in the process of networked multilateralism did not mean the privileging of an open-door diplomacy. Although frequently visible at the cutting edge, much of the details of the *mesa* process remained hidden from view. Even if it did open up more space for a variety of actors in the non-state domain, the architecture of the initiative was designed to promote efficiency and order, not equity of representation. To compensate for the closed nature of the *mesa*, some participants continued to grandstand in order to attract media attention. Excluded outsiders challenged the legitimacy of the process. Individuals with small electoral bases of support (such as Paniagua) were thrust into the spotlight at the expense of more established figures.

Finally, highlighting the achievements of the OAS High-Level Mission to Peru is not to lose sight of the persistent democratic consolidation challenges faced by Peru. That is, the approach taken in Peru, like previous OAS missions, once again fits under the rubric of "firefighting" rather than preventing democratic instability. The OAS High-Level Mission was officially terminated in February 2001, arguably before democracy had been permanently consolidated in Peru. Problems of social exclusion, political party fragmentation, corruption, national reconciliation, and a relatively weak civil society persist. While all these constitute domestic concerns, undoubtedly the UPD and the OAS, at Peru's invitation, could have played a much stronger, longer-term role in supporting the country's still fragile configuration of democratic actors and institutions. This is certainly a complementary step to the "Peru model" in strengthening the collective defense-of-democracy paradigm promoted by the OAS.

To signal these problems, though, is not to give them greater credence than they deserve. As a channel for the transition from the April/May 2000 presidential elections to the exit of Fujimori, the OAS High-Level Mission to Peru and its *Mesa de Diálogo* were indispensable. The *mesa* filled the institutional vacuum and solved the political impasse caused by the polarization of political forces in Peru following the May elections. It became the locus of real decision-making power during the final days of the Fujimori government and before the Peruvian opposition could win control of Congress and form an interim government. On the opposition side, it allowed space and opportunities for fragmented and alienated groupings to be reintegrated into institutionalized political life. On the government side, it provided an attractive route for the constellation of forces loosely coalesced around Fujimori to reinvent and relegitimate itself. Peru's political elites were motivated to work together on a problem-solving basis wherein the only alternatives were likely state repression, a coup d'état, or civil war.

As a model for future OAS missions[25] a number of lessons from the Peru initiative stand out. Notwithstanding all its obstacles, the initiative was a much-needed catch-up in diplomatic method in the Americas. Contrary to its traditional concern with territorial integrity, the OAS and the inter-American community made sovereignty the subject of bargaining. The Peru experience has furthered the gradual altering of the notion of sovereignty itself; territorial inviolability, non-intervention, and self-determination are rights enjoyed only by freely elected governments of the hemisphere.[26] Part and parcel with these changes, regional diplomacy and the domestic political process are no longer insulated from each other. The enduring credibility of this form of networked multilateralism rested not only on inter-state relations but also on how well it was able to coax the political system inside Peru.

What is more difficult to come to terms with is the exceptional quality of the Peru case. If the OAS took advantage of a learning curve from other initiatives, both in the context of regional experience and the wider maturation process after the end of the Cold War, structural determinants do not explain everything about the OAS mission. Situational contingencies played a vital role as well. The Peru crisis became a symbol of the state of democracy in the hemisphere. Diverse sources of agency came into play. The internal shocks opened up space for the salience and ongoing reshaping of the *mesa* process. OAS intervention complemented not contradicted the privileging of "made in Peru" solutions to the crisis.

CHAPTER FIVE

The Making of the Inter-American Democratic Charter: The Apex of Networked Multilateralism

The making of the Inter-American Democratic Charter elevated the level of OAS commitment to networked multilateralism. As initially brought to life within the OAS, the pattern of conducting affairs through multilateral means—or "deep organizing" principles[1]—developed according to set club rules. To balance the fear of U.S. interventions the norms of sovereignty and non-intervention were highlighted as defensive mechanisms.[2] To reinforce the notion of organizational equality, the institutional culture—or rules of conduct—that developed in the OAS accorded great weight to consensual decision-making. Both tenets reinforced the "top-down" state-centric nature of the architectural design. The OAS traditionally argued that as long as its decisions were made in an inter-governmental forum, it had a solid democratic legitimacy to speak for the inter-American system as a whole. Under this mantra, the OAS did not consider it necessary to question the closed nature of its decisional structures, or to think about the inclusion of civil society organizations in debates.

As witnessed by the evolution of the Inter-American Democratic Charter the pattern of new or networked multilateralism conflates with a much richer organizational dynamic. On the involvement of actors, this mode of multilateralism brought with it a sense of heightened participation of civil society—more specifically NGOs. By allowing greater access to forces that have been historically muted—if not entirely voiceless—it also extended in a dramatic fashion the "bottom-up" process already embedded in the OAS initiative on Peru.

In terms of intensity the contrast between club and networked multilateralism became even more pronounced in the making of the Inter-American Democratic Charter. Because of its concern with organizational maintenance, the diplomacy of the OAS injected historically a measured, slow-paced approach. Conversely, an essential component of the type of diplomacy propelling the Inter-American Democratic Charter is a "just in time" quality. Indeed this emphasis on speed is taken to be a necessary part of the search for a new diplomacy.[3] Club rules that allow a hesitant and opaque mode of decision-making, an obsession with consensus, and a willingness to settle for lowest denominator outcomes were subordinated to rapid (albeit sometimes erratic) moves as well as the search for ad hoc routes to deliver results on an extended list of subjects.

The normative character of the charter adds to the impression of new or networked multilateralism reaching beyond its previous limits within the hemisphere of the Americas. In addition to offering a synthesis of the existing legal instruments at the regional level, the Democratic charter marks a clear evolution of the nature of the commitment of the states included in the inter-American system to include the collective defense of democracy within the region.[4] In its Article 1, the charter solemnly affirms that "The people of the Americas have a right to democracy and their governments have an obligation to promote and defend it." Going well beyond the formal mechanisms traditionally associated with the operation of a democratic order, the new definition of democracy comprises a number of original references to human rights, poverty, and development. Finally, the charter institutionalizes the will of the American states to answer collectively in cases of "alteration" of the constitutional order vis-à-vis countries of the area, and to take the step of suspending non-democratic states from the ambit of activities within the inter-American system.[5]

Though Peru took the lead in promoting the initiative, the charter was not a solo run. Other secondary powers acted as willing followers through the enterprise, playing a variety of constructive—if selective—roles.[6] More dramatically, the societal orientation of this diplomatic initiative gradually shone through the process of negotiation. At odds with the closed operating style long privileged by the OAS, the transparency expanded through the negotiations dealing with the charter. In doing so, the charter process captured much of the complexity of state–society relationships deemed vital to the process of networked multilateralism.

Breaking away from the familiar constraints of the inter-American system, the Inter-American Democratic Charter stands out for the speed with which it was negotiated. Framed by a number of key events—the challenge and fall of the Fujimori government in Peru through 2000, the Quebec Summit in April 2001, through to the San José, Costa Rica OAS General Assembly meeting in June 2001, and eventually the Lima meeting in September 2001—the process sped forward at an impressive pace. Although at times it may be said to have complicated proceedings, the very intensity of the momentum that took the charter from initiation to conclusion in well under a year may be said to be a good part of its recipe for success.

Yet, for all of these connections between the Inter-American Democratic Charter and an ascendant form of complex[7] or networked multilateralism, the vision of diplomatic innovation and regional transformation should not be exaggerated. Even though much of the grip of the traditional club-like atmosphere of the OAS has been lifted, the emergence of the charter demonstrates that some of the residue of past habits remain. The multilateralism featured in the initiative of the charter—although reaching the apex of success for a new type of multilateralism—remains a mix of the old and the new.

This chapter elaborates on this theme by looking more closely at the in-between—or hybrid—status of the multilateralism showcased through the negotiating of the charter. Whereas one part of the character of the charter negotiations fits the criterion of emergent multilateralism, another part contradicts this impression. The initial burst of speed with which the initiative got off the ground ran up against both technical and bargaining imperatives. The diplomatic process benefited from agility in terms of response time and delivery on a bottom-up basis. But this re-jigging of leadership did not mean that the United States—or even an established middle power such as Canada—abdicated responsibility. Nor did the ability of NGOs to provide a check on the value of the ideas emanating from the negotiating process translate into a ceding of decision-making authority. While the NGOs were not only facilitated and legitimized but also accommodated, the mode of multilateralism featured on the Charter remained "a far cry from society centred multilateralism."[8]

The viewpoints of the NGOs were taken into account largely to offset state-based resistance. What is more, underlying tensions appeared between different constituencies within the NGO community, most notably between Northern- and Southern-based NGOs. This gap in turn reflected serious differences between delivery and outcome. What some groups treated as an opportunity to expand the normative basis for the advancement of democracy in the Americas, other groups criticized as a deeply flawed document.

The Initial Burst of Speed

In filling out the contours of how the Inter-American Democratic Charter was made, an initial burst of speed—or intensity—remained an essential ingredient. The speed involved in the take-off of the charter process can be captured in an extended chronology of the evolution of the charter. The initial call for a democratic charter came on December 11, 2000 in an address to the Peruvian Congress by the former UN Secretary-General Javier Pérez de Cuéllar, the new foreign minister and president of the Cabinet of Ministers in the transitional (Valentín Paniagua) government that took office subsequent to the fall of the Fujimori government.[9] There was a constitutional requirement for a presentation of a plan to Congress by the new government and Pérez de Cuéllar fulfilled this mandate by speaking of the need to expand and systematize the inter-American regime—and rules—for the promotion and defense of democracy. Diplomatically, the initiative received its first audience in February 2001, first through a presentation on February 2 at the OAS by Ambassador Manuel Rodríguez Cuadros,[10] the Peruvian permanent representative to that body, and subsequently on February 21 by Diego García Sayán, the Peruvian minister of justice, to an OAS-sponsored conference on multilateral/regional organizations and the defense and protection of democracy.[11]

Another stage moved the multilateral process from the presentation of a first draft at the OAS Summit Implementation Review Group (SIRG), to the first real debate on the proposal at another session of the SIRG held in Barbados, and then to its eventual perusal by heads of state/government at the April 2001 Quebec City Summit of the Americas.[12]

One sign that the old club-like mode of operation (and image) was changing involved the instructions included in the Summit Declaration from the heads of state/government to their foreign ministers that they adopt an Inter-American Democratic Charter at the forthcoming June 2001 meeting of the General Assembly of the OAS, although the full text of that charter was absent in their discussions at Quebec. The Peruvian delegation, led by Pérez de Cuéllar (who went instead of the transitional President Paniagua, because of travel restrictions on the head of government) did present a proposal for the charter.[13] But this proposal consisted of only a very preliminary draft. Therefore, obtaining a paragraph on the charter included in the Quebec Declaration in these circumstances was a major achievement in itself, in light of the cautious culture embedded in the inter-American system and the open-ended nature of the mandate.

A second feature of note was the way the negotiations at Quebec on the charter caught up and superseded the multilateral negotiations on a "democracy clause." The introduction of such a clause had proved a protracted affair, given the high stakes involved.[14] The focus of the clause on language such as "unconstitutional alteration," "interruption of the democratic order," and "insurmountable obstacle" to participation pointed toward a more robust regime of sanctions. Yet, faced with opposition from a number of member states, the clause adopted remained ambiguous on a number of counts after Quebec.[15] First of all, heads of state/government were obligated to consult only about interruptions of democracy. Secondly, the details about why, how, and in what order the clause was to be adopted was left unclear.

The rationale behind the urgency and the momentum with which the charter moved can be explained in a number of ways. For the Peruvians, in particular, the charter served two fundamental purposes. At one level it served as a means of "democratic reinsertion" into the inter-American community.[16] At another level it provided a more effective means by which collective action could move into the fuzzy (or disguised) areas between classic coups and anti-democratic actions by established governments. For the inter-American system as a whole, the charter provided a new and graduated means of problem solving in difficult cases such as the 2000 crisis in Peru and the imbroglio in Haiti where the secretary-general had had to resort to ad hoc measures. These mechanisms, however, put the onus on political rather than legal techniques—allowing consensus to take shape (or not) on a case specific basis.

As a triggering effect the notion that the charter was an idea whose time had come should not be underestimated. After all it evolved in a way that not only incorporated some aspects of the Democratic Clause, but also included suspension from the club at the top of the list of progressively tougher measures in response to "any unconstitutional alteration or interruption." It moved well beyond the formal mechanisms traditionally associated with the inter-American system by linking development and poverty with the problems associated with democratic consolidation.[17] The charter also made at least the declaratory acknowledgement concerning the importance of the promotion of a "democratic culture."[18]

A "Made in Peru" Document

The heavy Peru imprint on the Inter-American Democratic Charter came about through a combination of that country's own experience with the OAS and the pattern of networking built up by key Peruvians with international forces. As noted, the success of the OAS's application of its defense of democracy repertoire in the Peru episode was achieved neither instantly nor completely.[19] The OAS intervention in 2000 only came after the failure of Resolution 1080 as a response to Fujimori's earlier 1992 *autogolpe* or self-coup. Norm development at the declaratory level did not match the capacity for decisive action.

From a more instrumental perspective the OAS still lacked the necessary formal mechanisms to handle threats to democracy that did not take the shape of traditional coups. As showcased by the Peru case, democracy in the region remains primarily defined by free elections and an open competition between political parties. The OAS has found itself without the means—and the will—to intervene under conditions where there has been slippage from democratic norms, whether through the curtailment of basic rights such as the right of assembly and the right to freedom of expression, the suspension of the legislative capacity, the replacement of judges in the Supreme Court, and government by decree. As suggested by Robert Pastor, the OAS has found itself stymied in ambiguous situations, or gray zones, in which democracy is threatened but not to the extent of featuring a coup d'état.[20]

These insights into the limitations of the OAS mode of operation propelled key members of the Peruvian transitional government to take up the challenge of instituting the charter. In procedural terms, their motivation was to deliver the charter while the Peruvian crisis was still on the minds of the inter-American community (and while the Peruvians themselves retained a high degree of moral or normative authority).[21] In principled terms their priority was to use the charter to fill the gap—showcased by the backsliding of the Fujimori regime—of the OAS's defense of democracy paradigm. As Pérez de Cuéllar put it in his address to the Peruvian Congress in December 2000, the perceived need was for the charter to be the centerpiece of a new and effective set of rules within the OAS framework that would combine with the extant mechanisms and instruments used in the promotion of democracy.[22]

The Peruvian experience created the logic, pressure, and target for a "norms cascade" democratic to be directed through this Andean country.[23] The extensive international network built up through an impressive set of actors who eventually took up key roles in the post-Fujimori government acted as the conveyor belt for the delivery of the charter. The fundamental import of the quality and quantity found in these contacts was first signaled by the attendance of prominent Peruvian critics at the Windsor OAS General Assembly. An excellent example of this phenomenon was the presence of Diego García Sayán, not only an ascendant opposition politician in the struggle against the Fujimori regime but also a figure with extensive experience in NGOs and epistemic communities (as illustrated through his experience as executive director of the Andean Commission of Jurists, and in 1992 as director of the Human Rights Division of the United Nations Observer Mission in El Salvador (ONUSAL)). Another notable example featured the role of Sofía Macher, the executive-secretary of the Peruvian National Human Rights Coordinator (CNDDHH), who had forged an extensive network with the wider human rights community through the Americas including a cluster of groups within Washington, DC.[24]

This accentuated pattern of networked multilateralism became more systemized through the workings of the table of dialogue, or *Mesa de Diálogo*. The establishment of this *mesa* is significant not only for the degree of representation from civil society contained within it, but also because it facilitated contact between representatives of national and international NGOs.

It also allowed extensive networking to develop between the members of Peruvian civil society and state officials from a variety of countries sympathetic to the defense of democracy in Peru. The networking between Canadian state officials—a secondary state that in an earlier diplomatic initiative had worked in support of a similar norm-driven campaign against apartheid in South Africa[25]—and members of the extensive Peruvian NGO community was especially strong. The strong Canadian-Peruvian connection that developed through the OAS intervention that facilitated networking transcended both national and state/societal boundaries during the charter process. This contact was particularly evident between Marc Lortie as the coordinator and Prime Minister Jean Chrétien's personal representative at the Quebec Summit, and Peter Boehm (who chaired the SIRG in the Summit process devoted to the democracy basket) with García Sayán and Rodríguez Cuadros. Both of these Peruvian notables consulted closely with Boehm concerning his presentation to the OAS-sponsored conference on multilateral/ regional organizations and the defense and protection of democracy in February 2001.

Instead of trying to play too robust a role in the extension of networked multilateralism, Canada was content to support Peru in its efforts to negotiate the charter. Such support came in many forms. Canadian officials supplemented Peru's own diplomatic efforts to formulate a supporting coalition of "like-minded" states. They gave special attention to questions of timing, including setting the dates for the special General

Assembly held in Lima to finalize the charter. When a variety of state and society sources attempted to try to block the charter, Canada worked hard to overcome these obstacles in tandem with Peru. What it did not want to do was to seek or expect ownership of this initiative. As played out in the OAS intervention on Peru, Canadian participation on the charter was selective and consistent with a team approach.

The United States: Neither the Maker nor the Breaker of the Charter

As reiterated throughout this book, the United States serves from many angles as an ambiguous (or even hypocritical) advocate of democracy in the Americas. To the extent that democracy in the hemisphere has figured significantly in the administration of George W. Bush, it is almost exclusively as a reaction to the problems within the Americas that have potentially serious repercussions for U.S. security interests, whether drug-trafficking or illegal immigration.[26]

The public perception of the close links forged between the Fujimori regime with the Central Intelligence Agency and the Drug Enforcement Agency[27] further constrained the U.S. efforts to be an effective catalyst for collective action in the specific case of the charter. Try as it might, the United States could rally little in the way of support for this campaign. The U.S. response to subsequent events in the unraveling of the Fujimori regime confirmed this convenient attitude. The most serious of these concerned the response given by the United States to the issue of asylum for Vladimir Montesinos, Peru's notorious intelligence chief. Worried about the possibility of a military coup, the United States took a narrow problem-solving line on this question: viewing a soft-landing for Montesinos as an acceptable cost for clearing the imbroglio on the way to democratic reform. An authoritative journalistic account depicts this approach: "The U.S. worked the phones to find a country that would take Montesinos."[28]

Yet, amidst these signs of disjunction, the United States remained indispensable in the making of the charter. The United States continued to possess the most leverage on a bilateral basis with all the other countries of the Americas. The United States also maintained a stranglehold on the crucial function of chief financier of democratic development, together with a wealth of experience and knowledge on democratic institution building. For mainly bureaucratic reasons the United States assumed a secondary position in the early part of the negotiations on the charter. The initiative coincided with a whole-sale change in bureaucratic personnel, with key figures such as Luis Lauredo, the U.S. permanent representative to the OAS, Peter Romero, the acting assistant secretary, Bureau of Western Hemispheric Affairs in the State Department, and Arturo Valenzuela at the NSC being replaced by Roger Noriega and Otto Reich respectively. Under these distracting conditions, the United States did not play a role commensurate with its structural position within the Americas. At the June 2001 OAS General Assembly meeting in Costa Rica, for example, the United States made do with a small team, with little in the way of institutional memory (except for Tom Shannon, an experienced State department official later promoted as Assistant Secretary of State for the Western Hemisphere) and consisting of only a single lawyer. In a telling signal at the hemisphere's ranking in the hierarchy of U.S. priorities, Secretary of State Colin Powell cancelled his trip to San José to focus on Middle East diplomacy.

If not the maker of the Charter process the United States was not the breaker either. President Bush and his advisory team did not hold up the paragraph on the charter at the April 2001 Quebec Summit as to the lack of a text. On the contrary the United States perceived the benefits of having the charter in place not only to lock in representative democracy in countries such as Peru but also to use it as another potential tool in any crowbar diplomacy directed in different ways at Haiti, or potentially Venezuela or Cuba.[29]

From the perspective of civil society, U.S. groups were in the forefront of the monitoring (and lobbying) effort to strengthen the wording of the charter. Jennifer McCoy, the director of the Latin American and Caribbean program at the Carter Center in Atlanta, was arguably the most prominent of these U.S.-based activists.[30] As the process of consultation took shape, this campaign was joined by the National Democratic Institute and 17 other NGOs.[31]

From a state-centric perspective, Secretary of State Powell made the decisive contribution when it mattered the most. Although he was not present in the long prelude to the special OAS meeting finalizing the charter on September 11, 2001, Powell did what was necessary to bring the charter into existence amidst the unfolding specter of tragedy in the United States. Instead of leaving right away for Washington, DC, Powell stayed in Lima for the number of hours it took to have the charter passed with decisive and unanimous approval. For a moment at least the need for an endorsement of a multilateral commitment—and democratic solidarity with the United States—trumped over all other priorities.

Bottom-Up State Leadership and Constraints

One of the striking paradoxes about the making of the charter is how secondary states provided both the driving force and the brakes for the negotiating process. The earliest and most persistent source of opposition came from the regime of President Hugo Chávez Frías in Venezuela.[32] Venezuela stood out at the Quebec Summit as the one country ready and willing to go on record as having reservations about the charter. This stance was in large part politically motivated, as Chávez and his government perceived the United States as being one of the main candidates calling for an intervention on this basis. The United States and other opponents of the Chávez regime depicted Venezuela as having slid toward authoritarianism with large-scale rule by decree and a concentration of power in the executive branch.

By voicing this competing normative claim the Chávez regime began to build a counter-consensus to the charter. Because of the speed with which this initiative was promoted, the determination and attractive discourse expressed by the champions of the charter and the timing of the initiative to coincide with the reemergence of democracy in Peru, Chávez could not block the charter through any sort of veto (as it found to its detriment at the Quebec Summit). What Chávez and his state officials could do with some other allies, however, was to bog down the negotiating process in protracted negotiations.

What transformed the contours of this struggle was the willingness of a strong contingent of Caribbean states to join with Venezuela in this offside position. One important root of this widened resistance was the embedded support for the tenets of sovereignty and non-intervention due to the Caribbean countries' own unique historical experiences. Besides Mexico and Suriname, Antigua and Barbuda, Dominica, the Dominican Republic, Grenada, Haiti, Jamaica, Saint Kitts and Nevis, Saint Lucia, and Trinidad-and-Tobago remained the only countries not to have ratified the Protocol of Washington—with its threat of suspension to member states—by mid-2001.[33]

The same group of countries also had both a deep set of linkages (including substantial oil and gas transactions) and some political sympathy with the outlook of the Venezuelan regime. To give just one illustration, Saint Lucia proposed a number of amendments to the draft, as it proceeded from the OAS Permanent Council to—and beyond—the General Assembly meeting in San José, which tried to balance the claims of representative and participatory democracy. One proposed amendment stated that: "[t]he peoples of the Americas have a right to democracy since democracy has proven to be the best way to achieve human and social development, which on the basis of free and universal electoral processes, requires the daily and constant participation of all citizens in the permanent task of its enhancement and renewal." Another added, "Citizenship participation in decisions regarding their own development is a fundamental condition for the legitimate and effective exercise of democracy. It is therefore necessary to develop conditions conducive to the genuine exercise of participatory rights while also eliminating obstacles that prevent, hinder, or inhibit this exercise."[34]

On top of these other sources of opposition, the Caribbean countries possessed a vigorous determination to show that they had a legal pedigree distinctive from the Latin Americans. Anxiety flared up about the implications of any constitutional changes (for example, the end of the connection with the British monarchy or the decision to opt out of the Commonwealth). Further, they were not easily convinced of the distinction between a legal instrument and a political statement. This issue of blurring the distinction between the two was particularly sensitive given the controversy in some Caribbean countries over their obligations under the inter-American system of human rights. Specifically, Trinidad-and-Tobago withdrew from the American Convention on Human Rights to protect its right to uphold the death penalty. More generally, the Caribbean countries have mooted the idea of creating a distinctive Caribbean Court of Justice.

Through to the Quebec Summit the proponents of the charter had considered the mix of norms, networks, and intensity to be enough to deliver the charter. As the entrepreneurial and technical bar for success rose, however, these promoters realized the imperative of expanding their diplomatic base. The modification in tactics was most clearly witnessed by the informal partnership that developed between a cluster of like-minded countries on the charter, namely Peru, Canada, the United States, Argentina, and Costa Rica. To be sure, this group served as a sounding board for the draft developed by the Peruvian state officials before the text was presented to the Permanent Council post-Quebec.[35]

It should be acknowledged though, that amidst these advantages there were also risks to this widening-out approach. From the perspective of Venezuela (and for that matter, Cuba) the image of this cohort was not a gathering of a coalition of the like-minded but rather a group dominated by the United States.[36] Nor did this image dissipate entirely with the inclusion of other countries (above all, Mexico as represented by the new Fox/Castañeda team) into the mix. Both the Venezuelan government and the Castro regime alluded to a muscular grouping of countries, centered on the United States but containing other countries such as Mexico and Costa Rica, throwing its weight around.[37] Moreover the inclusion of Mexico also complicated matters in other ways. As pointed out by at least one astute commentator, the presentation by the Mexican ambassador of an alternative draft produced another "difficult period" until it was withdrawn.[38]

Having said that, the major point on which some supporters and constructive members of the opposition camp could coalesce was the need for a more appropriate schedule for negotiation. The speed—and the apparent asymmetry—of the process as it had raced through Quebec simply magnified the objections of those forces that opposed the charter. Conversely, a slowing down of the process reduced the pressure. Paul Durand, the incoming Canadian ambassador to the OAS summarized the sentiments: "The unrealistically short time span between the Quebec City Summit (April 2001) and the regular OAS General Assembly (June, 2001, in San José, Costa Rica) made the negotiations even more challenging. While every effort has been made to bring all member states to the point of consensus before the GA, many felt that the process was rushed and that insufficient time had been granted for consultation."[39]

Societal Support and Resistance

Another compelling paradox concerning the negotiation of the charter relates to the difference in attitude between Northern- and Southern-based NGOs. The model of a new or networked multilateralism is based on the premise of a unified stance among NGOs. In the Peru case, targeted societal groups received not just moral but also financial support from both state and societal sources. At the time of the 2000 elections, for example, Canada gave financial support both at the bilateral level and through the UPD for infrastructural support and aid via Peruvian organizations monitoring the election. Key individuals such as García Sayán had privileged access to influential forums such as the Study Group on Western Hemisphere Governance established by the Inter-American Dialogue in Washington, DC (a body on which Pérez de Cuéllar served as chair emeritus).[40]

What was different was the presence of highly visible and contentious cleavages that emerged within the wider NGO community in the Americas over the merits of the Inter-American Democratic Charter. The state-based opposition to the charter was premised on the notion that this mechanism was too intrusive. The problem for the society-based opposition, or at least for the resistance that emerged from groups located in North America, was the reverse. That is to say, the fundamental concern of this quarter was the lack of clarity and substance in the draft text. Confronting the state officials who gathered at the San José for the June 2001 OAS General Assembly, these groups acted as both an institutional check and a form of hemispheric conscience for making the charter a more meaningful document.

The vigor of this dissent from Northern-based NGOs caught state officials unaware because they had considered the draft presented by the group of five like-minded states at San José to be a credible document. As Graham notes in his excellent review of the negotiations, "[m]easures to address both abrupt and subtle breaks or alterations of the 'Constitutional Order' were addressed, as were circumstances in which the secretary-general could conduct investigative visits. The draft incorporated references to the human rights of hemispheric citizens, a link to the Human Rights Commission and to the Inter-American Court of Human Rights. It also made a connection to the basic requirement of free and fair elections."[41]

These improvements, nonetheless, did not meet the raised expectations of the assembly of NGOs gathered in Costa Rica. On substance, one main focus of the Northern-based NGOs' criticism related to the lack of a clear definition of democracy. As Warren Allmand, President of the Montreal-based Rights & Democracy group (that, along with several other groups, the Canadian government had opened up a dialogue with on the Charter) declared, the phrases "representative democracy," "the democratic order," and "the democratic institutional process," were trotted out, without clarification: "Without a concrete definition of democracy, the Charter could be applied differently on different days."[42]

A second fault outlined by the Northern-based NGOs was the absence of linkage between the charter and the negotiations on the FTAA in the summit process. Though some state delegations expressed concern that a decision by an OAS body to suspend a member from the summit process under the charter would be ultra vires because of the disconnect between the two frameworks (a problem rectified at San José by stating that the sanctions under the charter would be related only to participation in the OAS forums), the NGOs were wary of any backsliding on their assumption that the charter would contain a provision for sanctions to allow the exclusion of states deemed undemocratic from economic integration.[43] A related concern stemmed from the vagueness the Northern-based NGOs perceived in the set of conditions that would trigger action through the charter. As McCoy extended the argument,

"I would spell out the conditions that threaten democracy. Granted, an enumeration also runs the risk of the failure to anticipate all possible scenarios in which the clause might be implemented, but the hemisphere should begin to enumerate some of the basic acts that would constitute an 'unconstitutional alteration.' "[44]

On process, the continued exclusion of civil society during the negotiations perpetuated the traditional perception of the OAS as a closed club.[45] Through one lens, this procedural issue conjured up the familiar image (highlighted by the tussle at San José) of the state delegates locked inside the negotiating arena and the NGOs outside using press conferences and media interviews, among other means, to get attention. Through another lens, furthermore, this gap was understood by the NGOs to have enormous implications for the enforcement of the charter. According to Article 13 of the draft charter, only member states or the secretary-general could require immediate convocation of the Permanent Council of the OAS in order to make a collective assessment of the democratic condition of a targeted country. This wording, groups such as Rights & Democracy argued, did not make it possible for citizens—including representatives of minority parties, minority races, or minority religions—to trigger pro-democracy operations.[46] Often states and governments are the "principal violators of democracy and human rights," Allmand voiced: "Enforcement of the Charter should not be left just to states."[47]

Instead of presenting a protracted obstacle to the closure of the multilateral negotiating process on the charter, it must be emphasized, the disruptions that were centered on the San José meeting proved a valuable pause for reflection and improvement in the ascendancy of networked multilateralism. Since final agreement had not been reached within the short time-span of the San José meeting,[48] the General Assembly instructed a working group headed by Colombia's permanent representative to the OAS, Humberto de la Calle, to come up with the final text for a special session of the General Assembly to be held in Lima in September 2001. Between June and September 2001, Ambassador de la Calle undertook an impressive amount of work to get the charter into acceptable form. This included an unprecedented inclusive process in which citizens across the hemisphere were invited to submit written opinions concerning the charter. Over 8000 civil society organizations participated, effectively assuming a more comprehensive form of ownership of the charter.

The differentiated responses of U.S.- and Canada-based NGOs and those based in Latin America, particularly in the "home" of the charter (Peru), must at the same time be highlighted. The North American NGOs continued to act, as the cliché goes, as the proverbial bad cop of the exercise, cajoling the states to do better in the negotiations. In the multilateral process leading up to the special General Assembly meeting convened in Lima, Rights & Democracy with other groups pushed for the "essential elements" contained in other parts of the document to be made part of the definition in Article 3, a further clarification of the mechanisms for evaluation and enforcement, and an expansion of the standards and sanctions to include not only the OAS but also the summit process.[49]

In complete contrast, while providing considerable input about how the charter could be improved, Peruvian NGOs adopted a more sympathetic tone in their input—becoming in effect the good cop. A large number of respected individuals and representatives of Peruvian NGOs took part in a major dialogue session hosted by *Asociación Civil Transparencia* on July 5, 2001. Among the participants were Enrique Bernales, director of the Andean Commission of Jurists, Sofía Macher, executive-secretary of the CNDDHH, and Rafael Roncagliolo, secretary-general of *Transparencia*.[50] Transnationally, many of the same groups not only contributed written submissions to the OAS consultation process, they also attended en masse at the Lima General Assembly.

With respect to process, this concerted support to the charter by Peruvian NGO representatives owed much to the sense of ownership displayed by the transitional government in which the core Peruvian troika of state officials behind the Charter (Pérez de Cuéllar, Rodríguez Cuadros, and García Sayán) were embedded. Although their positions were subsequently transformed with the election of the Alejandro Toledo government (with Pérez de Cuéllar becoming the Peruvian ambassador to France, Rodríguez Cuadros moving to the position of vice/deputy minister and secretary-general of the Ministry of Foreign Affairs, and García Sayán shifting from Justice to the position of foreign minister), their continued commitment in the creation of the charter was maintained. Appreciation with respect to this activity concomitantly came in a variety of forms, such as the selection of García Sayán to chair the OAS meeting in Lima.

This translation of ideas into purposeful action was an extension as well as penetration of the post-Fujimori government by former NGO leaders. García Sayán once more stands out in this category. But the same trend can be seen in the appointment of Sofía Macher to head the Truth and Reconciliation Commission as well as many other appointments. Arguably the most defining feature of the immediate post-Fujimori era was the positioning of former NGO representatives as state officials while these individuals maintained their contacts—and flow of thinking—with their previous associations. This pattern allowed the state to tap into the accumulated knowledge and networks built up by selected NGOs over the course of agenda setting. It removed some of the barriers between horizontal and vertical organizational structures. And it provided seamless access by committed change agents to the decision-making process—albeit at the expense of formalizing their links to government and the political process.[51]

With respect to substance, as a final document, the charter included some of the concerns of the NGO community—especially in the North. For one thing, in Articles 3 and 4, the charter furnished what approaches a fuller definition of democracy, that is, with a list of "essential elements" that can be used as yardsticks and/or criteria for strengthening democratic governance. For the sake of balance, however, the charter addressed concerns that the OAS was promoting a single model of democracy, as the list is flexible enough to permit a wide degree of variation in terms of idiosyncratic institutions and practices across countries.

In a similar vein, the same search for balance can be found in other parts of the document. The operational clauses contain a spectrum of provisions, from the constructive to the punitive. This graduated approach is not unlike the provisions contained in Chapters 6 and 7 of the UN Charter, which promote the exhaustion of pacific measures and the use of force only in the last instance. On the constructive end of the spectrum, Articles 17 and 18 provide the basis for preventive and proactive collective action, advancing self-help for countries that request assistance as well as establishing the notion of community watch or collective vigilance. With sensitivities concerning sovereignty in mind, these articles enshrine the "by invitation only" or prior consent principle as a requirement for preventive action. The same principle is further found in electoral assistance provisions in Articles 23–25.

On the opposite side of the scale, Articles 19–21 provide more punitive actions. Article 19 reaffirms the democracy membership criterion. Most importantly, it rectifies the main weakness of 1080: that it only applies to coup d'état situations. As outlined above, in a critical precedent, Article 19 establishes a crucial distinction between the unconstitutional "interruption" (coups) versus the unconstitutional "alteration" (incumbent backsliding) of the democratic order. It is made clear that a country's membership in the OAS is jeopardized on both accounts. What remains unclear is precisely what these "alterations" consist of and/or when they occur.

In the tradition of Resolution 1080, Article 20 of the charter provides a mechanism for rapid response to democratic crises. Akin to Resolution 1080, it is an open-ended clause that authorizes the OAS to take such decisions as it deems appropriate. Unlike 1080, however, the threshold for invoking Article 20 is even lower. Since it addresses unconstitutional alterations, OAS collective action can be launched before an actual coup (unconstitutional interruption) takes place. At the top end of the scale, consistent with the Washington Protocol, Article 21 provides for the suspension of an undemocratic state's membership from the OAS.[52] What is missing amidst this emphasis on graduated levels of punitive action is a sustained discussion about the contents of the OAS toolkit as constructive measures for creating appropriate democratic rules of the game—through the use of dialogue tables, the UPD, and the creation of a system of "democracy traffic lights."[53]

Finally, in no small part, thanks to the pioneering efforts of the Stein mission, we also see for the first time the enshrinement of an electoral observation role for the OAS with some bite to it. Even though the prerequisite that ". . . the electoral observation mission shall be carried out at the request of the member-state concerned" is underlined in Article 24, for the first time in Article 25 we observe an official sanctioning of OAS actions that may contravene member-state sovereignty. Article 25 states: "The electoral observation missions shall advise the Permanent Council, through the General Secretariat, if the necessary conditions for free and fair elections do not exist."

The Importance of the Inter-American
Democratic Charter

In conceptual terms, the diplomacy on the Inter-American Democratic Charter confirms the flexible and often contradictory nature of new or networked multilateralism. The imperative of speed (doing something, doing it quickly, and to be seen to be doing it) stands out as the first hallmark feature of the charter initiative. This sense of urgency emerges in the declaratory statements (and the actions) of even those personnel most familiar with the cautious and incremental culture located in the OAS and the inter-American system. As Secretary-General Gaviria put it at the Lima special General Assembly, the need was for a bold move to wrap a democratic cloak around the hemisphere: "By adopting this democracy Charter, you are putting on notice all of an authoritarian bent that there would be no tolerance towards those who would over-throw governments, seek to subvert the constitutional order, or undermine political control."[54]

Yet, when we step back from the process and look at it, this impression of zeal and breakneck speed is offset by the complexity of the negotiating process. Although the charter came into being in less than a year, the document went through numerous (17 or more) draft versions. Furthermore, this very intensity necessitated a time of reflection after the San José General Assembly to get a second wind before the final burst of activity leading up to and encompassing the Lima meeting. The charter process was no marathon. But neither was it a short—and uninterrupted—sprint. Speed was matched and compensated for by an appreciation of the technical qualities and the sheer complexity of the process.[55]

A second dominant image of the expression of networked multilateralism vis-à-vis the charter is that of a bottom-up process as opposed to a top-down process. The driving force behind and ownership of the charter remained with a decidedly secondary power (Peru) having diplomatic backup from Canada and other middle or smaller states. As in the case of the land mines campaign and the International Criminal Court (ICC) initiative, where new multilateralism has come to the fore at the global level basis, smaller powers not only possessed good ideas[56] but—with support and the fortune of circumstances—also the means to bring those ideas into being.

Gaps in the image of the charter as a model of bottom-up multilateralism relate to both the retention of the dominant power (the United States) as part of the coalition and the degree of state centrism by which it was developed in Peru. At odds with the experiences of both the land mines and ICC campaigns, the United States was neither antagonized nor self-excluded. Such bridging behavior lead to Powell's decisive intervention at the September 11 meeting in Lima. While NGOs and their representatives played a significant role in shaping and modifying the charter, state officials in Peru and other countries remained at the core of the process. The attitudes and pressures of the NGOs were taken into account, absorbed, and deflected. But, as witnessed in other significant areas of multilateral diplomacy there was no sign of states ceding final authority to non-state actors.[57]

To nuance the claims of a new societal-led multilateralism is not to reject the robust and innovative partnership based on extensive links formed between states and NGOs as well as those between like-minded states. Indeed this is the construct that is at the heart of the networked multilateralism found within the charter initiative. The charter process allowed an interface between state and societal-centered supporters based on a common interest in communication, the sharing of information, and negotiation between themselves as well as with the resisters of the making of the charter. The partnership that developed outside of the Peru context, however, was not the result of a smooth or uniform process. Nor, as witnessed by the disagreements at San José, did it mean that state officials and NGO representatives moved anywhere close to the point of sharing a common discourse or agenda.[58]

In the minds of NGO representatives (especially those based in the North) state officials—even those on side with the initiative—remained locked within the mindset of bureaucratic pragmatism and calculated ambiguity. If these same sympathetic officials admired the commitment and energy of the NGOs, they continued to be frustrated at their lack of appreciation of what was possible to negotiate in the setting of an inter-governmental organization.

A final connecting image of the multilateralism featured on the Inter-American Democratic Charter is the public dimension of the exercise. In tandem with the concentrated process came a great deal of media coverage reminiscent of the land mines and ICC cases. Yet again this image is somewhat misleading. True, the charter was effectively launched amidst the clamor and publicity attached to the Quebec Summit (both inside the meeting and on the streets). And the culmination of this exercise became intertwined in a most unanticipated manner with the shock and horror of September 11. But if the attention given to the charter was both vivid and amplified because of its intersection with these events, it was also surprisingly localized and short-lived. Even at the launch and at the culmination of the process the charter had to struggle to get attention of people other than the most committed observers. There was also an uneven quality to this focus of attention, with a particularly keen interest shown in the negotiations involving some Latin American countries (Peru in particular), with Canadian and U.S. media outlets content with making small bursts of commentary on the charter. Unlike the land mines case (or other cases such as the Jubilee 2000 antidebt campaign), there was not one popular champion (or a transcending personality with a global star quality such as Princess Diana, Bono, or even Pope John Paul II!) with whom the Northern mainstream media could identify.

Although the charter passed its first operational test, in the case of Venezuela in April 2002, numerous other questions were left open (discussed in the next chapter). At least some mention must be made of the fact that the crisis orientation of the charter still bypassed the deeper problems of democratization. Despite the targeting of the problems of poverty in the charter, inequality, social exclusion, corruption, and the role of paramilitary groups have remained untouched by its implementation. Even Peru the "home" of the charter witnessed a release of a massive backlash in the form of the 2002 "Arequipa effect" against the trajectory of public policy and the flow of information by the democratically elected government of President Toledo.

As an illustration of multilateral activity the case of the Inter-American Democratic Charter stands at the apex of something new while retaining standard features associated with older forms of OAS diplomacy. Driven by the power of norms and networks, accepted methods of working within the regional framework of the OAS and the inter-American system were modified on an improvised basis. The line between domestic and the international contexts became increasingly blurred. The innovative quality of this "new" multilateralism, however, should not be exaggerated to the point of distortion. Intensity was mixed with the discipline of sustained engagement at both the state and societal level. A greater voice for civil society coexisted with the primacy of an inter-governmental system. Crosscutting coalitions bent the culture of consensus but established institutions were not circumvented through "end runs" as in the land mines case. In combination the push and pull of these different ingredients meant that the initiative retained an awkward quality, full of compromises and controversy, and some unexpected detours. But this complex dynamic also allowed a built-in sense of equipoise between innovation and entrenched habits and modes of behavior, a balance vital to the successful delivery of the Inter-American Democratic Charter.

CHAPTER SIX

Passing the (First) Test? The Venezuelan Coup of April 11, 2002

If Peru served as the stimulus for a flurry of networked multilateral activity surrounding the Inter-American Democratic Charter, Venezuela's crisis presented a crucial first test for the updated democratic solidarity paradigm. Up to and including the Peruvian political crisis in 2000, the OAS had responded to periodic threats to democracy among member states mostly when they were already full-blown crises, rather than taking steps in advance to prevent them. This earned the OAS the reputation for "firefighting," instead of thwarting fires from catching in the first place.[1] As we have discussed previously, in no small part, this tendency reflected the limits of club multilateralism.

As related in the last chapter, the Inter-American Democratic Charter provided two sets of provisions that in theory gave the OAS the means for preventive or proactive diplomacy. Article 17, the "self-help" clause, furnished the basis for member states under duress to request the assistance of the secretary-general or the Permanent Council in finding a solution to their crises. Article 18, the "community watch" clause, gave other member states and/or the secretary-general, with the consent of the host government, the ability to arrange visits or other actions to assess the situation, prepare a report for the consideration of the Permanent Council, and undertake measures necessary to defend democracy.

Haiti had the distinction of almost becoming the first test case under the newly minted Inter-American Democratic Charter. Following an armed attack on December 17, 2001 on the National Palace and a rapid escalation of political violence and conflict thereafter, the secretary-general convened a special meeting of the Permanent Council on January 15, 2002 to consider the OAS's response. The Permanent Council did discuss invoking Article 18 of the charter. However, an invitation by the Haitian government to invoke Article 18 of the charter was not forthcoming. Neither Haiti nor the member states of the Caribbean Common Market (CARICOM) supported invoking the charter. Ironically, the clauses of Permanent Council Resolution 806 adopted on January 16 were very much consistent with the charter (although it was not actually invoked), including instructions for the secretary-general to monitor events in Haiti and for the Inter-American Commission on Human Rights to conduct an onsite visit.[2]

The adoption of Resolution 806 leads to the question of why the charter was not invoked. The common perception among many member states was that invoking the charter was tantamount to taking a punitive measure that carried a huge stigma. Nobody wanted to be the charter's first test case. Additionally, conscious of a history of U.S. intervention in the region, Haiti and other Caribbean states were concerned that the defense of democracy under the charter could be a pretext for hidden motives. The Bush administration, for example, had been very critical of the Aristide government. Efforts to promote the use of the newly minted charter thus were trumped by suspicions that had long underpinned OAS behavior. Finally, some suggest that the charter was not used because the OAS had hinted to Aristide that it would invoke the charter as a ploy to extract concessions from the Haitian government, namely official consent to a special mission.[3] If this was the case, the ruse certainly reinforced the perception of the charter as a punitive, rather than a constructive instrument.

Venezuela thus became the charter's first formal trial. Long regarded as an exemplar of successful democracy in the Americas, built on the so-called *Puntofijo* model, Venezuela by the millennium had become one of the region's political problem cases. Following a general strike against the government that culminated in the shooting deaths of at least 14 protestors and the wounding of more than 100 others, on April 11, 2002, a coup coalition led by business leader Pedro Carmona and a group of high ranking military officers arrested President Hugo Chávez and seized power.

In what follows, we analyze closely the OAS multilateralism–democracy nexus as it unfolded in the Venezuelan crisis. As in Peru, here too we encounter the recurrence of two problems for which the Inter-American Democratic Charter was supposed to provide the necessary countermeasures: crisis prevention and sustained engagement. Again, we also find that innovation in multilateralism was essential for overcoming built-in resistance to pro-democracy activism within the OAS. Networked multilateralism, albeit with some awkwardness, came once more to the fore. In this chapter, we examine the initial foray of the OAS into Venezuela in the context of the April 2002 coup. As in the Peru case, the next chapter recounts what would become the patent of OAS embedded engagement on the frontlines of crises: OAS-facilitated democratic dialogue tables.

The Origins of the April 11 Coup

The deterioration of events in Venezuela that culminated in the 2002 coup was a far cry from the days when the *Puntofijo* political system was held up as a model of democracy in the Americas. Constructed in 1957–1958, *puntofijismo* was the end product of a series of elite pacts. The goal of these elite agreements was the ouster of dictator Marcos Pérez Jiménez (1952–1958) and the creation of a political system that facilitated both the sharing of economic and political power among Venezuelan elites, as well as elite alternation and circulation of power under democratic auspices. That is, instead of fighting for power, particular ipating elites agreed to share the pie. The system crystallized in the peaceful electoral competition between two groups of elites and their political parties: the social democratic Democratic Action Party (*Acción Democrática*) and the social Christian Committee of Independent Electoral Political Organization (COPEI). Venezuelan oil wealth provided the economic means to sustain the elite compromise and build clientelistic and electoral support for the emerging two-party system.[4]

As the *Puntofijo* system consolidated, Venezuela projected its newfound democratic values abroad. The Betancourt Doctrine, named after Rómulo Betancourt, one of the founders of the *Puntofijo* system and the first *Puntofijo* president (1959–1964), became a cornerstone of Venezuela's foreign policy. Long before it was enshrined as a hemispheric principle in the Washington Protocol, this doctrine denied Venezuelan diplomatic recognition to any government, whether left or right leaning, that came to power by undemocratic means.[5]

The April 11 coup had its origins in both the longer-term decline of the *Puntofijo* political system and the more immediate events of 2001 and early 2002.[6] With respect to the former, what were originally the strengths of the model, an economy based on oil exports and elite pact-making, were ultimately also its weaknesses. For almost 25 years the political system had operated successfully on a foundation of petroleum-led economic growth. However, in 1982 international oil prices plummeted, exacerbating the government's growing difficulties in honoring its external debt payments. On "Black Friday," February 18, 1983, President Luis Herrera Campíns announced a major devaluation of the bolivar. Venezuela's economy never fully recovered from the severe economic stagnation and inflation that ensued. Black Friday shattered the myth of seemingly limitless oil wealth for all and raised growing questions about what had happened to all of the country's oil earnings.[7]

The downturn in Venezuela's oil-based economy exposed the extent of the country's growing poverty and inequality. While times were good, *Puntofijo* appeared gradually to spread the benefits of oil-led growth to the middle and popular classes. Following Black Friday however, oil proceeds declined and had to be diverted increasingly into debt servicing, leaving fewer resources for poverty alleviation. Nevertheless, not all Venezuelans suffered equally from economic setbacks. While the ranks of those excluded from the benefits of oil wealth increased, the *Puntofijo* elite continued to enjoy them and were able to maintain their standard of living.

In 1989, "bait-and-switch" tactics by newly elected president Carlos Andrés Pérez exacerbated tensions between the *puntofijista's* "haves" and the "have nots." Leading the electorate to believe that he would return the country to the days of prosperity during his first presidency (1974–1979), Pérez abruptly announced an IMF-sponsored structural adjustment program soon after assuming his second term as president. The price hikes that resulted from the neoliberal plan triggered mass riots in Caracas and the infamous *Caracazo* across the country on February 27. As many as 1000–1500 people died as a result of police and military efforts to terminate the rioting.[8] The *Caracazo* violence put an ugly face on *puntofijismo*: a privileged elite prepared to resort to force to protect its interests against the growing legions of disadvantaged. The growing disrepute of the *puntofijista* elites went from bad to worse in May 1993 when Pérez became the first president in Venezuelan history to be impeached for corruption.

Without adequate oil income to build popular support bases through corporatism and clientelism, Venezuela's crisis of economic exclusion became a political one as well. The corporatist and clientelist underpinnings of the *Puntofijo* system were undermined, and the elite pact-making that had underpinned the system became deficient.[9] From a product of inclusionary thinking and consensus politics, the aging *puntofijista* elite gradually became exclusionary in the context of economic decline. Alongside clamors for greater wealth sharing, Venezuela's middle and popular classes increasingly demanded greater political representation.

The rise of Hugo Chávez, a former parachutist officer, coincided with the discrediting of the *Puntofijo* system and its two principal political parties: *Acción Democrática* (AD) and COPEI. Though Chávez's first attempt to seize power through a coup d'état on February 4, 1992 failed, his blistering verbal attacks on the corrupt, elitist *Puntofijo* system increasingly resonated among the Venezuelan population. In December 1998, Chávez swept to victory on an electoral campaign platform where he vowed to obliterate the decrepit *Puntofijo* system in favor of a new pro-poor program of direct democracy, economic redistribution, and nationalism, a program that he called the Bolivarian Revolution.[10]

The link between the longer-term origins of the 2002 coup and its more immediate antecedents is precisely the old guard, the former *puntofijista* elites who lost institutional political power and privileges as a result of Chávez's assumption of the presidency. Unlike the *Puntofijo* arrangement where AD and COPEI would share power, irrespective of which party won the previous election, Chávez systematically excluded former elites and AD and COPEI party faithfuls from state positions and perks in what Jennifer McCoy has called the end of Venezuela's "partyarchy."[11] Chávez's breaking with the traditions of *Puntofijo* triggered an intense intraelite existential struggle between the old guard and the new Chávez elites.[12] AD, COPEI, affiliated oil and business elites, as well as the AD-affiliated Confederation of Venezuelan Workers (CTV) were key actors in the opposition to Hugo Chávez.

During the first few years of the Chávez presidency, opposition was fragmented. On one hand, it reflected the fact that many Venezuelans who were one-time supporters of the old established parties were supportive of the need for political change and thus were willing to give the new president a chance. Undoubtedly this followed the gradual fragmentation of the two-party *Puntofijo* system that occurred during the 1990s, a trend that worsened when former president Rafael Caldera split from COPEI to run as an independent candidate leading a coalition called National Convergence in the 1994 presidential election. By the 1998 presidential election, AD and COPEI were but two declining parties in a numerically expanding political party system.[13]

A series of occurrences during 2001 and early 2002 galvanized and united the opposition. First, the Bolivarian Revolution failed to deliver many tangible goods during the first few years of the Chávez presidency. Instead, the economy grew worse during 2001 from a combination of capital flight and slumping oil prices. The economic downturn contributed to the growth in the numbers of disenchanted across the country.

Second, in November 2001, President Chávez used special powers to issue a series of 49 far-reaching decrees, including controversial land reforms and the introduction of laws affecting the oil sector and fisheries. Opponents of the decrees charged that there had been no debate over the content of the decrees, as required by Chávez's own constitution, and that legal private property was under assault. The business community criticized the new laws for scaring off foreign investment.[14] Dissatisfaction with the new decrees came on top of other growing grievances, such as the perceived "Cubanization" of education and health through the introduction of legions of Cuban teachers and physicians, Chávez's increasingly confrontational stance towards the United States, and the government's determined efforts to win control over the Confederation of Venezuelan Workers (CTV).

On December 10, the opposition launched a one-day general strike that effectively shut down the country. For the first time, the fragmented opposition was united. Resistance to Chávez brought together an unlikely alliance of actors, including the umbrella organization for national business, FEDECAMARAS, and its usual adversary, the CTV. Additional support for the strike came from the traditional political parties, sectors of the Catholic Church, and most of the media. The protestors demanded Chávez's resignation.[15]

Third, in early February 2002, elements of the military joined the opposition in demanding that Chávez resign. On February 7, Air Force Colonel Pedro Soto criticized the politicization of the armed forces under Chávez. Shortly afterward, Captain Pedro Flores of the National Guard and Rear Admiral Carlos Molina Tamayo added their voices to Colonel Soto's call for Chávez to step down.[16]

Behind the scenes, the growing resistance to Chávez had its impact within the ranks of *Chavistas*. Splits occurred among Chávez elites on the issue of how to deal with the opposition and its mobilization. Moderates argued the need for dialogue and compromise with the opposition. Hardliners in the government advocated not backing off and instead responding in kind to opposition protests with similar demonstrations of popular support for Chávez. Key players, such as the moderate Luis Miquilena, Chávez's interior minister until January 2001, defected. On the day of the coup, Miquilena severely criticized the Chávez government for its alleged role in the shootings of protestors.[17]

The final blow in a sequence of destabilizing events was Chávez's April 6 announcement of the firing of seven executives from *Petroleos de Venezuela, Sociedad Anónima* (PDVSA) and their replacement by *Chavistas*.[18] Control over Venezuela's state oil monopoly, both in terms of its petroleum workers' union and its executive, had become a key issue of contention between government and opposition.[19] Chávez issuing dismissals served to strengthen further the strategic alliance between PDVSA management and unionized workers.

On April 9, Carlos Ortega, the leaders of the CTV, and Pedro Carmona Estanga, president of FEDECAMARAS, led another general strike to protest the dismissals. What was originally meant to last one day dragged on for three. On the third day of the strike, upon reaching the headquarters of PDVSA at Chuao, which was the original destination of the march, the organizers with help from the media encouraged the multitude of some 200,000 protestors to press onward to the presidential palace of Miraflores and oust Chávez. In the course of the march toward the palace, opposition protestors encountered throngs of Chávez supporters in the center of the city. Shots broke out from unidentified gunmen located on the bridges in the vicinity of the march, killing at least 10 protestors and wounding nearly 100.[20]

Shortly thereafter, on the evening of April 11, various military officers were prompted by the violence to make televized calls for civil disobedience against the Chávez government. Then, in the early hours of April 12, General Lucas Rincón Romero announced on television that President Chávez had resigned. Subsequent television footage showed Chávez being put under arrest at Fort Tiuna.[21] Pedro Carmona Estanga, president of FEDECAMARAS, was sworn in as Venezuela's president, even though the constitutionally established line of succession was through the vice president and then the head of Congress.

The OAS Response

Returning to our main theme, it must be mentioned that in the months immediately prior to the April 11 coup d'état, there was recognition within the OAS of the increasingly precarious state of Venezuela's democratic order. However, apart from an expression of concern by Secretary-General Gaviria criticizing Colonel Pedro Soto for attempting to incite military rebellion,[22] the OAS did not take any actions to stem the tide of events in Venezuela leading up to the coup. As we know from chapter five, far from being an advocate of the Inter-American Democratic Charter, Chávez was a staunch opponent of any intrusions on sovereignty. Accordingly, neither did the Chávez government seek assistance through Article 17, the "self-help" clause of the Democratic Charter, nor did the secretary-general or Permanent Council invoke

Article 18, the "community watch" clause. In Chávez, the OAS confronted an interesting anomaly; while promoting participatory democracy at home, he used one of the long-standing prerogatives of club membership—executive sovereignty. Coupled with Chávez's own denial of the seriousness of the situation, the OAS effectively had little hope of invoking the charter before a full-blown crisis occurred.

Fortunately for the OAS, other regional actors provided an immediate external response to Chávez's ouster. The Rio Group coincidentally happened to be meeting in San José, Costa Rica that very same day. The assembled foreign ministers hastily and unanimously issued the declaration of the Rio Group on the situation in Venezuela.[23] The declaration condemned the interruption of the constitutional order in Venezuela and requested that the secretary-general immediately convene a special session of the Permanent Council under Article 20 of the charter in order to undertake a collective assessment of the situation and adopt whatever measures were deemed necessary.

Interestingly, since information at the time seemed to indicate that Chávez had resigned, the Rio Group made no request for his return to power as part of the efforts to restore constitutional order. The Rio Group declaration drew attention to a noteworthy contradiction within the charter text. In its condemnation of the interruption of the constitutional order in Venezuela, the declaration seemed to acknowledge that a coup had occurred in the country. Nevertheless, the declaration requested invoking Article 20 of the charter, which pertains to unconstitutional alterations (authoritarian backsliding by an elected leader) rather than unconstitutional interruptions (coups). The more punitive Article 21, and not Article 20, deals specifically with unconstitutional interruptions, yet it was not invoked. On the other hand, Article 20, in a fashion similar to that of Resolution 1080, allows, where Article 21 does not, for a collective assessment by the Permanent Council of the situation. Certainly conflicting pieces of information from Venezuela constrained the ability of the Rio Group foreign ministers to properly assess the situation, add to this the wording explaining the differences between unconstitutional alterations and interruptions contained in Articles 20 and 21 seemed to confuse the matter somewhat.

An encouraging sign that the new regional democracy norms had been internalized in key national contexts came from Mexico. Mexican President Vicente Fox came out strongly saying Mexico would not recognize Venezuela's new government until elections were held. Fox's statement was a signature departure from previous Mexican leaders who had routinely defended the right of self-determination, as well as the

Estrada Doctrine: automatic recognition of any de facto government irrespective of its political stripe or the means by which it had come to power. For their part, the leaders of Argentina and Paraguay labeled the Carmona government illegitimate, while Peru, notwithstanding a statement by President Alejandro Toledo to the effect that he had little time for Chávez, offered an equally strong condemnation. Other Latin American governments urged Carmona to organize new elections for the National Assembly.[24]

Despite a widespread dislike for Chávez, Latin American leaders united in their refusal to condone the coup. In part, this important consensus reflected many leaders' collective sentiment that any future coups in their own countries ought to be strongly condemned by all. On another level, Latin American leaders were acutely concerned about their international image and therefore felt the need to dispel and move decisively beyond the old international stereotypes of uncivilized brutal banana dictatorships. More importantly, the consensus reflected the fact that Latin American elites on the whole have come to reject coups as a legitimate form of political change. Impressively, senior military leaders contacted their respective heads-of-state in San José to condemn the coup.

The United States once again revealed its ambiguity toward the defense of democracy. In stark contrast to the Latin American states mentioned above, the United States appeared to support the overthrow of Chávez. Senior Bush administration officials had met several times with key opposition figures in the months prior to the coup. White House spokesman Ari Fleischer and National Security Adviser Condoleezza Rice remarked that Chávez had provoked his own downfall and that his government had suppressed a peaceful demonstration. Though the U.S. government was understandably upset with the Chávez government for policies, such as its harsh criticism of the U.S. fight against terrorism, its close ties with Cuba, its apparent support for the FARC in Colombia, and its refusal to allow the United States to fly drug interdiction flights over Venezuelan territory, the apparent support of the United States for the coup was at odds with the widespread sentiment expressed elsewhere in the region.[25]

While the OAS had said or done little in the months leading up to the coup, it responded rapidly to the outburst of violence hours before the coup transpired. On April 11, Secretary-General Gaviria issued a statement on the situation in Venezuela, deploring the violence of that day and calling on both protestors and the government to conduct themselves peacefully and with respect for democracy and the rule of law.[26]

An even more rapid, initial response was delayed for several practical reasons. First, the secretary-general delayed convening an emergency session of the Permanent Council on Friday, April 12 while awaiting the outcome of the Rio Group meeting in San José. This approach made sense because the OAS permanent representatives from Latin America took their cue from their foreign ministers anyway. Second, the speed of the OAS response also depended on a reliable flow of information from Venezuela. In the heat of the crisis, there were significant information gaps concerning whether Chávez had resigned or been forcefully removed from office.

When the Permanent Council finally met for the first time that Friday evening under Article 20 as requested by the Rio Group, it joined the Rio Group in treating Chávez's resignation as a fait accompli. Under pressure from the new Carmona government, the decision was thus taken to exclude the incumbent Venezuelan ambassador, Jorge Valero, to his great frustration and anger. However, considering the fluid situation in Venezuela and the conflicting reports coming out of the country, the Venezuelan representative was permitted to attend the marathon session that began the following morning. Indeed, at the April 13 meeting, the Venezuelan permanent representative argued that since a classical coup had occurred, the OAS needed to invoke the Inter-American Democratic Charter's Article 21 that called for the suspension of a member state. Despite this plea though, confusion reigned for many hours. Had Chávez resigned or had he been forced out by a coup? Given the lack of reliable information, the council therefore decided for the time being against invoking Article 21.

The United States (with Colombia) appeared at the beginning of the Permanent Council session to endorse the coup, albeit through a stance couched in very diplomatic language. The United States, however, became more flexible when Chávez was restored to power later the same day. The U.S. permanent representative, Roger Noriega, played a very low-key role throughout much of Saturday, not even addressing the council until the very end of the session on Saturday night.

In the midst of the deliberations, Secretary-General Gaviria fueled controversy when he mentioned that he was in touch by telephone with Carmona, feeding speculation that he supported the coup and/or accepted Carmona as de facto head of state of Venezuela. He was quickly taken to issue by the representatives from Brazil and Barbados on this point. Canada's representative stressed that the Carmona provisional government had no democratic legitimacy either in the way it assumed power or in its anti-democratic actions since assuming power. For their part, most Rio Group members made their views clear from the outset: they condemned what took place in Venezuela as a coup d'état. Caribbean representatives were generally more cautious about labeling what took place as a coup. In overall terms, most countries felt that the situation was so fluid and that available information was of such questionable reliability that a wait-and-see position was necessary until more was found out through a fact-finding mission. By the late evening of Saturday, April 13 into the early hours of April 14 much of this preceding debate was laid to rest by reports that began to filter in from Venezuela that Chávez had been restored to power.

At the end of its deliberations, the Permanent Council adopted Resolution 811.[27] The resolution called for the application of the mechanisms within Article 20 of the charter. It condemned the coup or, in wording adopted from the charter, the "alteration" of the constitutional order in Venezuela. Interestingly, in the discourse of the Inter-American Democratic Charter, "alteration" would presumably refer to some form of anti-democratic action by the incumbent elected government, whereas "interruption" would indicate a coup d'état. It is unclear why the word "alteration" was adopted in Resolution 811 under circumstances that by Saturday evening, April 13, clearly suggested a coup d'état had occurred.

Resolution 811 authorized an urgent mission led by Secretary General Gaviria for the purposes of fact finding and promoting the normalization of Venezuela's democratic order through his position's good offices. The resolution called for a special session of the General Assembly to be convened on April 18 at which Gaviria would deliver his mission report and the assembly would adopt whatever measures it deemed appropriate.

A combination of internal divisions within the coup coalition, popular resistance within Venezuela, and a lack of international support resulted in a coup government that lasted barely 36 hours. First, various authors suggested that a "coup within a coup" had occurred.[28] The organizers of the demonstrations convened by the political opposition and many social organizations on and prior to April 11 were apparently different from those who usurped power, detained President Chávez, and attempted to establish a provisional government. Despite an alliance prior to the coup with organized labor under the CTV, Pedro Carmona hastily formed a new government that was almost exclusively right wing, including ultraconservative business interests and military officers. This action angered many initial supporters, especially those in the labor sector, who expected a more broad-based coalition government.

The new government's initial decisions upon taking power caused among *Chavistas* and its sympathizers a great concern that its intention was to do away with democracy altogether. President Carmona alienated numerous moderate, more democratic anti-*Chavistas* on April 12 by issuing a series of anti-democratic decrees characteristic of a classic coup d'état, and not of a democratizing government of salvation: suspending the constitution, dissolving the National Assembly, firing Supreme Court judges, and ordering the arrest of key members of the Chávez government. Many who were otherwise glad to see the end of Chávez thus felt duped by a transitional government that clearly was acting in its own narrow interests. Many of the same high ranking officers who had initially lent their support to Carmona began to demand restoration of the constitution and the National Assembly.

Simultaneously, once the word spread that Chávez had been forcefully ousted, thousands of *Chavistas* from the poorer areas of Caracas mobilized in front of Miraflores Palace demanding his restoration. Key military units at the air force and military base of Maracay, such as the paratrooper battalion that Chávez had formerly commanded, declared their support for Chávez. Faced with the prospect of defending an unpopular interim president, military officers who had hitherto supported Carmona called for his resignation. *Chavista* militants and paratroopers were eventually able to reestablish control over the presidential palace during the afternoon and evening of April 13, prompting Carmona to flee. At 3 am on April 14, Chávez returned by helicopter from a naval base on the island of Orchila where he had been held captive.[29]

Externally, the strong support Carmona and company likely expected from the United States was not forthcoming and the OAS-Rio Group tandem declarations delivered a strong condemnation of the coup. Poor timing also did not help Carmona: the coup occurred on the very same day as a meeting of foreign ministers of the Rio Group. As in the case of Fujimori's demise in 2000 in Peru, the combination of powerful domestic resistance and international isolation proved decisive in quickly undermining the legitimacy of the interim government.[30]

Pursuant to the instructions of Resolution 811, Secretary-General Gaviria embarked on a fact-finding and diplomatic mission to Venezuela during April 15–17. He was accompanied by the permanent council chair, Ambassador Margarita Escobar of El Salvador, and the Belize ambassador and CARICOM spokesperson, Lisa Shoman. In another unforeseen factor that slowed down the OAS's rapid response capacity, the mission was delayed by a day because of a cancelled commercial flight to Venezuela. By the time Gaviria, Escobar, and Shoman reached Venezuela on April 15, the presidency was once again firmly in the hands of Hugo Chávez. Consequently during their visit, the delegation

focused on meeting with a broad cross-section of Venezuelan government and society representatives in an effort to conduct an effective crisis
postmortem and identify continued threats to Venezuelan democracy.
On the evening of April 18, the region's foreign ministers or their
representatives met at a special session of the General Assembly to
receive the secretary-general's mission report and discuss the situation in
Venezuela. Of course, by the time this event convened, the restoration
of Chávez four days before had reduced its significance. Still, Gaviria's
report deserves attention for focusing on many of the problems in
Venezuelan democracy and offering recommendations for addressing
them.[31] In doing so, Gaviria criticized the Chávez government for
actions that had weakened democracy and polarized political forces in the
country. In reply, the Venezuelan foreign minister defended the Chávez
government's democratic and human rights record and its sovereign right
to strengthen democracy without external interference.[32] U.S. Secretary
of State Colin Powell then launched a thinly veiled attack on the Chávez
government's use of undemocratic methods. However, in somewhat of
a reversal from earlier Bush administration statements at the time of the
coup, he condemned the blows to Venezuela's constitutional order and
called for the OAS to examine how it could have used the mechanisms
of the charter before April 11 to support Venezuelan democracy more
effectively. Powell also proposed that the General Assembly give the
secretary-general a mandate to facilitate national dialogue in Venezuela.[33]

The Persistent Challenge of Follow-Up

Articles 26 and 27 of the Inter-American Democratic Charter provide
the potential basis for OAS follow-up or oversight after the end of an
immediate political crisis. They furnish the OAS with a justification for car-
rying out programs and activities to promote and strengthen democracy.
However, once Chávez was back in power, any effort to provide OAS
follow-up, oversight, or assistance to strengthen democracy in the wake
of the crisis depended on the willingness of the Venezuelan government
to request or endorse it. Not surprisingly, the Venezuelan foreign minister did not issue any such invitation.

Nevertheless, Resolution 1 that came out of the special session of
the General Assembly on April 18 did manage to establish a certain
degree of oversight/monitoring via a previously planned Inter-American
Commission on Human Rights (IACHR) onsite visit to the Venezuela
scheduled for early May. As this visit had come from an official invitation

from the Venezuelan government much earlier in September 1999,[34] the Venezuelans were not in a position to refuse an onsite visit. In addition, the resolution commissioned the Permanent Council to produce a comprehensive report on the situation in Venezuela to be presented at the next General Assembly that was to be held in Bridgetown, Barbados in early June. In terms of OAS follow-up then, the IAHCR onsite visit of May 6–10 provided a narrow window of opportunity to keep the OAS involved in Venezuela. The report that the IAHCR delegation issued identified a host of continuing threats to the country's democratic order.[35]

The OAS subsequently convened a Permanent Council meeting on May 28 to consider the situation in Venezuela. The highlights of the meeting were a document presented by the Venezuelan representative providing a government update of the situation and the release of the Permanent Council report as mandated by General Assembly Resolution 1 on April 18. In an address from its representative to the council, the Venezuelan government made clear that it had already received the most important help that it required from the OAS, namely political support for the Chávez government and a condemnation of the coup. It concluded that it was capable on its own of resolving its problems and did not require additional assistance.[36] As for the Permanent Council report,[37] it served as little more than a compilation of the text and documents of the proceedings of the special session of the General Assembly on April 18. Though the U.S. permanent representative responded to the Venezuelan intervention in an attempt to press for a more active role for the OAS in strengthening democracy and national reconciliation in Venezuela, there was no follow-up discussion on what further actions needed to be taken.

At the Bridgetown, Barbados, annual General Assembly held on June 4, the OAS adopted the *Declaration on Democracy in Venezuela*, presented originally by Venezuela.[38] As with Resolution 1, the declaration once again offered the OAS's assistance for democratic consolidation and national dialogue and reconciliation, reiterating the organization's rejection of the use of violence as a means of replacing a democratic government in the hemisphere and its intention to continue applying the charter in the preservation and defense of representative democracy.

A Passing Grade for the Democratic Charter?

Without question the swiftness and decisiveness of the OAS response to the Venezuelan crisis had a strong psychological influence on the resolve of that country's coup plotters. The charter did deliver in a number of ways. First of all, it provided both a first recourse and an automatic response to the crisis. Secondly, the response to the Venezuelan test crystallized what the charter really means in practical terms. Thirdly, the "right to democracy" presented in Article 1 provided a mantra for rallying a defense from both inside and outside Venezuela. Fourthly, the charter proved flexible enough to respond to the peculiarities of the Venezuela situation.

Though in many ways it was a success during its first major test, many of the lessons have been unintended ones. In terms of its target country, the charter has had not only its most critical opponent, but also its most grateful beneficiary. In terms of application, the combination of external pressure (through both multilateral forums and the international media) and internal popular resistance in the Venezuelan case reinforced each other just as they had in Paraguay (1996) and Peru (2000). In terms of ambiguity in the doctrine of democratic solidarity, the behavior of the United States stands out. At odds with the declaratory statements offered by Secretary of State Powell on September 11, 2001 in Lima that democracy had to be defended in times of crisis, the U.S. actions on Venezuela lost it a lot of credibility in the region as a defender of democracy and even in its broader struggle against terrorism.

Yet, when framed in the larger context, the U.S. position simply underscored the degree to which the Americas stood together. The inter-American sense of solidarity during the Venezuela crisis showed that the system had come a long way in its maturation. Long considered a rubber stamp for U.S. actions, the OAS in combination with the Rio Group provided a salient force with respect to intra-multilateral coordination and complementarity. Faced with this force, the United States found itself awkwardly to be on the defensive. Out of step with the prevailing consensus, United States officials found themselves with little choice but to fall back into line with their Latin American counterparts.[39] In fact, in the months following the coup, the United States issued strong statements warning Venezuelans against any violent, unconstitutional attempts to depose Chávez.[40] The Venezuelan case reveals that the defense of democracy in America has been led collectively by the Americas.

The Venezuelan test case underscores the persistent sovereign limits of the charter. Venezuela's coup crisis illustrates that the ability to invoke preventive or follow-up diplomacy, despite provisions for such within the charter, remains poor because of its wedding to the sovereignty norm of "by invitation only." Responding effectively before a political crisis flares up or sustaining engagement to strengthen democracy once the immediate crisis subsides continue to be largely outside the OAS's capabilities. As we have stressed, the charter was born with the birthmarks of club multilateralism. As we see in the next chapter, only circumstances that significantly weaken a host government's authority, and therefore its recourse to executive sovereignty, open up possibilities for networked multilateralism.

CHAPTER SEVEN

In Between Club and Networked Multilateralism: The Quest for a Solution to the Venezuelan Political Crisis

As we left off in the last chapter, sustaining an OAS presence on the ground following Chávez's restoration to power appeared uncertain, despite the seeming fragility of the political situation. In this chapter, we trace how the OAS overcame initial resistance to its continued presence and ultimately lodged itself in the daily political life of Venezuela, as it had done so in Peru. As in the Peruvian case, an OAS-facilitated *mesa* or table became the principal means by which the OAS sought to promote democratic dialogue and national reconciliation in Peru and Venezuela among polarized key domestic actors as well as to bring about a negotiated, peaceful resolution of the crisis. At each *mesa*, an OAS official served as the "facilitator," moderating discussion among the Peruvians and Venezuelans assembled at the table. If such a thing as an OAS "*mesa* model" of third-party mediation exists though, the Peruvian and Venezuelan experiences demonstrate that there were significant variations across tables in terms of origins, size, composition, and agenda. Importantly, the Peruvian *Mesa de Diálogo* and the Venezuelan *Mesa de Negociación y Acuerdos* showed important differences in terms of their outcomes and success in strengthening democracy and resolving conflict.

In the period from the immediate aftermath of the April 2002 coup to the August 15, 2004 presidential recall referendum, we observe the emergence of a more complex, networked multilateralism from the traditional club style. From the vantage point of the OAS and other international actors intent on defending democracy in Venezuelan, networking multilateralism was a creative approach to problem-solving. Significantly, for the first time, the OAS combined forces with a prominent non-state actor, the Carter Center, as well as the United Nations Development Program (UNDP) to form a tripartite working group. In terms of domestic actors in Venezuela, the Chávez government and the Venezuelan opposition grouped together in the *Coordinadora Democrática* (Democratic Focal Point) attempted to seize the opportunity provided by the OAS-Carter Center-UNDP "triumvirate" to extend the terrain of their struggle into the multilateral sphere. The *mesa*, as the hub of multilateral efforts, became another locus to advance their political agendas in their existential struggle. Where Chávez had previously resisted international intervention on traditional sovereignty grounds, in the period covered in this chapter he grew more accepting of an OAS role and used networked multilateralism when it suited him. The opposition adopted a similar opportunistic/pragmatic approach to international actors. Whatever the calculus or motivations, the longer-term effect of this dynamic was both to strengthen and legitimize the networked direction of OAS multilateralism for democracy.

Origins of the
Venezuelan *Mesa de Negociación y Acuerdos*

Despite repeated offers of assistance from the OAS in the months immediately following the April coup, the Chávez government clung to its sovereign prerogatives under club multilateralism. It opted to go it alone in terms of promoting national dialogue and reconciliation. However, these efforts failed to engage the opposition. Undoubtedly, attempts by the government to restore its authority by pursuing the perpetrators of the coup instilled fear within the opposition ranks and raised doubts concerning the sincerity of government-brokered reconciliation talks. The political situation remained tense and polarized.

Over time, the advantages for the Chávez government to turn from club to networked multilateralism grew. His government had some incentive to entertain some form of international involvement/oversight in the process of "national dialogue" that they convoked in the post-coup context. Symbolically, such an initiative allowed the government to take the moral high ground and improve its international image in a display of its own democratic credentials vis-à-vis the recent anti-democratic tactics of a good many of its opponents. It also provided the government with an extended cloak of legitimacy that it could use in the global arena, particularly as it sought solidarity with anti-globalization forces fighting democratic deficits and lack of transparency. More pragmatically, this tactic bought time for the government as it endeavored to consolidate its domestic position amidst all the aftershocks of the coup.

The Chávez government initially turned to those it considered its international friends for third-party mediation, namely the Carter Center, issuing a formal invitation to former president Jimmy Carter to facilitate a process of national dialogue on June 4. Rightly or wrongly, Chávez deemed Carter to be both a sympathetic and credible interlocutor. Undoubtedly Carter's more progressive leanings as well as his recent visit to Cuba impressed Chávez. In hindsight, we can see Carter as a crucial bridge between the old and the new; as a former high ranking and respected member of the club himself, he could use his cachet and contacts to open up multilateralism of a more networked variety. His club credentials allowed him to do so without the defenders of the club realizing that multilateralism was being changed.

Beyond the Venezuelan government's own failure to kick-start national dialogue with the opposition, there was a connected logic to the Chávez government's willingness to seek an international presence—but not directly or exclusively vis-à-vis the OAS. To target Jimmy Carter and the Carter Center as a fundamental component of this strategy was an inspired move of diplomacy. A personal invitation appropriated the Carter presence—and reputation—over to the Chávez side. It defused the impression that Chávez was an international troublemaker, an image created because of his close ties with the leaders of pariah states. What is more, it allowed Chávez to position Carter as the "good guy" versus the "bad guys" in the Bush administration who were widely perceived to have supported the April 2002 coup.

Carter attempted during a visit in early July to get both sides of the Venezuela stand-off to agree to conditions and an agenda for dialogue. Ultimately, his efforts were unsuccessful.[1] Opposition representatives from the fledgling *Coordinadora Democrática* refused to meet with members of the government in any government building. They also snubbed a subsequent invitation by Carter to meet together with him and President Chávez at his hotel in Caracas. At this point in time, various opposition figures viewed Carter as being partial to the Chávez government because it had invited him and therefore refused to accept him as go-between. Distrustful of the government, they insisted that the OAS instead must facilitate any dialogue between the two sides. Coming on the eve of a massive demonstration in which at least 600,000 protested, the opposition certainly felt little urgency to enter into talks with the government it despised.

The rapid turn of events in Venezuela shortly after the Bridgetown General Assembly compelled the Venezuelan government to reconsider its polite but firm rejection of the OAS's formal offers of support for national reconciliation and democratic strengthening. Instead of opposition demobilization, Chávez once again began to encounter mass demonstrations of the sort that pre-dated the coup in April. Equally worrisome, on August 14, 11 Supreme Court magistrates, many of whom were former *Chavistas*, dismissed charges against 4 senior military officers for their involvement in the April 11 coup.

After Carter's initial efforts in July failed, Gaviria's chief of staff, Fernando Jaramillo, Carter Center representatives Jennifer McCoy and Francisco Diez, and UNDP representative Elena Martínez remained on the ground in Venezuela to engage government and opposition in an attempt to kick-start an internationally facilitated dialogue process. As we have also acknowledged in the Peru case, these kinds of actors become crucial in the evolution of networked multilateralism. Their efforts gradually paid off as Venezuelan Vice President José Vicente Rangel extended formal invitations to the OAS and the UNDP in August to join the Carter Center in facilitating dialogue. Concurrently, in a symbolic act challenging the government's sovereignty, the opposition extended its own invitation to the two organizations. Approved on August 14, 2002, Permanent Council Resolution 821 provided the formal mandate for the OAS and the tripartite mission (comprised of the OAS, the Carter Center, and the United Nations Development Program) to assume a facilitation role. As in the case of Resolution 1753 for the OAS High-Level Mission in Peru, Resolution 821 also provided a mandate that was sufficiently broad and vague enough to allow for significant mission creep.[2]

The Actors at the Table

It is through the inter-action of multiple actors both Venezuelan and international that we come to appreciate the changes occurring in multilateralism. Secretary-General Gaviria himself personally assumed the position of lead facilitator for the tripartite mission. Unlike the low-key role played by Latorre in Peru, Gaviria was intentionally placed in the public eye. Based on an agreement between the Venezuelan government and opposition, his role as international facilitator of the *mesa* defined him also as its official public spokesman.³ In the succeeding months this link with the media would prove very useful for Gaviria to make announcements that helped prevent *mesa* members from reneging on agreements.

Gaviria's leadership begs the question why he and not some former head of state or ex–foreign minister, as in the case of Latorre in Peru, took personal charge of facilitating the Venezuelan *mesa*. After all, Gaviria was the former president of Colombia, a country with which Venezuela had considerable tensions over recent Colombian guerrilla operations along their shared border. Additionally, as secretary-general, Gaviria raised the stakes. The outcome of his efforts as chief facilitator would potentially put the OAS's credibility on the line. His role as facilitator also added enormously to his already heavy workload in Washington, leading some to doubt his ability to devote his undivided attention to Venezuela.

For his critics, his rationale was taken to be self-promotion, either in terms of a bid for the Nobel Peace Prize, a high UN position, or (in an even more far fetched manner) reelection as secretary-general. But for his supporters, the reasons combined a genuine concern with the promotion of a "new" OAS and a fear of the spillover effect in the hemisphere (the Andean region in particular, including Colombia) of the breakdown of order in Venezuela. In Peru the original intention was to strengthen Peruvian democracy over a 3–5 year time frame and in a context where regime breakdown seemed unlikely under Fujimori. A former foreign minister thus seemed a suitable choice for the context. However, in Venezuela, the potential for political violence and disorder appeared much higher after the *Caracazo* of 1989 and the recent bloodshed of April 11, 2002, and there were also clear signs of the spread of weapons among the general population. Hence the need for a facilitator of Gaviria's stature existed. In case any doubts remained about his personal commitment to the mission, the secretary-general moved physically and psychologically to Caracas for approximately six and half months.

Chávez insisted on a tripartite mission that, alongside the OAS, also included the Carter Center and the UNDP. In so doing, whether consciously or unconsciously, Chávez pushed multilateralism from a state-centric club style into an innovative direction. In this sense, OAS facilitation was more complex in Venezuela than in Peru. What Chávez could not have anticipated is that this "triumvirate" would actually strengthen the OAS's efforts, rather than hinder them. While the UNDP adopted a largely logistical and technical role, the Carter Center provided an added ingredient to the facilitation process that was not enjoyed by Latorre in Peru. As a pure facilitator bound by a pledge of impartiality and respect for Venezuelan sovereignty as well as beholden to the member states of the Permanent Council, Gaviria had little leeway to present proposals to the government and opposition. Jimmy Carter and his capable team on the ground, however, were not bound by the same restrictions. Carter and company acted not only as facilitators but also as mediators and advisers that could and did present proposals. Additionally, the Carter Center could exploit this dual role because it enjoyed the Chávez government's confidence. Carter publicly proposed two possible solutions to Venezuela's political impasse, a constitutional referendum to enable early elections through a shortened presidential term or a recall referendum in August 2003 to determine whether the Chávez government should complete the remainder of its term in office. These proposals refocused the energies at the *mesa* at a crucial juncture.[4]

Moreover, whereas Chávez's ties with Carter and his team were excellent, relations between Chávez and Gaviria had always been strained. This was particularly true in December 2002 when relations turned especially sour between Chávez and Gaviria. Public remarks made by Gaviria criticizing Chávez's government for media intimidation allegedly infuriated Chávez. In the months that followed leading up to the May 23 agreement, Carter and his team were able to sustain vital behind-the-scenes discussions with Chávez while relations with Gaviria remained acrimonious.

In both Peru and Venezuela, it is worth mentioning that both facilitators were aided by highly capable teams on the ground. This team approach was characterized on both occasions by the prominent role played by Gaviria's own chief of staff, Fernando Jaramillo. In Venezuela, Jaramillo worked closely with the OAS local representative as well as with Jennifer McCoy and Francisco Diez from the Carter Center and Elena Martínez of the UNDP.[5] This team accomplished an enormous amount of preparatory work for the *mesas* and engaged in crucial behind-the-scenes discussions with *mesa* members. They were valuable envoys at times when government and opposition were otherwise not in direct communication with one another.

Although Gaviria and Jaramillo originally considered applying the Peruvian *mesa* model, the Venezuelan government would have no part of it. The protracted presence of the fugitive Peruvian ex–security chief Vladimiro Montesinos in Venezuela prior to his arrest had soured relations between the two countries, curbing enthusiasm of the Chávez government to adopt the Peruvian *mesa* model. Additionally, whereas the Peruvian *mesa* contained multiple voices from diverse sectors of society, in its Venezuelan counterpart opposition members attempted to promote the Democratic Focal Point (*Coordinadora Democrática*), to which they all belonged, as the single legitimate interlocutor and united front of the opposition against Chávez. Indeed, the Democratic Focal Point's creation on July 5, 2002 from a very fractious, heterogeneous opposition was prompted by the perceived need to have a single voice in dealings with the Carter Center and the OAS. In the Venezuelan case, the six opposition participants at the *mesa* also resembled a shadow cabinet that seemed to match the positions and attitudes of the government representatives at the table.

The Venezuelan *mesa* was smaller than its Peruvian predecessor: six participants for each side for a total of twelve members. Each side was further permitted one on-hand adviser. The design deliberately incorporated three key sets of actors: government ministers, pro-government and opposition members of congress, and civil society representatives. The Venezuelan *mesa* also contained state governors on both sides, giving it a reach beyond the capital city of Caracas.

Once the *mesa* took shape, the Chávez government took its presence very seriously. Indeed, by buying into the *mesa*, Chávez reinforced networked multilateralism. The government assigned six of its most senior members to take up the positions allocated to it at the table. This group included José Vicente Rangel (the vice president), Roy Chaderton Matos (foreign minister), Aristóbulo Istúriz (minister of education, culture and sports), María Cristina Iglesias (minister of labour), Ronald Blanco La Cruz (governor of the state of Táchira), and Nicolás Maduro (National Assembly deputy). As adviser at the table, the government had first Jorge Valero (permanent representative to the OAS) and later, Omar Meza Ramírez (National Assembly deputy).

As in Peru, the *mesa* contained a strong presidential imprint. For all of the high-profile representation on the government side of the *mesa*, Chávez ultimately held veto power over the results of the proceedings. This came out clearly in the attempt to work out a preagreement between the government and opposition in April 2003. An agreement that Gaviria thought had been sealed unraveled when President Chávez said he wanted to see the text. Instead of saying no outright, Chávez dragged out the proceedings saying he was too busy with other events. Weeks elapsed before a counter-proposal was issued on April 24, when the government issued a new text (and a request that that the entire agreement be submitted for approval by the political and social forces supporting the government). A similar scenario played out in the drafting of the final agreement. Although numerous advisers were brought into the process to provide technical expertise, the final say was left personally to Chávez.

The opposition presence at the Venezuelan table included: Timoteo Zambrano from the *Alianza Bravo Pueblo*, a breakaway party from the old *Acción Democrática*; Alejandro Armas, a deputy in the National Assembly; Eduardo Lapi, governor of the state of Yaracuy; Manuel Cova, the secretary-general of the Confederation of Venezuelan Workers (CTV); Américo Martín, a civil society representative; and Rafael Alfonso from the executive of FEDECAMARAS, Venezuela's national federation of chambers of commerce. Finally, Juan Manuel Raffalli (*Primero Justicia*, a political party) was the group's designated adviser at the *mesa*.

Through the lens of networked multilateralism, the opposition's challenge was to compress the Democratic Focal Point's 19 political parties, 79 civil society organizations, and 16-member executive into a workable group of 6 *mesa* members and one adviser. The *mesa* design allowed different opposition representatives to match up with their government counterparts. Armas (a former Chávez supporter) provided a counterpoint to the militancy of Rangel. Cova matched up well with the labor minister, María Cristina Iglesias. Zambrano's speaking skills compensated for the strength on the government side.

In contrast to Peru, the Venezuelan *mesa*'s weakness was the lack of civil society representation, to some degree at odds with the recent effervescence in civil society activism throughout the country.[6] In Venezuela, the composition of opposition participation suggested the dominance of *Puntofijo* political elites within the Democratic Focal Point over newer civil society actors.

The task of selecting civil society representation was particularly arduous in Venezuela. Unlike in the case of Peru, it was hard to differentiate politicians from representatives of civil society. Nor had select members of Venezuelan civil society become thoroughly transnationalized allowing them to be singled out by the OAS or the Carter Center for consideration. In part this can be explained by the fact that Venezuelan civil society was relatively young. It was precisely Chávez's presidency that was the catalyst for much of the stirring of Venezuelan civil society. The 1999 constitution promoted popular political participation. Civil society also galvanized through popular resistance to his rule. Moreover, the OAS's lack of familiarity with Venezuelan civil society leaders was compounded by the fact that the Democratic Focal Point also had access to considerable resources. It was backed by powerful sectors of the business elite. For example, the expensive computer stations and electronic network that the opposition had set up across the country during the various phases of the national referendum process illustrated the impressive financial resources that it had at its disposal. Pro-opposition elites also owned most of the national television, radio, and print media in the country, giving the Democratic Focal Point a powerful weapon in its information politics against the Chávez government. The Venezuelan opposition clearly depended less on external actors for economic resources or media access than their Peruvian counterparts.

Allowed the responsibility for self-selection, Venezuelan civil society ran into a dead-end trying to pick a representative from among its ranks. There were simply too many groups and individuals with too many agendas and interests to do so by consensus. More precisely, there was a huge variation between human rights groups in terms of their responses to the political situation. The compromise choice was Américo Martín, a former guerrilla who had drifted into the center right of politics.

The dearth of authentic civil society representation had its repercussions. One problem for the Venezuelan case arose in the process of setting up working groups. Because of its relatively large size, the Peruvian *mesa* could effectively diversify through this route, building trust and deliverables through the interfacing of its members in smaller working-group settings. These working groups also facilitated the inter-action of *mesa* members and technical experts in the labor intensive design of political reforms. The Venezuelan case found it much harder to move in this direction. While the Venezuelan *mesa* had access to formal advisers, including Raffalli on the opposition side and Valero and later Ramírez on the government side as well as a host of informal advisers, its relative small size prevented it from dividing into smaller working groups.

One advantage possessed by the OAS's pro-intervention advocates was the initiative's *indirect* association with the United States. The United States was certainly heavily involved in both Peru and Venezuela although it avoided taking direct leadership of the OAS interventions. Diplomatically, the big difference between the two cases of U.S. involvement was its entry into the Group of Friends of Venezuela that lent diplomatic backing for the *mesa* process. Such a grouping did not exist in the Peruvian case. Created on January 15, 2003 in Quito, Ecuador, by several Latin American presidents attending the inauguration of Ecuadorian president Lucio Gutiérrez, the group consists of six members: Brazil, Mexico, Chile, Spain, Portugal, and the United States.[7] Their motives for forming the group certainly went beyond being good neighbors and international citizens. The group formed at the height of a crippling two-month national strike by petroleum workers opposed to the Chávez government when the danger of spillover effects from this destabilization was real.

In part, the United States took one of the leads in this group to ward off what could have been a far different grouping. The Venezuelan leader would have preferred the so-called Friends of Chávez—including Cuba, Algeria, and Russia to provide a forum that is both sympathetic and competing to Secretary-General Gaviria and the *Mesa de Negociación y Acuerdos*. The United States was also concerned about securing a reliable strategic oil supply in the context of its plans to go to war with Iraq. Undoubtedly the United States also sought to balance the role of Brazil, which took the central leadership position within this group.

Reacting to the impasse at the *mesa*, Brazil chaired a number of meetings of this alternative grouping in Washington, Caracas, and Brasilia. While this group did not produce a breakthrough in the dialogue, its pressure did help keep both sides at the *mesa*. The Group of Friends of Venezuela also served as another form of watchdog to prevent both the government and the opposition from crossing the line to unacceptable behavior. Through our conceptual lens, Brazil's leadership of the group is worthy of attention. As a quintessential club member, Brazil could lend its regional influence to the push for a diplomatic solution in Venezuela while containing both the potential spillover of the conflict into its territory and the bending of club multilateralism in directions that it considered problematic.

The *Mesa* Agenda

Another important dimension of this form of networked multilateralism was agenda-setting. The invitation formally extended by the Chávez government and the Democratic Focal Point to the so-called tripartite mission of the OAS, Carter Center, and UNDP delegated the authority to set the agenda and rules for dialogue to the invitees.[8] Political circumstances dictated a very different agenda for the Venezuelan table. Though the Peruvian *mesa* focused on a multipoint agenda aimed at substantially overhauling the country's political system, despite initial efforts by the tripartite mission to fashion a detailed 12-point agenda for the Venezuelan *mesa*, they failed to obtain agreement from government and opposition. In contrast to Peru then, much of the effort at the Venezuelan table was directed toward getting both sides to agree to a set of "rules of the game" for a peaceful, democratic, electoral, and constitutional solution to the crisis.

Unlike the list of 29 points for strengthening democracy that the OAS fashioned as the basis for dialogue in Peru, in the Venezuelan case the tripartite mission's early facilitation efforts could not produce such a detailed, multipoint agenda. It could get the two sides to agree to three basic rules of the game, as laid out in the *Declaration of Principles for Peace and Democracy in Venezuela* and the *Operational Synthesis* and a dialogue that would be focused on three key issues: the strengthening of the electoral system, the establishment of a truth commission to investigate the violence of April 11–13, and civilian disarmament.[9]

The *mesa* formally got under way on November 8, 2002. Progress on the agenda points was very slow at the outset. As in Peru, the *mesa* was not viewed as the only game in town for key participants. In Venezuela, neither government nor opposition originally channeled their full energies into the *mesa* process. For the Chávez government, the international presence enhanced its legitimacy and dissuaded any would-be coup conspirators. It possessed a majority in Congress so the *mesa* had no particular use as a parallel congress. The opposition participated in the OAS-facilitated dialogue process as but one of several tracks in a multitrack strategy to oust the Chávez government. The opposition continued to maintain pressure on the government through highly confrontational means including mass demonstrations, an attempted rebellion by anti-Chávez military officers, a "consultative referendum" that purportedly gathered over two million signatures, and a two-month general strike led by the petroleum workers that paralyzed the country during December 2002 and January 2003. Indeed, in a tit-for-tat power struggle, the government seized control over the pro-opposition Metropolitan Police of Caracas following the opposition's attempt to hold a constitutionally questionable "consultative referendum" against Hugo Chávez. This in turn provoked the *Coordinadora Democrática* to launch a general strike in December 2002. So long as the elements grouped together under the Democratic Focal Point continued their pursuit of street tactics, the *mesa* advanced little on its three-point agenda. Instead, it served as a valuable communication link between two polarized sides that otherwise were not communicating during this period of heightened mobilization.

Just as in Peru, it took a turn of events that dramatically altered the domestic structure of political power to galvanize the *mesa* into action. In Venezuela, there were no detonating events such as the Vladivideo exposé in Peru to undermine government or opposition. Rather, it was the outcome of the two-month opposition-led general strike in December 2002 and January 2003 that determined the future course of the *mesa*. While the petroleum sector-led stoppage did severe damage to the Venezuelan economy and resulted in record numbers of business bankruptcies and an alarming rise in unemployment, the Chávez government managed to outlast its opponents and emerge victorious from the confrontation. Indeed, it emerged more powerful than prior to the strike. Thanks to the strike, the Chávez government seized control of the state oil monopoly PDVSA, firing the executive and 19,000 employees. With the addition of PDVSA, Chávez now had a formidable power base that also included control over the state and the military, as well as mass support among Venezuela's urban and rural poor. As the prolonged strike also bankrupted or weakened many businesses across the country, the economic base of the opposition was hurt, throwing many of its militants into personal financial difficulty. It effectively tipped the balance in the conflict in favor of the *Chavistas*.

From February 2003 onward, the *mesa* became a much more interesting option to an opposition weakened and divided by the strike. The peaceful, democratic, electoral, and constitutional exit out of the crisis that the tripartite mission had advocated all along, all at once became much more attractive and opposition energies were henceforth channeled toward pushing for a recall referendum as provided for under Article 72 of the Venezuelan Constitution.

At the height of the strike, some timely help came from Jimmy Carter. He proposed that government and opposition adopt one of two options to exit out of the crisis: a recall referendum after the halfway point of the president's term on August 19, 2003 or a constitutional amendment to enable early elections through a shortened presidential term.[10] With Carter's dual proposal, Secretary-General Gaviria was able to direct dialogue back to the original 3-point agenda. Eventually both sides agreed to the recall referendum as the only solution to the crisis, something that the Chávez government had advocated all along. They turned to Gaviria and his facilitation team to prepare a working document, "Procedural Issues on the Recall Referendum for Discussion in the Forum for Negotiation and Agreement," as the basis for negotiating an eventual agreement on a recall referendum.[11]

By early April, both sides at the table reached agreement on a "preagreement" (*pre-acuerdo*).[12] Reverting to an executive prerogative, all that was missing was Chávez's endorsement as president of Venezuela. Chávez's approval, however, was not immediately forthcoming. In these circumstances, some skilful maneuvering was still required by the OAS facilitation team in order to seal an agreement. Fernando Jaramillo, operating as acting facilitator in Gaviria's temporary absence, formally announced to the Venezuelan press on April 11, 2003 that the government and the opposition had reached a deal on the preagreement as a way to force Chávez's hand. In a timely move, the Group of Friends of the secretary-general traveled to Caracas to throw their weight behind the deal. In an official communiqué issued on April 15, the Group of Friends praised the preagreement of April 11.[13] Chávez, no doubt furious because of Jaramillo's and the group's gambit, was put in an awkward position that made him look domestically and internationally like a negative force in a dialogue process that was finally appearing to reach an agreement. On April 24, Chávez put forward an alternative proposal for an agreement through the government representatives at the table.

Eventually Secretary-General Gaviria and his team were able to get government and opposition *mesa* members to back a formal accord on May 23, 2003.[14] Of special note, Carter's representatives, Jennifer McCoy and Francisco Diez, met with President Chávez to revise the agreement text to his satisfaction. Chávez recognized the publicity value for his government of having an agreement in hand on the eve of the 17th summit of the heads of state and government of the Rio Group in Cusco, Peru. With minutes to spare before Chávez boarded his plane to Cusco, the final wording of the May 23 agreement was adopted. Wherever Gaviria and Jaramillo met obstacles, Carter's team was able to take advantage of having privileged access to President Chávez to facilitate an agreement behind the scenes.

Beyond the *Mesa*: The Recall Referendum

Although embedded in the Venezuelan political system, the *mesa* process did not provide a novel outcome to the crisis but rather reaffirmed a constitutional route that had always existed. Whereas the Peruvian *mesa* contributed to the dramatic overhaul of the Peruvian political system, its Venezuelan counterpart had a somewhat more limited impact in reinforcing the recall referendum path set out in Article 72 of the Venezuelan constitution as the only viable exit out of political crisis. The success of Venezuela's *mesa* can be measured along two lines: the May 23 agreement and its impact on political process.

The crowning achievement of the Venezuelan *mesa*, the May 23 agreement, appears modest in comparison to its Peruvian counterpart. It did not lead to major institutional changes as it did in Peru. Its importance, however, should not be underestimated. The heart of the agreement was found in Article 12 that simultaneously bolstered respect for the constitution and effectively channeled both sides' energies into a democratic, electoral route out of crisis through a recall referendum.

The OAS and the tripartite mission also succeeded in getting both sides to agree formally in writing to their continued role as guarantors of the May 23 agreement. This stands in contrast to the situation immediately following the April 2002 coup when the OAS was unable to obtain the Chávez government's invitation to continue its presence in the country in order to promote national dialogue and reconciliation. The *mesa's Operational Synthesis*, the *Declaration Against Violence and for Peace and Democracy* and Articles 18 and 19 of the May 23 agreement provided for international follow-up, oversight, and technical assistance for the implementation of the recall referendum process, including continued facilitation by a post-*mesa* permanent follow-up liaison mechanism called the *Comisión de Enlace*. This guarantor role was ultimately embodied in the sustained presence and involvement of the OAS and Carter Center throughout the lengthy recall referendum process from 2003–2004.

The *mesa* also made an important contribution by way of political process. For example, during the tensest days of the national strike of December 2002 and January 2003, it kept crucial lines of communication open between the mutually hostile *Chavistas* and the opposition. This helped prevent misunderstandings that might have escalated the conflict into violence. In the midst of the strike, on February 18, 2003, Secretary-General Gaviria succeeded in getting both sides at the *mesa* to sign a declaration in which they pledged to avoid the use of violence.[15] Almost miraculously, the highly confrontational two-month strike did not erupt into mass violence and disorder. As Gaviria himself subsequently remarked, "One of the most important achievements of the Forum for Negotiation and Agreements had been to serve as an open channel of communications, especially during those heated moments, and as a factor for moderation and restraint of political passions . . ."[16]

As mentioned above, the OAS and the Carter Center remained active in Venezuela throughout the entire recall referendum process. Interestingly, their role became more complex. With the initiation of the referendum process, their activities now included not only third-party facilitation, but as international elections monitors they now also potentially served as "judges" in the last instance to oversee whether or not the recall referendum met international standards of freedom, fairness, and transparency. In the highly volatile atmosphere in which the recall referendum process unfolded, it was no easy challenge for the OAS and Carter Center to maintain appearances of impartiality as simultaneous facilitators and arbiters. As Carter Center official Francisco Diez remarked in hindsight, "it was a big challenge and the source of some tension, because a facilitator or mediator can't judge, while an observer is obligated to judge, in a way . . . I know in the eyes of some, the roles were not separate, but one and the same . . ."[17]

According to Article 72 of the Venezuelan constitution, any elected official in the country was potentially subject to a recall referendum after serving half of their elected term in office. In the case of President Chávez, the opposition was required to collect signatures from 20 percent, or 2,436,083, of registered voters in order to trigger legally a recall referendum against him. For their part, *Chavistas* also attempted to invoke Article 72 to recall various elected officials from the opposition.

The constitutional requirements of a recall referendum, occurring in the context of a high stakes, "existential" struggle between government and opposition, resulted in a protracted four-part process.[18] First, the two sides engaged in a formal signature collection process from November 28 to December 1, 2003. Just days beforehand, the OAS and the Carter Center received formal invitations from the National Electoral Council (CNE) to assemble a joint mission to monitor the signature collection and verification processes. On December 19, the opposition delivered to the CNE approximately 3.4 million signatures gathered during the formal collection period.

The collection exercise triggered the second phase of the process: a lengthy exercise of counting and verifying the signatures that began formally on January 13, 2004. This stage was arduously slow and fraught with tension. Between February 27 and March 4, a series of clashes between opposition demonstrators and the National Guard resulted in at least 14 deaths and almost 300 cases of injuries.[19] Against this backdrop, the signature counting and verification process was rife with controversy. To begin with, the opposition accused the CNE executive of having all along been partial to the government. On August 29, 2003, after the National Assembly had failed in its deliberations, the Supreme Court named, as stipulated in the constitution, the five-person executive of the CNE. Two of the five directors selected were pro-opposition, two were pro-government, and the fifth was ostensibly independent. However, in crucial executive votes, the so-called independent director casts his tie-breaking vote almost always consistent with the pro-government position. Moreover, since no existing detailed legislation or constitutional provisions existed for implementing a recall referendum, the CNE found itself practically inventing the rules as it went along.[20] To the opposition, these seemingly arbitrary decisions by the CNE smacked of government manipulation. CNE President Carrasquero in turn accused the OAS and Carter Center of being partial to the opposition.[21] For their part, *Chavista* militants of the electoral organization *Comando Ayacucho* accused the opposition of submitting fraudulent signatures.

The aforementioned violence coincided with the most contentious moment in the signature verification process, when the CNE president, Francisco Carrasquero, announced preliminary verification results on March 2, well after the 30-day verification period established in the constitution. The CNE's initial results invalidated over 900,000 signatures for "similar handwriting." That is, during the official signature collection process at the collection stations across the country, thousands of signatories had their personal data filled in on their signature forms by CNE-appointed opposition collection agents, instead of the signatories themselves filling in the information. The infamous name attached to these forms with similar handwriting was *"planillas planas."* Nonetheless, these signatories did sign and place their fingerprints on the forms. To Chávez's supporters, these forms filled in with similar handwriting amounted to fraud.

The CNE came under intense pressure simultaneously but separately, locally from the opposition and internationally from the OAS and the Carter Center. In Peru during the April and May 2000 elections, an informal transnational coalition was formed in criticism against Fujimori and the ONPE's electoral manipulations. While the CNE's recent actions triggered a backlash, it did not necessarily result in a similar transnational coalition being formed in Venezuela. In a sharp rebuke of the CNE, the OAS and the Carter Center publicly stated that the expressed will of the opposition signatories should take precedence over the problem of the *planillas planas* and that their signatures should therefore be respected.[22]

The CNE announced its final verification results on April 23. The CNE declared 1,910,965 signatures valid and 375,241 completely invalid. Under pressure both domestic and international, the CNE declared that an additional 1,192,914 signatures were invalid but that a third phase of the recall referendum would take place in which opposition supporters whose signatures had been rejected would be given a chance to "repair" them.[23]

With no precedent whatsoever for a signature repair process, the CNE and the political parties accepted the OAS and Carter Center's suggestion to negotiate and agree upon a set of procedures. With the partial help of OAS-Carter Center facilitation, the two sides agreed to give signatories the right to confirm or remove their signatures. The ability to remove their signatures and not just to authenticate them implied that the opposition potentially stood to lose signatures and not only to gain them. The signature repair process formally took place on May 28–31, 2004. On June 3, the CNE announced that the opposition had succeeded in obtaining the required number of signatures to trigger the recall referendum.

More than eight months after signatures had been collected, the fourth and final phase of the recall referendum process, the recall itself occurred on August 15, 2004. An impressive 70 percent of the electorate turned out to vote. In the early hours of August 16, the CNE announced that President Chávez had defeated the opposition bid to oust him via referendum by a vote of 5,800,629 to 3,989,008, or 59 percent versus 41 percent of the vote. Following the qualitative monitoring and a secret quick count of the referendum, the OAS and Carter Center electoral observation mission corroborated the CNE result, concluding that the official tally reflected the true will of the Venezuelan electorate.

However, the opposition was not so convinced. Many in the opposition ranks, most notably much of Venezuela's mainstream media, were quick to condemn the referendum as fraudulent, directing much of their assault not only at the Chávez government but also at the OAS and the Carter Center. In an abrupt reversal, opposition turned from their earlier admiration of the international observers to contempt for them. Extra security had to be brought in to protect international observers from a potentially violent reaction from protestors planted outside their two hotels in Caracas. In contrast, many *Chavistas*, albeit grudgingly, found new respect for the Carter Center and the OAS after harboring suspicions that the international observers were somehow agents of an imperialist Bush government.

Many of the largely unsubstantiated fraud allegations surrounded the use of brand new, sophisticated touch-screen voting machines connected to an electronic network with a mainframe computer in Caracas, as well as new fingerprint machines to create a national fingerprint database against fingerprint fraud. At the conclusion of the voting process, each of the voting stations communicated to Caracas its vote count from the voting machines electronically. With highly restricted access to the mainframe computer in Caracas, the opposition cried electronic fraud.[24]

One of the checks built into the new electronic voting machines, however, was the automatic printing out of a paper ballot each time a voter registered his/her vote on the touch-screen. The voter could then confirm on the ballot that his/her vote had been recorded correctly and then deposit it in a sealed ballot box. There was thus a paper trail for every single vote registered electronically.

With approval from the CNE, the OAS and the Carter Center held a special audit three days after the referendum in an effort to test the reliability of the electronic voting result and in so doing hopefully dispel opposition accusations. Under close coordination among the CNE, OAS, and the Carter Center, a random sample of 150 polling stations with 359 voting machines was selected to compare the paper ballots with the electronic tallies the machines produced. The selection was done in a way that ensured that nobody within the military (*Plan República*) guarding the ballot boxes had any knowledge of which of them would be chosen for the audit prior to the arrival of international observers to collect the boxes. International observers continuously stayed within the presence of the selected ballot boxes for the entire duration of the audit, from the military bases where they were collected through their delivery to a central CNE warehouse in Caracas, including the three-day long audit process. The exhausting audit process determined that there was only a 0.01 percent discrepancy between the electronic count and the corresponding paper ballot count, further confirming that the voting machines had indeed registered the will of the electorate.[25] Unfortunately, the opposition boycotted this audit and refused to recognize its results.

Following the recall referendum, the opposition that was once united in the *Coordinadora Democrática* soon fragmented. Within weeks, key defections from the CD occurred, including FEDECAMARAS, *Alianza Bravo Pueblo, Causa R, Primero Justicia,* and *Proyecto Venezuela.* Even *Acción Democrática* eventually bailed out of the CD, its leader announcing that it was severing its links with the oligarchy and reorienting its efforts toward its historic roots in the popular classes.[26]

In the days following the debacle, opposition stalwarts began assigning blame among themselves for their loss. The chance to oust Chávez had been the incentive that had sustained a marriage of convenience among many political parties and civil society organizations that otherwise had few compelling grounds for cooperating. The referendum result divided the opposition among hard-liners intent on boycotting looming regional and municipal elections in October 2004, those intent on radicalizing the struggle to get rid of Chávez, and the pragmatists who grudgingly accepted defeat and advocated refocusing energies on the pending October elections and ultimately on winning the presidential election of 2006.[27] No doubt many suffered the fatigue that came with protracted mobilization from before the April 2002 coup.

Many recognized, albeit quietly, that for all the suspicions of fraud, the opposition had only itself to blame for failing to present a single charismatic leader as the presidential challenger to Chávez. Instead, the "united front" that was the Democratic Focal Point was led by a group of leaders many of whom aspired to be Chávez's successor, yet none of whom had his charisma or popular appeal. Additionally, whereas the *Chavista* electoral organizations of *Comando Ayacucho* and afterward *Comando Maisanta* fanned out across the country to rally the "No" vote, the opposition had failed to establish a presence and run an effective campaign on the ground beyond the middle- and upper-class neighborhoods where they drew most of their support.

Ultimately, a social movement perspective reveals that the political opportunity structure that had favored the rise of the Democratic Focal Point abruptly took a negative turn after the recall referendum loss.[28] Leaders and militants alike had little incentive to sustain their voluntarism in the wake of a decisive defeat at the polls. With the passing of the recall referendum, the Democratic Focal Point's continued reason for existence died.[29]

Defending Democracy in Venezuela: Advances, Limits, and Unanticipated Consequences

As mentioned in chapter five, the Inter-American Democratic Charter was inspired by the lessons learned from the OAS's efforts to defend democracy in Peru. Accordingly, the charter provided provisions for preventive or proactive diplomacy, for dealing with both coups d'état (unconstitutional interruptions) and authoritarian backsliding by incumbent elected leaders (unconstitutional alterations), as well as for crisis follow-up and oversight.

The Venezuelan crisis, from the April 2002 coup to the August 15, 2004 recall referendum, demonstrated the ongoing difficulty in putting the OAS's emerging regional democracy norms, now codified in the charter, into practice. While innovations pushed multilateralism in a networked direction, the hold of club multilateralism persisted. The OAS was not able to undertake any significant preventive action prior to the April 2002 coup, despite signals of a rapidly deteriorating political situation. Once again, "firefighting" was the order of the day. By the same token, once Chávez was restored to power, the OAS was unable to obtain consent from the Venezuelan government to maintain its presence on the ground in the interest of promoting democratic dialogue and national reconciliation. The OAS acquired an invitation to do so only after the political situation had once again deteriorated during the summer of 2003.

While the Venezuelan experience signified the ongoing limits of the OAS's collective-defense-of-democracy, as in Peru, it also represented a further elaboration of both the democratic dialogue mode of intervention and networked multilateralism. Unlike Peru, the Venezuelan *Mesa de Negociación y Acuerdos* did not result in any far-reaching democratic reforms in the Venezuelan political process. However, as an innovation in networked multilateralism, the *mesa* was in itself not a guarantee for a sustained solution to Venezuela's crisis. Nonetheless, during the more than two years that the OAS and its partner, the Carter Center, were present in Venezuela, vital lines of communication between government and opposition were sustained and a mass outbreak of political violence and/or civil war was averted.

The outcome of political conflict in Venezuela during this time was not a lasting peace agreement or additional strengthening of democracy. Indeed, while the OAS and the Carter Center were focused on facilitating and observing the recall referendum process during 2003–2004, it can be argued that Chávez was busy at work weakening democracy on other fronts. He simultaneously initiated legislation to increase the number of Supreme Court judges and potentially undermine horizontal accountability in the country through partisan appointments.[30]

With the benefit of hindsight, we can now see that the presidential recall referendum advocated by the May 23 agreement was perhaps unrealistic as a means of resolving conflict. As borne out by events surrounding the August 15 vote, a yes or no plebiscite is inherently divisive rather than unifying.[31] As discussed above, the Democratic Focal Point rejected the CNE's official result, despite the OAS and Carter Center's authentication of Chávez's commanding victory. The country remained polarized with 41 percent of the population voting against Chávez. Moreover, among many in the opposition, the performance of the CNE during the entire process did not instill confidence in Venezuela's electoral institutions.

Inadvertently though, the OAS and Carter Center presence did make an important difference. In the time that they were on the ground in Venezuela, the Chávez government was finally able to consolidate its power and authority in Venezuela via nonviolent, electoral means. From a precarious position in the aftermath of the April 2002 coup, President Chávez incrementally gained control over the military, the petroleum sector, and the National Assembly. The August 15, 2004 referendum confirmed once and for all his popular mandate to govern. In a high stakes gamble, the opposition lost badly, leading ultimately to the demise of the Democratic Focal Point and leaving President Chávez in a commanding position to implement his Bolivarian Revolution with a democratic seal of approval.

CHAPTER EIGHT

Intervention Without Intervening?

In this book we tell the story of the recent evolution of multilateral efforts by the OAS to defend and promote democracy in the Americas. Our case studies examine the OAS's attempts to resolve the political crises in Peru and Venezuela. Two principal themes underpin our analysis. On a broader conceptual level, from an older club-style multilateralism, we trace the evolution of networked multilateralism in its relation to an emerging regional democratic solidarity paradigm. Tied in with the first theme at a more specific, detailed level is a novel form of intervention in the Americas—the OAS dialogue tables, the ascendancy of which we analyse.

The "tale of two *mesas*" at the center of this book points to the significant variation in the recent OAS interventions in Peru and Venezuela in terms of actors, agendas, and achievements. For the purposes of replication in other crisis contexts in the Americas and elsewhere, it is therefore difficult to speak of a single coherent "*mesa* model" of third-party mediation to defend democracy. Notwithstanding their differences, the two *mesas* crystallize the persistent challenges that entail operationalizing the declaratory principles of the OAS's democratic solidarity paradigm.

We can, however, speak of a novel mode of intervention. Laurence Whitehead has identified three historical forms of intervention or "imposition" to advance democracy in the Americas: incorporation, invasion, and intimidation.[1] These, of course, are all hard or forcible modes of intervention.[2] By contrast, the OAS missions in Peru and Venezuela, with the dialogue tables at their center, constitute a new, promising, and softer mode of intervention: *intervention without intervening*. That is, through the *mesa*-focused, intra-elite dialogue processes, the OAS presence (together with the Carter Center and the UNDP in Venezuela) in these countries inserted itself into their domestic politics with minimal intrusion into their political decisions. The OAS effectively moved inside the political life of two of its member states, all along treading softly. At the same time, the OAS left the details of political change to the Peruvian and Venezuelan elites themselves. The OAS agents at the table were neutral, impartial dialogue *facilitators* as opposed to mediators or arbiters with the authority to make decisions or recommendations. Even with these constraints, this soft mode of intervention does not mean that the OAS was powerless. Although their role was on the whole a restrained one, the OAS facilitators enjoyed certain subtle but potentially powerful soft power resources to influence the dialogue process without participating in the actual decision-making.[3] First, in both Peru and Venezuela they played a pivotal role in establishing the agenda for discussion by domestic elites as well as the rules for their participation at the table. Second, in both instances the OAS also gave crucial input for the selection of the actors chosen to sit (or not sit) at the *mesas*. The inclusion of certain actors and not others had an important legitimating/de-legitimating effect. Third, *mesa* participation no doubt also influenced the political fortunes of some. Valentín Paniagua, for example, rose to become interim president of Peru, in no small part thanks to the enhancement of his profile through his involvement in the *mesa*. Fourth, in the Venezuelan case, the OAS facilitation process helped prompt the fragmented opposition forces to unite and articulate the *Coordinadora Democrática* as the only legitimate interlocutor before the Chávez government. Fifth, in the Venezuelan context, the facilitator was also the *mesa*'s official spokesperson, whose public announcements could be used potentially as a tool to keep both sides committed to agreements made at the table. Finally, as the concrete local embodiment of an inter-American commitment to defend democracy with the weight of the international community behind them, the OAS facilitators and their teams were a constant reminder to domestic elites that undemocratic means of resolving any crisis were unacceptable options. Paradoxically then, intervention without intervening could potentially mean both treading softly and leaving lasting imprints.

Charles Sampford and Margaret Palmer have identified three good reasons why a country's own officials and citizens should take the lead in defending democracy. First, it is *their* democracy. Second, international support can be notoriously fickle. Finally, we must consider each country's particular history and circumstances. As Sampford and Palmer point out, domestic responses must be the first line of defense against threats to democracy.[4]

Unfortunately in the cases of Peru and Venezuela, domestic political actors were alarmingly polarized. Armed conflict and political violence seemed a more likely prospect than domestically driven multiparty and multisectoral dialogue and reconciliation. Under these circumstances, the OAS's intervention without intervening was a sort of happy medium. Foreign facilitators enabled nationals to address their own political crisis, something they would not likely have been willing or able to do without a helping external hand.

OAS Intervention in Peru and Venezuela: Success or Failure?

The outcomes of the two *mesas* were very different. Whereas the Peruvian *mesa* contributed to the dramatic overhaul of the Peruvian political system and the restoration of democracy, its Venezuelan counterpart helped to coax divided elites to channel their energies into a recall referendum that in the end failed to resolve the country's bitter divide. When the OAS High-Level Mission to Peru departed in January 2001, the country's democratic prospects looked promising. When the OAS mission in Venezuela closed shop following the August 15, 2004 referendum, government and opposition had still not made amends. Nonetheless, a semblance of political stability had been restored as Chávez emerged stronger, his power more consolidated than ever while the Democratic Focal Point quickly lost influence and fell apart.

How do we judge the relative successes and failures of OAS intervention in Peru and Venezuela? Success can be measured along two lines: any achievements in the form of concrete agreements or reforms as well as strengthening or stabilizing political processes. These factors underline the importance of also gauging success in terms of the counterfactual: what might have happened in these two countries in the absence of OAS intervention?

The Peruvian table is perhaps more impressive in terms of tangible achievements. Peruvian elites gathered at the *mesa* reached agreement on 16 of the 29 agenda items, including reforms that ensured the independence of the judiciary from governmental interference, eliminated the sinister SIN that had terrorized so many Peruvians, as well as instituted electoral reforms and the selection of new electoral authorities that would help guarantee the transparency of the April 2001 elections.

The crowning achievement of the Venezuelan *mesa*, the May 23 agreement appears more modest by comparison. It did not lead to major institutional changes as it did in Peru. Its importance, however, should not be underestimated. Centered in Article 12, the agreement effectively channeled both sides' energies into a democratic, electoral route out of the crisis through a presidential recall referendum that simultaneously bolstered respect for the constitution. Essentially, the OAS and international presence in Venezuela prevented an escalation of the crisis so that the opposition finally realized that its best chance all along for defeating Chávez was not through general strikes, mass demonstrations, or military rebellions but via the constitutional route of recall referendum as provided for under Article 72 of the constitution. As it had advocated from the beginning, the OAS got both sides to agree to a peaceful, democratic, electoral, and constitutional solution to the crisis.

The OAS and the tripartite group also succeeded in getting both sides to agree formally in writing to their continued presence as guarantors of the May 23 agreement. The *mesa*'s *Operational Synthesis*, the *Declaration Against Violence and for Peace and Democracy* and Articles 18 and 19 of the May 23 agreement provided for international follow-up, oversight, and technical assistance for the implementation of the recall referendum process, including continued facilitation through a post-*mesa* follow-up body called the *Comisión de Enlace*. Elaborating an important follow-up, oversight role was particularly significant in light of the OAS's broader objectives, as captured in the Inter-American Democratic Charter, to expand its more traditional firefighting tendencies toward a longer-term, more forward looking democracy strengthening capacity. In effect, the OAS, Carter Center, and the UNDP continuously remained on the ground in Venezuela until after the August 15, 2004 referendum. Keeping both sides committed through all phases of the contentious referendum process was a significant achievement in itself.

Sadly, the referendum did not prove to be the complete resolution of Venezuela's political crisis hoped for by the OAS or as captured in the May 23 agreement. The Democratic Focal Point rejected the National Electoral Council's official results (that pronounced Chávez the winner with a 59 percent share of the popular vote) and denounced the referendum as fraudulent. In so doing, the opposition also refused to accept the endorsement by the OAS and Carter Center's own electoral observation of the official results. Indeed, many in the opposition-controlled media suggested complicity by the OAS and the Carter Center in manufacturing Chávez's victory. Instead of restoring confidence in the country's institutions and in the democratic process, the referendum further increased distrust and division among Venezuela's elites and the greater population. As the OAS mission wound down following the referendum, a solution to the impasse seemed more elusive than ever.

We must acknowledge the unintended consequences of international efforts in Venezuela. While the discord between government and opposition was not alleviated, Chávez successfully consolidated his power. Inadvertently, with Chávez more solidly installed in office, the prospects for stability in Venezuela's immediate future were enhanced.

Since success is normally gauged by outcomes, it is easy to ignore the important contribution made by OAS efforts to political life in both countries in terms of political processes. For example, the insertion of OAS-led dialogue processes at moments of extreme political polarization and instability had a crucial moderating and restraining effect on politics. As was made particularly clear in the Venezuelan case, the weight of the OAS, its Inter-American Democratic Charter, the tripartite group, and the Group of Friends of Venezuela made any undemocratic and unconstitutional measures during the crisis by government or opposition alike politically unacceptable. For instance, in October 2002, Secretary-General Gaviria strongly criticized the unconstitutional and insubordinate actions of a group of Venezuelan soldiers who attempted to incite a barracks revolt and civil disobedience. The international facilitation efforts also paid off in convincing both sides to repudiate the use of political violence via formal agreements, at the outset of *mesa* negotiations and most crucially following the tensest moments of the opposition-led general strike.[5] The *mesas* also sustained open lines of communication between otherwise mutually hostile political elites, an additional contribution toward moderating political conflict in the two countries.

Counterfactually, we must ask what might have happened were the OAS not on the ground. One can only imagine the extremes to which the two crises might have gone in the absence of OAS facilitation efforts. In Peru, the power vacuum and political instability caused by the chain of events beginning with the Vladivideo exposé in September 2000 might well have led to a military coup or civil war had not the OAS dialogue process with strong international backing been in place at the time. Similarly, the isolated incidents of violence that occurred in Venezuela during heightened periods of opposition and pro-government mobilization before and during the general strike of December 2002 and January 2003 could have been much worse had not the tripartite group with its international support not kept both sides communicating at the table at the most difficult moments of the crisis.

As a channel for the transition from the April–May 2000 presidential elections to the exit of Fujimori, the OAS High-Level Mission and its *mesa* were indispensable. The *mesa* filled the institutional vacuum caused by the polarization of political forces in Peru following the May elections. It became the locus of real decision-making power during the final days of the Fujimori government, acting almost as a parallel congress before the Peruvian opposition could win control of Congress and form an interim government.

The *mesa* experience in Peru suggests that the process emphasized there might even have contributed to valuable political cultural change. The intra-elite dialogue begun at the *mesa*, with its emphasis on consensus, multi-sectoral representation, inclusionary decision-making, and pluralism continued following the restoration of democracy in the country long after the *Mesa de Diálogo* ceased operations in December 2000. A certain positive momentum was carried forward from the *mesa* process for Peruvian political and civil societies. Political parties, civil society organizations, and individual citizens, for example, actively participated in the elaboration of their government's draft proposal for the Inter-America Democratic Charter. The new ethos of intra-elite dialogue and consensus-building culminated in an important effort to establish a new set of democratic rules of the game, the National Political Accord of July 2002. Fittingly, OAS Secretary-General Gaviria was on hand to witness the signing of this historic document.

The OAS in Peru and Venezuela: Strengthening Democracy?

Assessing the successes and failures of OAS intervention in Peru and Venezuela would not be complete without addressing the question of their impact on democracy. What kind of democracy did the OAS promote? Did the interventions resolve the root problems of Peruvian and Venezuelan democracy?

Rhetorically at least the OAS had a good sense of what type of democracy it was trying to promote. For the first time, in articles 3–6 the Inter-American Democratic Charter laid out an extensive set of definitional criteria for what it meant by "representative democracy." While permitting considerable institutional and procedural variations across countries, the "essential elements of representative democracy" identified in the Inter-American Democratic Charter could be used as benchmarks both for gauging authoritarian backsliding and for strengthening democracy.

In practice, intervention without intervening was not a form of intervention that leant itself readily to promoting many of the charter's democratic criteria. To recap, OAS intervention in Peru and Venezuela was largely predicated on domestic elites finding for themselves made-in-Peru and made-in-Venezuela solutions to their respective countries' political problems. It was not about imposing a political model on a target population.

Moreover, there were really two objectives in the crises. One was certainly to strengthen and defend democracy. The other concerned conflict resolution and national reconciliation between polarized elites. While these dimensions were certainly intertwined, it was by no means a given that conflict resolution and national reconciliation through intra-elite dialogue would take a path that strengthened democracy. Elite compromise could possibly have taken many different forms over which OAS facilitation might have little real influence.

Nonetheless, as suggested above, we should not underestimate the potentially powerful and far-reaching influence of the intervention-without-intervening mode on democracy. To reiterate, the OAS could exercise considerable soft power in the form of agenda-setting. This was particularly evident in the Peruvian case, where Secretary-General Gaviria and the Canadian Foreign Minister Lloyd Axworthy's capable teams assembled a 29-point agenda for strengthening democracy after consulting widely with Peruvian elites. In Venezuela on the other hand, the tripartite group simply could not get the opposing sides to agree to a multipoint agenda. Instead, government and opposition eventually agreed to a 3-part agenda: strengthening the electoral system, the establishment of a Truth Commission to investigate the violence of April 11–13, and civilian disarmament. Even here in this more limited agenda-setting, the OAS could potentially channel elite energies into democratic ends.

Another potentially powerful OAS prerogative was the giving of voice through the overseeing of the selection of representatives at each *mesa*. The exercise of *mesa* member nomination could effectively determine how representative the democratic dialogue would be. The OAS had the delicate task of reconciling representation with task orientation: a large number of members might be more representative but less efficient in terms of covering the agenda, and vice versa.

Interestingly, the two *mesas* tackled the representation-task orientation tension differently. The Peruvian *mesa* had a larger number of members that represented both political society and civil society more amply. Then again, political society and civil society were on an unequal footing at the *mesa* since political party representatives had both voice and vote while civil society representatives had voice but no vote. The Peruvian *mesa* was also Lima-centric in its members' composition and thus was poorly representative of other parts of the country.

In Venezuela, the table was smaller in terms of its numbers but with more equal footing for political society and civil society representatives. The smaller numbers however meant that the *mesa* had a narrower representation of political society and civil society voices, particularly the latter. The Venezuelan *mesa* also had greater regional representation and was less Caracas-centric. From another angle, the *mesa* privileged representation from the Democratic Focal Point, particularly *puntofijista* elites, to the exclusion of independent, nonpartisan civil society in the country. This instantly legitimated this umbrella group as *the* interlocutor for opposition forces and reinforced the polarized government–opposition dyad in Venezuela at the expense of any more moderate, independent voices in the country. Finally, in both instances, it is worth noting that subaltern groups, such as Afro-Venezuelans or Peruvians of indigenous descent, were not directly represented at either *mesa*.

We see from this then that the OAS had a very powerful influence, whether intentionally or unintentionally, over who had voice and who was silenced. Ultimately, the OAS prerogative over member selection could to some degree either advance a status quo orientation or an anti–status quo bent.[6]

The OAS's pro- or anti–status quo orientation was reinforced even further by another subtle but conceivably powerful influence on democracy that the OAS could exercise through its facilitation of intra-elite dialogue: an implicit preference for pacted democracy. That is, through its facilitation of the *mesas*, the OAS favored the elaboration of elite-centered "pacts" or negotiated compromises that established the rules of governance over more mass-based, bottom-up alternative paths to democratization.[7]

In an acute sense of *déjà vu*, this was precisely the mode of transition to democracy captured in Venezuela's original Pact of Punto Fijo in 1958. While the *Puntofijo* elite pact successfully underpinned Venezuela's two-party political system for more than forty years, with the benefit of hindsight we can see that the system failed to distribute the benefits of the country's oil-driven economic growth beyond a relatively narrow segment of the population. When Venezuela entered into economic hardship in the 1980s and 1990s, popular support for the elitist *Puntofijo* system dwindled dramatically, leading to calls for its dismantling. Indeed, it was on this wave of popular discontent with the *Puntofijo* system that Hugo Chávez rode into office in 1998. *Puntofijistas* became a term of derision used by *Chavistas* against their political opponents.

If the implicit pact-making dimension of OAS democratic dialogue promotion is indeed neo-*puntofijismo*, than there is cause for concern for the longer-term democratic prospects of countries that achieve elite compromise through *mesa* processes. As Terry Lynn Karl has suggested, intra-elite agreements affect the crucial issue of *cui bono*: who gets what in the post-conflict political situation. Karl asserts that elite pact-making may carry a significant trade-off: the establishment of political democracy in the short term but at the cost of equity in the longer term.[8] If we look back at the demise of Venezuela's *Puntofijo* system, we certainly see in the end twin crises: a crisis of popular representation in an elitist political system and a crisis of accumulation or development that failed to distribute the benefits of the country's oil wealth to the vast, impoverished majority.

Counterfactually, of course, we must ask what the alternative to an elite-pacted resolution to the political crises in Peru and Venezuela might be. As we have indicated before, in all likelihood, increased political violence and even civil war might have been the alternative means to ending the crises in the two countries, with no guarantee (as we can infer from countries such as Colombia) for a successful resolution. The OAS's option therefore to facilitate intra-elite dialogue was certainly an imperfect one fraught with dilemma and even trade-offs.

The OAS's prerogative for selecting *mesa* membership as well as its influence on agenda-setting, nonetheless, contain within them the possibility of shaping elite pact-making in a less elitist way. Augmenting *mesa* membership to include increased representation of subaltern societal groups or putting some of their grievances on the agenda might well help address Karl's democracy-equity trade-off in the longer term. We should not underestimate, however, the enormity of the challenge of broadening intra-elite dialogue in an environment of the participation–task orientation tension, competing club and networked multilateralism, sovereignty considerations, and subaltern groups that often lack institutionalized forms of representation or well articulated grievances.

The State of the OAS Multilateralism–Democracy Nexus After Peru and Venezuela

There have been many positive developments in the evolution of the OAS multilateralism–democracy nexus stemming from the Peruvian and Venezuelan experiences. In a more general sense the hurdles presented by traditional club multilateralism inspired significant innovations in the direction of networked multilateralism. OAS efforts to defend democracy significantly expanded the existing set of players to include non-state actors. In contrast to the old cautious diplomacy, the newer multilateralism was distinguished by its flexibility, intensity, and speed. On the ground, the OAS demonstrated a remarkable ability to circumvent obstacles thrown up by sovereignty-oriented governments, adapt to changing circumstances, and seize opportunities for mission creep. At the forefront, the secretary-general was adept at expanding his good offices despite Permanent Council misgivings. The negotiation of the Inter-American Democratic Charter entailed a considerable public consultative process. Finally, networked multilateralism was driven by strong normative convictions about the need to defend democracy. Even as we acknowledge that the hold of club multilateralism has not been completely broken, these characteristics of a more networked multilateralism have proven their value and therefore must be taken seriously.

In a more specific sense, regional democracy norms and the OAS collective action repertoire expanded considerably as a result of the Peruvian and Venezuelan interventions. One important advance is the OAS's increasingly assertive external validation role,[9] mostly in the form of election monitoring. That is, the OAS has been prepared to use its electoral observation missions to criticize the host government when transgressions occur. In May 2000, mission leader Eduardo Stein's much publicized identification of grave electoral irregularities and shortcomings in the second round of elections caused serious damage to the Fujimori government's democratic credentials. Indeed, following the Stein Mission in Peru (and the equally critical OAS mission to the May 21, 2000 legislative elections in Haiti), Article 25 of the charter enshrined the obligation of electoral observation missions to advise the secretary-general and the Permanent Council when the conditions for free and fair elections do not exist. In the first few months of 2004, strong public criticism by Secretary-General César Gaviria and Jimmy Carter of the National Electoral Council's decision to nullify thousands of signatures collected by the opposition to demand a recall referendum no doubt had a strong influence on that body's decision to allow a signature "repair" process in May 2004.

The Peru and Venezuela experiences also helped hone the soft intervention diplomatic tools at the OAS's disposal. Secretary-General Gaviria expanded the use of his good offices more than any previous secretary-general. While technically beholden to member states, Gaviria exercised considerable situational leadership[10] both in Peru and Venezuela in a way that undoubtedly enhanced the prestige and authority of his office independent of the weight of member states behind him. In addition to numerous fact-finding and consultative trips as well as press statements, Gaviria expanded his good offices to include centering control over democracy defense and promotion activities in the Secretariat and personally taking charge of facilitating the Venezuelan dialogue process from November 2003 to May 2004.

As elaborated in detail throughout this book, the *mesa* mechanism was another important tool or rather set of tools added to the OAS's soft intervention repertoire. This included the creation of the facilitator role for the OAS in intra-elite democratic dialogue processes. The facilitator was ostensibly neutral and non-interventionist, while exercising considerable influence as mentioned above over agenda-setting and *mesa* participant selection. Then there was the *mesa* itself, which proved to be a dialogue mechanism that was adjustable in its shape and composition to the idiosyncrasies of different domestic political contexts.

The Peru experience, both for the Peruvian resistance to Fujimori and the OAS, proved to be the impetus behind the Inter-American Democratic Charter (IADC) signed on September 11, 2001. In addition to enshrining Resolution 1080 and the Washington Protocol, the IADC for the first time provided a set of definitional criteria for representative democracy. Moving beyond the OAS's traditional crisis response or reaction mode, the charter also contained clauses that created the basis for important roles for the OAS in crisis prevention and follow-up or oversight. From Peru came compelling grounds for developing a capacity to address not only coup but also non-coup scenarios. Accordingly, the charter explicitly acknowledged this in a language that differentiated between situations of unconstitutional interruption (coup) and alteration (authoritarian backsliding by incumbent elected leaders). The charter also allowed ample room for creative diplomacy, containing clauses that enabled the ratcheting up of diplomatic measures from the nonpunitive to the punitive.

Finally, through the Peru and Venezuela experiences, the OAS experienced a certain "coming of age" vis-à-vis the United States. The United States both ceded leadership to and adopted a supporting role behind the OAS in its efforts to find peaceful, democratic solutions to the Peruvian and Venezuelan crises. While undoubtedly this evolution can be explained by the interests of the United States itself, it is also a reflection of how far the OAS had come in terms of its efficacy and credibility in recent years. We also see in the response to the April 2002 coup against Hugo Chávez that OAS member state solidarity around the defense of democracy in that country put the U.S. government embarrassingly on the defensive.

Similarly, at the OAS General Assembly in Fort Lauderdale, Florida in June 2005, member states widely rejected a U.S. proposal to create a permanent, independent democracy monitoring and civil society consultative mechanism within the OAS. On one level the resistance was certainly reflective of the perceived threat to executive sovereignty. On another level, member states resented being pressured to support a proposal that was delivered to them barely a week before the General Assembly and that appeared to be a thinly veiled attack on Venezuela.[11] As Venezuelan President Hugo Chávez remarked, "The times in which the OAS was an instrument of the government in Washington are gone."[12] The United States can no longer, if it ever could, easily push the OAS around, certainly not in the issue area of democracy defense and promotion.[13] Indeed, the international response to the April 2002 coup against Chávez, the failure to impose its preferred candidate for the job of Secretary-General in early 2005, and the Fort Lauderdale debate suggest an important decline of U.S. influence and credibility in the Inter-American System.[14]

Nevertheless, there are still a number of persistent constraints and shortcomings in the OAS's democratic solidarity paradigm. One is the elusive goal of crisis prevention. The OAS's failure to stop the authoritarian transformation of Peru under Fujimori during the 1990s was one of the prime motivating factors behind the creation of the IADC. Even though the IADC contains provisions for preventive diplomacy, the OAS failed to prevent the Venezuelan coup of April 2002. Disturbingly, the OAS has also been unable to respond in a timely and effective manner to recent political crises in Ecuador and Bolivia, despite official offers of assistance.

The Friends of the Democratic Charter assert that the key obstacles to crisis prevention are design flaws within the Inter-American Democratic Charter itself. The charter fails to define the conditions that would constitute an unacceptable violation of the charter, it does not contain automatic responses to such violations, and the OAS lacks an effective early warning system.[15] These shortcomings are undoubtedly linked at a more profound level with what we have underscored in our analysis: the persistence of club multilateralism in the OAS with its traditional emphasis on executive sovereignty.

While external validation by the OAS has made important advances, it also has significant limits. Though the Stein Mission's assessment of the second round of elections in Peru in May 2000 helped undermine the Fujimori government's legitimacy, the OAS and the Carter Center could not convince the Venezuelan opposition that Chávez's recall referendum victory had indeed reflected the popular will. As a form of external validation, these contrasting experiences demonstrate that OAS elections monitoring is potentially very influential, although not necessarily so. Additionally, there are clear limits to how much external validation that OAS member states are willing to endorse. The Peruvian proposal to define in the IADC a role for the Inter-American Commission of Human Rights as a tool for monitoring and evaluating crises was flatly rejected. It is clear that OAS member states are extremely reluctant to support any form of peer review mechanism for non-electoral processes.

Despite the elaboration of such a noble document, there has been extreme reticence by OAS member states to invoke the Inter-American Democratic Charter. While preamble references have been made in various resolutions, neither in the Venezuelan nor the Haitian crises have we witnessed either besieged governments or other member states turning to the charter for assistance. Tellingly, Jean-Bertrand Aristide was ousted from office in February 2004 without the charter being invoked. It is also instructive that the IADC falls short of an international treaty, limiting its weight as an instrument of international law. For all the innovative advances in the direction of networked multilateralism, club multilateralism is very much alive in the region.

The IADC's seemingly tentative status suggests that regional democracy and intervention norms are still in an emergent state and fall short of what Finnemore and Sikkink call a norm cascade, or broad, uncontested norm acceptance.[16] In other words, converting many of the admirable principles contained in the IADC into practice continues to be difficult.

The aforementioned limits to OAS pro-democracy collective action indicate that sovereignty is alive and well in the inter-American system. In contrast to suggestions that sovereignty's prerogatives are shrinking in the Americas,[17] our study points to the persistent sovereign limits to OAS efforts to mount collective defenses of democracy.

The ultimate proof that sovereignty norms remain strong in relation to democracy and intervention norms is the stipulation that the OAS must be formally invited by host governments in order to pursue its pro-democracy activities within their borders. In keeping with Whitehead's inclination for alliteration,[18] intervention without intervening has yet another hallmark beginning with the letter "i": intervention by *invitation*. The OAS could not have launched its dialogue processes without the express consent of the Peruvian and Venezuelan governments. Certainly in the Peruvian case, this meant the consent of what was rapidly becoming a pariah government. In the Venezuelan case, the OAS together with the Carter Center and the UNDP received even a formal invitation from the Democratic Focal Point. While never formally issuing the OAS an invitation, the elected congressman and civil society representatives in Peru endorsed (albeit reluctantly at first) the dialogue process as well. Coming back to Sampford and Palmer,[19] intervention without intervening is a mode in which external actors on invitation help create a dialogue space for domestic political elites to wield their influence in directions that reflect domestic idiosyncrasies.

In sum, although the OAS has come a long way, its experiences in Peru and Venezuela underscore the real sovereign and institutional limits that continue to constrain its ability and demand its cunning and ingenuity in the promotion and defense of democracy.[20] Intervention without intervening indicates a multilateral defense and promotion of democracy regime that remains incomplete. As manifested in the Peruvian *Mesa de Diálogo* and the Venezuelan *Mesa de Negociación y Acuerdos*, this intervention was slow and arduous for making inroads into the political crises in Peru and Venezuela. It does not constitute a "quick fix" mode of intervention nor does it guarantee long-term political stability. Nor does the OAS solve the problem but rather provides the means for nationals to tackle their country's most pressing issues themselves. Notwithstanding their imperfections, these OAS interventions though ultimately proved more palatable than what might have happened in their absence. They were both highly effective in preventing a violent escalation of events over their duration, in maintaining open lines of intra-elite communication under polarized conditions, and in achieving consensus among diametrically opposed domestic political actors for nonviolent, democratic, electoral, and constitutional means to end the crisis. For all of these reasons, they are valuable additions to the expanding international collective action repertoire for confronting threats to democracy wherever they may arise in the Americas.

NOTES

Chapter 1 The Multilateral-Democracy Nexus: An Overview

1. Richard Bloomfield, "Making the Western Hemisphere Safe for Democracy? The OAS Defense-of-Democracy Regime," in *Collective Responses to Regional Problems: The Case of Latin America and the Caribbean*, ed. Carl Kaysen, Robert A. Pastor, and Laura W. Reed (Cambridge, MA: American Academy of Arts and Sciences, 1994, 15–28). (Also published in *Washington Quarterly* 17, no. 2 (Spring 1994): 157–169); César Gaviria, Address by César Gaviria, secretary-general of the Organization of American States, at the opening of the Conference of the Americas. Washington, DC, March 5, 1998. <http://www.oas.org/EN/PINFO/SG/305anoe.htm>; César Gaviria, Palabras del Secretario General de la Organización de los Estados Americanos, César Gaviria, in II Cumbre de las Américas. Santiago de Chile, April 18, 1998; César Gaviria, Palabras del Secretario General de la Organización de los Estados Americanos, César Gaviria, in Celebración del Cincuentenario de la Organización. April 30, 1998. Santafé de Bogotá. <http://www.oas.org/EN/PINFO/SG/418cumbr.htm>
2. Ellen L. Lutz and Kathryn Sikkink, "The International Dimension of Democratization and Human Rights in Latin America," in *Democracy in Latin America: (Re)Constructing Political Society*, ed. Manuel Antonio Garreton M. and Edward Newman (New York: United Nations University Press, 2001), 296. See also Karen L. Remmer, "External Pressures and Domestic Constraints: The Lessons of the Four Case Studies," *In Beyond Sovereignty: Collectively Defending Democracy in the Americas*, ed. Tom Farer (Baltimore, MD: Johns Hopkins University Press, 1996), 288.
3. Fernando Tesón, "Changing Perceptions of Domestic Jurisdiction and Intervention," in *Beyond Sovereignty: Collectively Defending Democracy in the Americas*, ed. Tom Farer (Baltimore, MD: Johns Hopkins University Press, 1996), 30–31.
4. Ibid., 30.
5. See Jon C. Pevehouse, "Democracy from the Outside-In? International Organizations and Democratization," *International Organization* 56, no. 3 (Summer 2002), 51; Jon C. Pevehouse, *Democracy from Above: Regional Organizations and Democratization* (Cambridge, UK: Cambridge University Press, 2005).
6. Phillipe C. Schmitter, "An Introduction to Southern European Transitions from Authoritarian Rule: Italy, Greece, Portugal, Spain, and Turkey," in *Transitions from Authoritarian Rule; Southern Europe*, ed. Guillermo O'Donnell, Phillipe Schmitter, and Laurence Whitehead (Baltimore, MD: Johns Hopkins University Press, 1986), 5.

7. Laurence Whitehead, "International Aspects of Democratization," in *Transitions from Authoritarian Rule; Southern Europe*, ed. Guillermo O'Donnell, Philippe C. Schmitter, and Laurence Whitehead (Baltimore, MD: Johns Hopkins University Press, 1986), 4–5.

8. Terry Lynn Karl, "Dilemmas of Democratization in Latin America," *Comparative Politics* 23, no. 1 (1990), 1–27. The "nativist" notion was coined in Philippe C. Schmitter, "The Influence of the International Context Upon the Choice of National Institutions and Policies in Neo-Democracies," in *The International Aspects of Democratization: Europe and the Americas*, ed. Laurence Whitehead, 2nd ed. (New York: Oxford University Press, 2001), 27.

9. Gerardo L. Munck and Carol Skalnik Leff, "Modes of Transition and Democratization: South America and Eastern Europe in Comparative Perspective," *Comparative Politics* 19, no. 3 (1997), 343–362.

10. Karen L. Remmer, "The Process of Democratization in Latin America," *Studies in Comparative International Development* 27, no. 4 (1992–1993), 3–24.

11. *Problems of Democratic Transition and Consolidation: Southern Europe, South America, and Post-Communist Europe*, ed. Juan J. Linz and Alfred C. Stepan (Baltimore: Johns Hopkins University Press, 1996); Jonathan Hartlyn, "Political Continuities, Missed Opportunities, and Institutional Rigidities: Another Look at Democratic Transitions in Latin America," *Politics, Society, and Democracy: Latin America*, ed. Jonathan Hartlyn (Boulder, CO: Westview, 1998), 101–120. Jonathan Hartlyn also conceives of international influences exclusively as context.

12. See Laurence Whitehead, "Three International Dimensions of Democratization," in *The International Dimensions of Democratization: Europe and The Americas*, ed. Laurence Whitehead, 2nd ed. (New York: Oxford University Press, 2001), hereafter cited as *Democratization: Europe and Americas*; Philippe C. Schmitter, "The Influence of the International Context upon the Choice of National Institutions and Policies in Neo-Democracies," in *Democratization: Europe and Americas*, ed. Whitehead, 26–54.

13. Laurence Whitehead, "Three International Dimensions of Democratization," in *Democratization: Europe and Americas*, ed. Whitehead, 9.

14. See e.g., Charles Powell, "International Aspects of Democratization: The Case of Spain," in *Democratization: Europe and Americas*, ed. Whitehead, 285–314.

15. Michael Waller, "Groups, Parties and Political Change in Eastern Europe from 1977," in *Democratization in Eastern Europe: Domestic and International Perspectives*, ed. Geoffrey Pridham and Tatu Vanhanen, 2nd ed. (London: Routledge, 1994), 50.

16. Kevin F.F. Quigley, "Democracy Assistance in South-East Asia: Long History/Unfinished Business," in *Democracy Assistance: International Cooperation for Democratization*, ed. Peter Burnell (London: Frank Cass, 2000); See also Laurence Whitehead, "Concerning International Support for Democracy in the South," in *Democratization in the South: The Jagged Edge*, ed. Robin Lucham and Gordon White (Manchester: Manchester University Press, 1996), 270.

17. See e.g., Hermann Giliomee, "Democratization in South Africa," *Political Science Quarterly* 110, no. 1 (1995), 83.

18. Philippe C. Schmitter, "The Influence of the International Context," 45, in Whitehead, *Democratization: Europe and Americas*.

19. Daniel C. Thomas, "Human Rights in U.S. Foreign Policy," in *Restructuring World Politics: Transnational Social Movements, Networks, and Norms*, ed. Sanjeev Khagram, James v. Riker, and Kathryn Sikkink (Minneapolis: University of Minnesota Press, 2002), 71–95.

20. See e.g., the political doctrine expounded by U.S. ambassador to the United Nations Jeane Kirkpatrick, a doctrine that advocates U.S. support of communist-opposing governments around the world. Jeane J. Kirkpatrick, *Dictatorships and Double Standards: Rationalism and Reason in Politics* (New York: Simon & Schuster, 1982).

21. See Jerome Slater, *The OAS as Antidictatorial Alliance: The OAS and United States Foreign Policy* (Columbus: Ohio State University, 1967).

22. Anthony Payne, "The United States and its Enterprise of the Americas," in *Regionalism & World Order*, ed. Andrew Gamble and Anthony Payne (London: Routledge, 1996), 97.

23. *Mexico's Political Economy: Challenge at Home and Abroad*, ed. Jorge Domínguez (Beverly Hills, CA: Sage, 1982), 13–14.

24. Lorenzo Meyer, "Mexico: The Exception and the Rule" in *Exporting Democracy: The United States and Latin America*, ed. Abraham F. Lowenthal (Baltimore: Johns Hopkins University Press, 1991), 217, 229.

25. Lutz and Sikkink, "The International Dimension of Democratization and Human Rights in Latin America," 294.

26. Philip Geyelin, *Lyndon B. Johnson and the World* (New York: Praeger, 1966), 254; Walter LaFeber, *Inevitable Revolutions: The United States in Central America* (New York: W.W. Norton & Company, 1993).

27. Fidel Castro in *Granma*, July 20, 1969, 5; Peter Binns and Mike Gonzalez, "Cuba, Castro and Socialism," *International Socialism Journal* 2, no. 8 (Spring 1980): 1–36.

28. For details of this episode see Piero Gleijeses, *Shattered Hope: The Guatemalan Revolution and the United States, 1944–1954* (Princeton, NJ: Princeton University Press, 1992).

29. See e.g., William I. Robinson, *Promoting Polyarchy: Globalization, U.S. Intervention and Hegemony* (Cambridge: Cambridge University Press, 1996).

30. Jorge Domínguez, "The Americas: Found, and Then Lost Again," *Foreign Policy* 112 (Fall 1998), 125–137.

31. Abraham F. Lowenthal, "The United States and Latin American Democracy: Learning from History," 263, in Lowenthal, *Exporting Democracy: The United States and Latin America*, 403.

32. Geoffrey Pridham, *Encouraging Democracy: The International Context of Regime Transition in Southern Europe* (New York: St. Martin's, 1991), 24.

33. Laurence Whitehead, "Democratic Regions, Ostracism, and Pariahs," in *Democratization: Europe and Americas*, 395.

34. For the case of Argentina, e.g., see Dominique Fournier, "The Alfonsín Administration and the Promotion of Democratic Values in the Southern Cone and the Andes," *Journal of Latin American Studies* 31 (1999), 39–74.

35. Guy Gosselin and Jean-Philippe Thérien, "The Organization of American States and Hemispheric Regionalism," in *The Americas in Transition: The Contours of Regionalism*, ed. G. Mace and L. Bélanger (Boulder, CO: Lynne Rienner, 1999), 175–194.

36. James Caporaso, "International Relations Theory and Multilateralism: The Search for Foundations," in *Multilateralism Matters: The Theory and Praxis of an Institutional Form*, ed. John Ruggie (New York: Columbia University Press, 1993); J.G. Ruggie, "Multilateralism: The Anatomy of an Institution," in *Multilateralism Matters; The Theory and Praxis of an Institutional Form*, 11.

37. For a complementary analysis that examines the United Nations as a conservative bureaucracy, see Michael Barnett and Martha Finnemore, *Rules for the World: International Organizations in Global Politics* (Ithaca, NY: Cornell University Press, 2004).

38. For a model of club membership of multilateral cooperation see Robert Keohane, *Power and Governance in a Partially Globalized World* (London: Routledge, 2002).

39. R. O'Brien, A.M. Goetz, J.A. Scholte, and M. Williams, *Contesting Global Governance* (Cambridge: Cambridge University Press, 2000).

40. Anne-Marie Slaughter, "The Real New World Order," *Foreign Affairs* 76, no. 5 (1997): 183–197; Anne-Marie Slaughter, *The Real World Order* (Princeton NJ: Princeton University Press, 2004). On the momentum towards networking in the global context see this source.

41. César Gaviria, secretary-general of the Organization of American States (Address at the opening of the "Conference of the Americas," Washington, DC, March 5, 1998), www.oas.org/EN/PINFO/SG/305anoe.htm.

42. David Mares, "Middle Powers under Regional Hegemony: To Challenge or Acquiesce in Hegemomic Enforcement," *International Studies Quarterly* 32, no. 4 (December 1988): 453–472.

43. Dominique Fournier, "The Alfonsin Administration and the Promotion of Democratic Values in the Southern Cone and the Andes," *Journal of Latin American Studies* 31 (1999): 39–74.

44. Maxwell A. Cameron, "Global Civil Society and the Ottawa Process: Lessons from the Movement to Ban Anti-Personnel Mines," in *Enhancing Global Governance: Towards a New Diplomacy?*, ed. Andrew F. Cooper, John English, and Ramesh Thakur (Tokyo: United Nations University Press, 2002), 68–89.

45. On the Friends of the Democratic Charter, see the Carter Center, "President Carter Delivers Keynote Speech to OAS Lecture Series of the Americas," January 25, 2005 <www.cartercenter.og/doc1995.htm>; Friends of the Democratic Charter, "It's Taboo To Say Our Democracies Are Weak," *Miami Herald*, May 2, 2005.

46. See Martha Finnemore and Kathryn Sikkink, "International Norm Dynamics and Political Change," *International Organization* 52, no. 4 (Autumn 1998): 887–917.

47. On trans-governmentalism, see Anne-Marie Slaughter, *A New World Order* (Princeton, NJ: Princeton University Press, 2004). Manuel Castells by way of contrast highlights a society-centered process of networking, inclusive of the networked enterprise, virtual networks, and identity-based societal movements. *The Information Age: Economy, Society and Culture Vol. 1: The Rise of the Network Society* (Oxford: Blackwell, 1996).

48. On "insider" and "outsider" non-state actors, see Roberto Patricio Korzeniewicz and William C. Smith, *Protest and Collaboration: Transnational Civil Society Networks and the Politics of Summitry and Free Trade In the Americas* North–South Agenda Papers No. 51 (Miami: North–South Center, University of Miami, September 2001); Roberto Patricio Korzeniewicz and William C. Smith, "Transnational Civil Society Actors and Regional Governance in the Americas: Elite Projects and Collective Action From Below," in *Regionalism and Governance in the Americas: Managing Unequal Power*, ed. Louise Fawcett and Mónica Serrano (New York/London: Palgrave, 2005).

49. G. John Ikenberry and Michael W. Doyle, *New Thinking in International Relations Theory* (Boulder, CO: Westview, 1997).

50. Laurence Whitehead, Postscript to *Democratization: Europe and Americas*, 443–454.

51. See also Hans Peter Schmitz, "Domestic and Transnational Perspectives on Democratization," *International Studies Review* 6, no. 3 (September 2004): 403–426.

52. In a similar vein, Keck and Sikkink have developed a network politics approach that analyzes the inter-actions between transnational advocacy networks and states. While our own work is inspired by Keck and Sikkink's rich analysis of non-state actors in their principled struggles against states across various issue-areas, we focus more on the multilateralism-democracy nexus. See Margaret E. Keck and Kathryn Sikkink, *Activists Beyond Borders: Advocacy Networks in International Politics* (Ithaca, NY: Cornell University Press, 1998).

Chapter 2   The OAS Democratic Solidarity Paradigm: Agency Innovation and Structural Constraints

1. Heraldo Muñoz, "Collective Action for Democracy in the Americas," in *Latin American Nations in World Politics*, ed. Heraldo Muñoz and Joseph S. Tulchin, 2nd ed. (Boulder, CO: Westview, 1996), 17–34; and Heraldo Muñoz, "The Right to Democracy in the Americas" *Journal of Interamerican Studies and World Affairs* 40, no. 1 (Spring 1998): 1–18.

2. Richard J. Bloomfield, "Making the Western Hemisphere Safe for Democracy? The OAS Defense-of-Democracy Regime," in *Collective Responses to Regional Problems: The Case of Latin America and the Caribbean*, ed. Carl Kaysen, Robert A. Pastor, and Laura W. Reed (Cambridge, MA: American Academy of Arts and Sciences, 1994), 15–28.

3. Arturo Valenzuela, *The Collective Defense of Democracy: Lessons from the Paraguayan Crisis of 1996* (A Report to the Carnegie Commission on Preventing Deadly Conflict, New York: Carnegie Corporation of New York, December 1999).

4. Domingo E. Acevedo and Claudio Grossman, "The Organization of American States and the Protection of Democracy," in *Beyond Sovereignty: Collectively Defending Democracy in the Americas*, ed. Tom Farer (Baltimore, MD: Johns Hopkins University Press, 1996), 148.

5. Bloomfield, *Making the Western Hemisphere Safe for Democracy?*, 164.

6. Organization of American States, *Charter of the Organization of American States* (Washington, DC: OAS, 1989), art. 3 (d).

7. 17th Meeting of Consultation of Ministers of Foreign Affairs of the OAS, OAS, Res/2, Ser/F II.17, Doc 49/79, Rev 2 (June 23) 1979.

8. Acevedo and Grossman, "The Organization of American States and the Protection of Democracy," 137–138; and Muñoz, "The Right to Democracy in the Americas," 7–8.

9. Joaquín Tacsán, "Searching for OAS/UN Task-Sharing Opportunities in Central America and Haiti," *Third World Quarterly* 18, no. 3 (1997), 495.

10. OAS, *Protocol of Cartagena de Indias*, February 26, 1986, OEA/Ser.P AG/doc.16 (XIV–E/85) rev. 2, 2.

11. OAS, *Serious Events in the Republic of Panama*, 1989, CP/Res. 534 (800/89).

12. Acevedo and Grossman, "The Organization of American States and the Protection of Democracy," 139–140.

13. OAS, *The Santiago Commitment to Democracy and the Renewal of the Inter-American System* (Adopted at the third plenary session, Santiago: Chile, June 4, 1991).

14. OAS, *Representative Democracy*, 1991, AG/RES. 1080 (XXI–O/91), 1.

15. Roland H. Ebel, Raymond Taras, and James D. Cochrane, *Political Culture and Foreign Policy in Latin America: Case Studies from the Circum-Caribbean* (Albany, NY: State University of New York Press, 1991), 121.

16. OAS, *Protocol of Amendments to the Charter of the Organization of American States "Protocol of Washington,"* December 14, 1992. 1-E Res.OAS Official Documents/Sec.A/2/Add 3—Treaty A-56, Amendment to Ch 3 of Art 9— at the 16th Special Session of the General Assembly of the OAS.

17. OAS, *Unit for Democratic Development*, 1990, AG/Res. 1063 (XX–O/90).

18. OAS, *Program of Support for the Promotion of Democracy*, 1991, CP/Res. 572 (882/91).

19. UPD, Permanent Council of the OAS Committee on Juridical and Political Affairs, *Work Plan of the Unit for the Promotion of Democracy* UPD–1999, February 4, 1999, OEA/Ser.G CP/CAJP-1436/98 corr.1, 1–2.

20. Randall Parish & Mark Peceny, "Kantian Liberalism and the Collective Defense of Democracy in Latin America," *Journal of Peace Research* 39, no. 2 (2002): 242; See also Rachel McCleary, *Dictating Democracy: Guatemala and the End of Violent Revolution* (Gainsville: University Press of Florida, 1999).

21. G. Pope Atkins, *Latin America in the International Political System*, 3rd ed. (Boulder, CO: Westview Press, 1995), 210. Forged in the context of recurring and/or threatened interventions by European states in order to protect their overseas residents or collect debts owed them, the Calvo and Drago Doctrines stressed absolute sovereignty and territorial inviobility as fundamental rights of states.

22. OAS, *Charter of the Organization of American States*, Chapter IV, Article 19. Bogotá, Colombia, 1948.

23. OAS, *Charter of the Organization of American States*, Article 20, Chapter IV. Bogotá, Colombia, 1948, December 13, 1951.

24. Joaquín Tacsán, "Searching for OAS/UN Task-Sharing Opportunities in Central America and Haiti," *Third World Quarterly* 18, no. 3 (1997): 498; See also Tom Farer, "Collectively Defending Democracy in the Western Hemisphere," in *Beyond Sovereignty: Collectively Defending Democracy in the Americas*, ed. Tom Farer (Baltimore, MD: Johns Hopkins University Press, 1996), 1–25; Fernando R. Tesón, "Changing Perceptions of Domestic Jurisdiction and Intervention," in *Beyond Sovereignty: Collectively Defending Democracy in the Americas* ed. Tom Farer (Baltimore, MD: Johns Hopkins University Press, 1996), 29–51; Thomas M. Franck,

"The Emerging Right to Democratic Governance," *American Journal of International Law* 86, no. 4 (January 1992): 46–91; and Muñoz, "The Right to Democracy in the Americas," 1–18.

25. OAS, Unit for Democratic Development, AG/Res. 1063 (XX-O/90), 1990.

26. Gordon Mace, Guy Gosselin, and Louis Bélanger, "Regional Cooperative Security in the Americas: The Case of Democratic Institutions," in *Multilateralism and Regional Security*, ed. Michel Fortmann, S. Neil MacFarlane, and Stéphane Roussel (Cornwallis: The Canadian Peacekeeping Press of The Lester B. Pearson Canadian International Peacekeeping Training Center, 1997), 123–146.

27. Alicia Frohmann, "Regional Initiatives for Peace and Democracy: The Collective Diplomacy of the Rio Group," in *Collective Responses to Regional Problems: The Case of Latin America and the Caribbean*, ed. Carl Kaysen, Robert A. Pastor, and Laura W. Reed (Cambridge, MA: American Academy of Arts and Sciences, 1994), 129–141.

28. Ibid.

29. Muñoz, "The Right to Democracy in the Americas," 9.

30. Arturo Valenzuela, "Paraguay: The Coup That Didn't Happen," *Journal of Democracy* 8, no. 1 (Spring 1997): 43–55; and Arturo Valenzuela, "The Collective Defense of Democracy: Lessons from the Paraguayan Crisis of 1996," *Latin American Weekly Report*, March 30, 1999.

31. Atkins, *Latin America in the International Political System*, 197.

32. Valenzuela, "Paraguay: The Coup That Didn't Happen," 54.

33. On the UN context see David Malone, *Decision-Making in the UN Security Council—The Case of Haiti 1990–1997* (Oxford: Clarendon Press, 1998).

34. OAS, *Weekly Report*, April 5, 1999: "OAS running out of money," *Financial Times* (London), June 8, 2000.

35. For an excelent analysis of the OAS's current finanacial woes, see John W. Graham, "La OEA Se Hunde: ¿Merece Ser Salvada?" *Foreign Affairs En Español* 5, 2 (April–June 2005).

36. UPD, *Work Plan of the Unit for the Promotion of Democracy (UPD)—1999*. Permanent Council of the OAS Committee on Juridical and Political Affairs. OEA/Ser.G CP/CAJP-1436/98 rev. 2 corr.1. February 4, 1999, Washington, DC.

37. OAS, *OAS Weekly Report*, April 12, 1999, Washington, DC.

38. OAS, *Key OAS Issues*, 2001, Washington, DC.

39. Summit of the Americas, *Declaration of Principles. Partnership for Development and Prosperity: Democracy, Free Trade and Sustainable Development in the Americas*, Plan of Action, First Summit of the Americas, Miami, December 1994, 1.

40. OAS, Office of the Secretary-General, "Financing the Inter-American Human Rights System," in *Cote Interamericana de Derechos Humanos, El Sistema Interamericano de Protección de los Derechos Hujmano en el Embral del Siglo XXI, Informe: Bases para un proyecto de protocolo a la Convención Americana sobre derechose humanos, para fortalecer su mecanismo de protección* (San José: Inter-American Court of Human Rights, 2001), 578. [Financing the Inter-American Human Rights System, A Report prepared by the Office of the Secretary-General of the OAS for the Ad Hoc Working Group on Human Rights, created by the Foreign Ministers meeting of November 22, 1999 held in San José, Costa Rica, April 28, 2000].

41. Robert A. Pastor, "The Clinton Administration and the Americas: The Postwar Rhythm and Blues," *Journal of Interamerican Studies and World Affairs* 38, no. 4 (Winter 1996): 99–128.

42. Jorge I. Domínguez, "The Americas: Found, and Then Lost Again," *Foreign Policy* 112 (Fall 1998): 135.

43. Pastor, "The Clinton Administration and the Americas: The Postwar Rhythm and Blues."

44. Andrew F. Cooper, Richard Higgott, and Kim Richard Nossal, *Relocating Middle Powers: Australia and Canada in an Evolving World Order* (Vancouver: University of British Columbia Press, 1993); and *Niche Diplomacy*, ed. Andrew F. Cooper (London: Macmillan, 1997).

45. Olga Pellicer, "La OEA a los 50 Años: ¿Hacia Su Fortalecimiento?" *Revista Mexicana de Política Exterior* 54 (June 1998): 19–36.

46. On Canada's foreign policy with respect to the Inter-American system, see Peter McKenna, *Canada and the OAS: From Dilettante to Full Partner* (Ottawa: Carleton University Press, 1995); James Rochlin, *Discovering the Americas: The Evolution of Canadian Foreign Policy Towards Latin America* (Vancouver: University of British Columbia Press, 1994); Andrew F. Cooper, *Canadian Foreign Policy: Old Habits and New Directions* (Scarborough, ON: Prentice Hall, 1997).

47. Andrew F. Cooper, "Waiting at the Perimeter: Making U.S. Policy in Canada," in *Canada Among Nations 2000: Vanishing Borders*, ed. Fen Osler Hampson and Maureen Appel Molot (Toronto: Oxford University Press, 2000), 27–46.

48. Bloomfield, Making the Western Hemisphere Safe for Democracy?, 169–171.

49. Gordon Mace, Guy Gosselin and Louis Bélanger, "Regional Cooperative Security in the Americas: The Case of Democratic Institutions," in *Multilateralism and Regional Security*, ed. Michel Fortmann, S. Neil MacFarlane, and Stéphane Roussel (Cornwallis: The Canadian Peacekeeping Press of The Lester B. Pearson Canadian International Peacekeeping Training Center, 1997), 123–146.

50. Joseph S. Tulchin, "Continuity and Change in Argentine Foreign Policy," in *Argentina: The Challenges of Modernization*, ed. Joseph S. Tulchin and Allison M. Garland (Wilmington, DE: Scholarly Resources, 1998), 163–197.

51. Alberto Van Klaveren, "Inserción Internacional de Chile," in *Chile en los Noventa*, ed. Cristian Toloza and Eugenio Lahera (Santiago: Dolmen, 1998), 149.

52. Parish and Peceny, "Kantian Liberalism," 237.

53. Oran Young, "Political Leadership and Regime Formation: On the Development of Institutions in International Society," *International Organization* 45 (1991): 302–303.

54. Alfred P. Montero, "A Delicate Game: The Politics of Reform in Brazil," *Current History*, 626 (March 1999): 111–115; and Michael Reid, "Brazil's Unfinished Search for Stability," *Washington Quarterly* 21, no. 4 (Autumn 1998): 79–92.

55. James Holston, and Teresa P.R. Caldeira, "Democracy, Law, and Violence: Disjunctions of Brazilian Citizenship," in *Fault Lines of Democracy in Post-Transition Latin America*, ed. Felipe Aguero and Jeffrey Stark (Miami: North-South Center Press, 1998), 263–296.

56. Bloomfield, *Making the Western Hemisphere Safe for Democracy?*, 168–169.

57. Jorge Chabat, "Mexican Foreign Policy in the 1990s: Learning to Live with Interdependence," in *Latin American Nations in World Politics*, ed. Heraldo Muñoz and Joseph S. Tulchin, 2nd ed. (Boulder, CO: Westview, 1996), 149–163; and Villicana Román López, "Mexico and NAFTA: The Case of the Ministers of Foreign Affairs," *Annals of the American Academy of Political and Social Science* 550 (March 1997): 122–129.

58. Ibid.

59. Ibid.

60. Chabat, "Mexican Foreign Policy in the 1990s: Learning to Live with Interdependence," 158.

61. Denise Dresser, "Treading Lightly and Without a Stick: International Actors and the Promotion of Democracy in Mexico," in *Beyond Sovereignty: Collectively Defending Democracy in the Americas*, ed. Tom Farer (Baltimore, MD: Johns Hopkins University Press, 1996), 322; and Carlos A. Heredia, "NAFTA and Democratization in Mexico," *Journal of International Affairs* 48, no. 1 (Summer 1994): 13–38.

62. M. Delal Baer, "The New Order and Disorder in U.S.–Mexican Relations," in *A New North America: Cooperation and Enhanced Interdependence*, ed. Charles F. Doran and Alvin Paul Drischler (Westport, CT: Praeger, 1996), 13.

63. Jorge G. Castañeda, secretary of foreign affairs, *Statement during the Joint Conference with the Secretary of the Interior* (Santiago Creel, Mexico City: Secretaría de Relaciones Exteriores, México D. F., February 7, 2002).

64. Guillermo O'Donnell, "Delegative Democracy," *Journal of Democracy* 5, no. 1 (Spring 1994): 55–69; James Petras and Steve Vieux, "The Transition to Authoritarian Electoral Regimes in Latin America," *Latin American Perspectives* 21, no. 4 (Fall 1994): 5–20; Carlos H. Acuña and William C. Smith, "The Political Economy of Structural Adjustment: The Logic of Support

and Opposition to Neoliberal Reform," in *Latin American Political Economy in the Age of Neoliberal Reform*, ed. William C. Smith, Carlos Acuña, and Eduardo A. Gamarra (New Brunswick, NJ: Transaction, 1994), 17–66; Eduardo A. Gamarra, "Market-Oriented Reforms and Democratization in Latin America: Challenges of the 1990s," in *Latin American Political Economy in the Age of Neoliberal Reform*, ed. William C. Smith, Carlos Acuña, and Eduardo A. Gamarra (New Brunswick, NJ: Transaction, 1994), 1–14; and *Fault Lines of Democracy in Post-Transition Latin America*, ed. Felipe Aguero and Jeffrey Stark (Miami: North–South Center Press, 1998).

65. For an excellent short summary of the on-going nature of these problems see Michael Shifter, "The Future of Democracy in Latin America," in *Freedom of the World 2003—The Annual Survey of Political Rights and Civil Liberties*, Freedom House (Lanham: Rowman & Littlefield Publishers, 2003).

66. Farer, "Collectively Defending Democracy in the Western Hemisphere."

67. Tesón, "Changing Perceptions of Domestic Jurisdiction and Intervention."

68. Ibid., 30.

Chapter 3   Defending Democracy?
The OAS and Peru in the 1990s

1. See, e.g., Terry Lynn Karl, "Dilemmas of Democratization in Latin America," *Comparative Politics* 23 (October 1990): 9–10.

2. See Julio Cotler, "Military Interventions and 'Transfer of Power to Civilians' in Peru," in *Transitions from Authoritarian Rule: Latin America*, ed. Guillermo O'Donnell, Philippe C. Schmitter, and Laurence Whitehead (Baltimore: Johns Hopkins University Press, 1986), 148–172; Philip Mauceri, "The Transition to 'Democracy' and the Failures of Institution Building," in *The Peruvian Labyrinth: Polity, Society, Economy*, ed. Maxwell A. Cameron and Philip Mauceri (University Park, PA: Pennsylvania State University Press, 1997), 13–36.

3. David Scott Palmer, "Collectively Defending Democracy in the Western Hemisphere," in *Beyond Sovereignty: Collectively Defending Democracy in the Americas*, ed. Tom Farer (Baltimore, MD: Johns Hopkins University Press, 1996), 272.

4. Cotler, "Military Interventions and 'Transfer of Power to Civilians' in Peru," 157; Cynthia McClintock, "Peru: Precarious Regimes, Authoritarian and Democratic," in *Democracy in Developing Countries: Latin America*, ed. Larry Diamond, Jonathan Hartlyn, Juan J. Linz, and Seymour Martin Lipset (Boulder, CO: Lynne Rienner, 1999), 323–324; Cynthia McClintock and Fabián Vallas, *The United States and Peru: Cooperation at a Cost* (New York and London: Routledge, 2003), 25–31.

5. On the popular mobilization that was inadvertently triggered by the Velasco regime's efforts to organize the poor, see Liisa North and Tanya Korovkin, The Peruvian Revolution and the Officers in Power, 1967–1976 (Montreal: Centre for Developing-Area Studies, McGill University, 1981).

6. Julio Cotler makes this same observation about the combined pressure of domestic opposition and international pressure weakening the regime but without delving into the theoretical implications. See Cotler, "Military Interventions and 'Transfer of Power to Civilians in Peru,'" 153.

7. Ibid., 165–166. On the broader brushstrokes of President Carter's human rights and democracy policy, see Kathryn Sikkink, *Mixed Signals: U.S. Human Rights Policy and Latin America* (Ithaca and London: Century Foundation/Cornell University Press, 2004); Thomas Carothers, *Aiding Democracy Abroad: The Learning Curve* (Washington, D.C.: Carnegie Endowment for International Peace, 1999).

8. 17th Meeting of Consultation of Ministers of Foreign Affairs of the OAS, OAS, Res/2, Ser/F II.17, Doc 49/79, Rev 2 (June 23) 1979.

9. See Terry Lynn Karl, "Dilemmas of Democratization in Latin America"; Terry Lynn Karl and Philippe C. Schmitter, "Modes of Transition in Latin America, Southern and Eastern Europe," *International Social Science Journal* 128 (May 1991): 269–284; Juan J. Linz and Alfred Stepan, *Problems of Democratic Transition and Consolidation* (Baltimore: Johns Hopkins University Press, 1996); Gerardo L. Munck and Carol Skalnik Leff, "Modes of Transition and Democratization: South America and Eastern Europe in Comparative Perspective," *Comparative Politics* 29, no. 3 (April 1997): 343–362.

10. On the *autogolpe*, see Gastón Acurio, et al, *Peru 1992: La Democracia en Cuestión* (Lima: North-South Center, Centro Peruano de Estudios Sociales, and Instituto de Estudios Peruanos, 1992); Maxwell A. Cameron, "Political and Economic Origins of Regime Change in Peru: The Eighteenth Brumaire of Alberto Fujimori," in *The Peruvian Labyrinth: Polity, Society, Economy,* ed. Maxwell A. Cameron and Philip Mauceri (University Park, PA: Pennsylvania State University Press, 1997), 37–69; Carlos Iván Degregori and Carlos Rivera, *Peru 1980–1993: Fuerzas Armadas, Subversión y Democracia* Working Paper No. 53 (Lima: Instituto de Estudios Peruanos, 1994); Eduardo Ferrero Costa, "Peru's Presidential Coup," *Journal of Democracy* (1993): 28–40; Cynthia McClintock, "Presidents, Messiahs, and Constitutional Breakdowns in Peru," in *The Failure of Presidential Democracy,* ed. Juan J. Linz and Arturo Valenzuela (Baltimore, MD: Johns Hopkins University Press, 1994), 360–395; Cynthia McClintock, "Peru: Precarious Regimes, Authoritarian and Democratic"; David Scott Palmer, "Collectively Defending Democracy in the Western Hemisphere"; Fernando Rospigliosi, *Montesinos y las Fuerzas Armadas,* especially Chapter 1 (Lima: Instituto de Estudios Peruanos, 2000); Susan Stokes, "Peru: The Rupture of Democratic Rule," in *Constructing Democratic Governance: Latin America and the Caribbean in the 1990s,* ed. Jorge I. Domínguez and Abraham F. Lowenthal (Baltimore, MD: Johns Hopkins University Press, 1996), 58–71.

11. According to a national survey taken just days after the April 6 self-coup, Fujimori's dissolution of Congress enjoyed an 88 percent approval rating while his plan to restructure the judiciary met with 94 percent approval. See Ferrero Costa, "Peru's Presidential Coup," 33. For additional survey statistics on the popular support for Fujimori's anti-democratic measures during the *autogolpe*, see Rolando Ames, Enrique Bernales, Sinesio López, and Rafael Roncagliolo, Situación de la Democracia en el Perú (2000–2001) (Lima: International IDEA and Pontificia Universidad Católicadel Perú Fondo Editorial, 2001).

12. Ferrero Costa, "Peru's Presidential Coup," 35.

13. Stokes, "Peru: The Rupture of Democratic Rule," 65.

14. Bernard Aronson in Maxwell Cameron, "Political and Economic Origins of Regime Change in Peru," 65.

15. For additional detail on the U.S. response to the self-coup, see Cynthia McClintock and Fabián Vallas, *The United States and Peru,* 136–141.

16. Ferrero Costa, "Peru's Presidential Coup," 34–35.

17. Ibid., 35.

18. The Rio Group consists exclusively of Latin American states. It does not have a secretariat or permanent body, and instead relies on yearly summits of heads of states.

19. *Representative Democracy.* AG/RES. 1080 (XXI-O/91), June 5, 1991.

20. See *The Situation in Peru.* CP/RES. 579 (897/92), April 6, 1992.

21. Cameron, "Political and Economic Origins of Regime Change in Peru," 66.

22. Ferrero Costa, "Peru's Presidential Coup," 35–36.

23. Margaret E. Keck and Kathryn Sikkink, *Activists Beyond Borders: Advocacy Networks in International Politics* (Ithaca: Cornell University Press, 1998).

24. On the National Human Rights Coordinator's efforts at transnational coalition-building, see Coletta A. Youngers and Susan C. Peacock, *Peru's Coordinadora Nacional de Derechos Humanos: A Case Study of Coalition Building* WOLA Special Report (Washington: Washington Office on Latin America, 2002).

25. Palmer, "Collectively Defending Democracy in the Western Hemisphere," 274.
26. Coletta A. Youngers and Susan C. Peacock, *Peru's Coordinadora Nacional de Derechos Humanos*, 19.
27. Human Rights Watch. *Peru: Human Rights Developments 1992.* http://www.hrw.org/reports/1993/WR93/Amw-09.htm#P536_256606
28. Ibid., 274.
29. See Kurt Weyland, "Neopopulism and Neoliberalism in Latin America: Unexpected Affinities," *Studies in Comparative International Development* 31, no. 3 (Fall 1996): 3–31; Kenneth M. Roberts, "Neoliberalism and the Transformation of Populism in Latin America: The Peruvian Case," *World Politics* 48 (October 1995): 82–116; Steven Levitsky and Maxwell A. Cameron, "Democracy Without Parties? Political Parties and Regime Change in Fujimori's Peru," *Latin American Politics and Society* 45, no. 3 (Fall 2003): 1–33; Steven Levitsky, "Fujimori and Post-Party Politics in Peru," *Journal of Democracy* 10, no. 3 (1999): 78–92.
30. Ferrero Costa, "Peru's Presidential Coup," 36.
31. Haggard and Kaufman's analysis of the impact of economic crisis on an incumbent authoritarian regime's relations with the business sector is highly relevant here. See Stephan Haggard and Robert R. Kaufman, *The Political Economy of Democratic Transitions* (Princeton, NJ: Princeton University Press, 1995).
32. For more detail see Peter Gourevitch, "The Second Image Reversed: The International Sources of Domestic Politics," *International Organization* 32, no.4 (1978): 881–912.
33. See Carlos Basombrío, "Civil Society Aid in Peru: Reflections from Experience," in *Funding Virtue: Civil Society Aid and Democracy Promotion*, ed. Marina Ottaway and Thomas Carothers (Washington, DC: Carnegie Endowment for International Peace, 2000), 269–290.
34. On the democratic conditionality phenomenon, see Philippe C. Schmitter, "The Influence of the International Context upon the Choice of National Institutions and Policies in Neo-democracies," in *The International Dimensions of Democratization: Europe and the Americas*, ed. Laurence Whitehead (Oxford: Oxford University Press, 2001), 26–54.
35. Diego García-Sayán, "El papel del multilateralismo en la defense y promoción de la democracia," <www.rree.gob.pe/cdioea/elpapel.htm>, November 8, 2002.
36. McClintock and Vallas, *The United States and Peru*, 142–147; Catherine M. Conaghan, "Troubled Accounting, Troubling Questions: Looking Back at Peru's Election," *LASA Forum* 26 (Summer 1995): 9–12.
37. Freedom House, *Freedom in the World: Peru* (New York: Freedom House, 2002).
38. See Human Rights Watch, *Peru: The Two Faces of Justice* 7, 9 (New York: Human Rights Watch, July 1995).
39. On the undermining of democracy and the establishment of authoritarianism under Fujimori, see *The Peruvian Labyrinth: Polity, Society, Economy*, ed. Maxwell A. Cameron and Philip Mauceri (University Park, PA: Pennsylvania State University Press, 1997); Carlos Iván Degregori, *La Década de la Antipolítica: Auge y Huida de Alberto Fujimori y Vladimiro Montesinos* (Lima: Instituto de Estudios Peruanos, 2000); Julio Cotler y Romeo Grompone, *El Fujimorismo: Ascenso y Caída de un Régimen Autoritario* (Lima: Instituto de Estudios Peruanos, 2000); Rolando Ames, Enrique Bernales, Sinesio López, and Rafael Roncagliolo, *Situación de la Democracia en el Perú (2000–2001)* (Lima: International IDEA and Pontificia Universidad Católica del Perú Fondo Editorial, 2001).
40. For a detailed analysis of the events surrounding the crisis, see Catherine M. Conaghan, *Making and Unmaking Authoritarian Peru: Re-Election, Resistance, and Regime Transition*, North–South Agenda Papers No. 47 (Miami: North–South Center, University of Miami, May 2001); and Andrew F. Cooper and Thomas Legler, "The OAS in Peru: A Model for the Future?" *Journal of Democracy* 12, no. 4 (October 2001): 123–136.
41. National Democratic Institute and the Carter Center, *Peru Elections 2000: Final Report of the National Democratic Institute/Carter Center Joint Election Monitoring Project* (Washington, DC: National Democratic Institute, 2000), 7.

42. OAS Electoral Observation Mission to Peru, *Executive Summary of the Final Report of the Chief of Mission*, OEA/Ser. P AG/doc.3936/00, June 5, 2000.

43. The OAS Electoral Observation Mission in Haiti: Chief of Mission Report to the OAS Permanent Council, July 13, 2000 <http://www.upd.oas.org/EOM/Haiti/haitichief%20of%20mission%20report.htm>.

44. Lewis Taylor, "Patterns of Corruption in Peru: The April 2000 General Election," *Crime, Law, and Social Change* 34 (2000): 406–407.

45. Conaghan, *Making and Unmaking Authoritarian Peru: Re-Election, Resistance, and Regime Transition*, 14.

46. Misión de Observacion Electoral, *Boletin No. 12*, May 25, 2000. <http://www.upd.oas.org/EOM/Peru/Boletin%20No.12.htm>.

47. The following analysis draws extensively on Andrew F. Cooper and Thomas Legler, "A Model for the Future? The OAS in Peru."

48. Executive Summary of the Final Report of the Chief of the Mission distributed as document AG/doc.3936/00 at the 30th Regular Session of the General Assembly in Windsor, Canada on June 4, 2000.

Chapter 4   Networked Multilateralism in Action: The OAS and the 2000 Crisis in Peru

1. Richard J. Bloomfield, "Making the Western Hemisphere Safe for Democracy? The OAS Defense-of Democracy Regime," in *Collective Responses to Regional Problems: The Case of Latin America and the Caribbean*, ed. Carl Kaysen, Robert A. Pastor, and Laura W. Reed (Cambridge, MA: American Academy of Arts and Sciences, 1994), 15–28.

2. Organization of American States Electoral Observation Mission (MOE/OEA), *Informe Final del Jefe de Misión. Misión de Observación Electoral, Elecciones Generales de la República del Perú, Año 2000* (Lima, Peru: June 2, 2000).

3. CNN, "OAS rejects U.S. Call For Action Against Peru Over Election," May 31, 2000.

4. "An Amber Light for Fujimori," *The Economist*, June 10, 2000: 36.

5. Veronique Mandal, "OAS Peru Mission Endorsed," *Windsor Star*, June 6, 2000.

6. Paul Knox, "Canada Pushes For Rights in Latin America," *Globe and Mail* [Toronto], June 5, 2000.

7. CNN, "OAS rejects U.S." May 31, 2000.

8. CNN, "Toledo Raises Idea of Sanctions: U.S. Softens Stance on Peru Elections," May 30, 2000.

9. Ambassador Luis J. Lauredo, Permanent Representative of the United States to the Organization of American States, "Remarks Concerning the OAS Electoral Observation Mission to Peru" (Address to the Special Session of the OAS Permanent Council, May 31, 2000), http://www.state.gov/www/policy_remarks/2000/000531_lauredo_oas.html.

10. Embassy of the United States of America in Lima, Peru, *Statement on Introduced Bills and Joint Resolutions* (March 28, 2000): S Res 43. See also the Joint Resolution of the U.S. Congress warning that "if the April 9, 2000 elections are not deemed by the international community to have been free and fair, the United States will modify its political and economic relations with Peru, including its support for international financial institution loans to Peru."

11. "OAS Welcome in Peru, But Election Stands," *Seattle Times*, June 6, 2000.

12. Andrew F. Cooper, *Canadian Foreign Policy: Old Habits and New Directions* (Scarborough, ON: Prentice Hall Allyn and Bacon, 1997).

13. For more detail about Vincent's role in this episode see James Bartleman, *On Six Continents* (Toronto: McClelland and Stewart, 2004); "The Canadian at the centre of Peru's hostage taking," CBC-National, December 19, 1996.

14. See César Gaviria, *A New Vision for the OAS*. Working Document presented to the Permanent Council, April 6, 1995 (URL: http://www.oas.org/EN/PINFO/nvindexe.htm).
15. Steven Pearlstein, "OAS Votes to Send Mission to Press Peru," *Washington Post*, June 6, 2000: A 20.
16. OAS General Assembly, *Resolution on Peru*, Released at the 30th OAS G A, June, 2000, Windsor: Canada, www.state.gov/www/regions/wha/00605_oasgares_peru.html.
17. Pearlstein, "OAS votes to send mission."
18. Veronique Mandal, "OAS Peru Mission Endorsed."
19. "OAS Welcome in Peru, But Election Stands." *Seattle Times*, June 6, 2000.
20. Peruvian Human Rights Groups and Canadian Churches, "Don't Betray The Peruvian People," press release, June 6, 2000, http://www.web.apc.org/~icchrla/Peru/PR-OASPeruMission-Jn00.htm; See also the open letter from Peruvian Human Rights Organizations to Foreign Minister Lloyd Axworthy with regard to the Imminent OAS Fact-finding Mission to Peru. Sofia Macher, executive-secretary, National Human Rights Coordinating Committee (CNDDHH), June 15, 2000, Lima.
21. Knox, "Canada Pushes for Rights."
22. Clifford Krauss, "O.A.S. Mission to Peru Says Intelligence Boss Must Go," *New York Times*, June 30, 2000.
23. Ibid.
24. Permanent Secretariat of the Organization of American States High-Level Mission to Peru, *Informe Final de la Secretaría Permanente de la Misión de Alto Nivel de la Organización de los Estados Americanos (OEA) en el Perú* (Lima, Peru: February 26, 2001).
25. Andrew F. Cooper and Thomas Legler, "The OAS Democratic Solidarity Paradigm: Questions of Collective and National Leadership," *Journal of Interamerican Studies and World Affairs*, 43 (Spring 2001). See this source for more details.
26. Joaquín Tacsán, "Searching for OAS/UN Task-Sharing Opportunities in Central America and Haiti," *Third World Quarterly* 18 (1997): 489–507; and Cooper and Legler, "The OAS Democratic Solidarity Paradigm."

Chapter 5   The Making of the Inter-American Democratic Charter: The Apex of Networked Multilateralism

1. John G. Ruggie, "Multilateralism: The Anatomy of an Institution," in *Multilateralism Matters; The Theory and Praxis of an Institutional Form*, ed. John G. Ruggie (New York: Columbia University Press, 1993), 3–50.
2. Guy Gosselin and Jean-Philippe Thérien, "The Organization of American States and Hemispheric Regionalism," in *The Americas in Transition: The Contours of Regionalism*, ed. Gordon Mace and Louis Bélanger (Boulder, CO: Lynne Rienner, 1999), 175–194.
3. Susan Strange, "States, Firms and Diplomacy," in *International Affairs* 68, no. 1 (1992): 1–15.
4. Early expressions of the notion of the right to democracy are found in Tom Farer, "Collectively Defending Democracy in a World of Sovereign States; The Western Hemisphere's Prospect," *Human Rights Quarterly* 15, no. 4 (1993): 716–750; and Thomas M. Franck, "The Emerging Right to Democratic Governance," *American Journal of International Law* 86, no. 1 (1992): 46–91. See also D.E. Acevedo and C. Grossman, "The Organization of American States and the Protection of Democracy." in *Sovereignty: Collectively Defending Democracy in the Americas*, ed. T. Farer (Baltimore, MD: Johns Hopkins University Press, 1996), 132–149; R.J. Bloomfield, "Making the Western Hemisphere Safe for Democracy? The OAS Defense-of-Democracy Regime." In *Collective Responses to Regional Problems: The Case of Latin America and the Caribbean*,

ed. C. Kaysen, R.A. Pastor, and L.W. Reed (Cambridge, MA: American Academy of Arts and Sciences, 1994), 15–28; and Heraldo Muñoz, "Collective Action for Democracy in the Americas," in *Latin American Nations in World Politics*, ed. by H. Muñoz and J.S. Tulchin, 2nd ed. (Boulder, CO: Westview, 1996), 17–34.; Heraldo Muñoz. "The Right to Democracy in the Americas," *Journal of Interamerican Studies and World Affairs* 40, no. 1 (1998): 1–18.

5. OAS, *Inter-American Democratic Charter (2001)*, September 11, 2001, OAS Doc.OEA/ Ser.P/AG/RES.1, XXVLLL-E/01, www.oas.org/charter/docs/resolution1_en_p4.htm.

6. For a fuller analysis of this concept see Andrew F. Cooper, Richard Higgott and Kim.Richard Nossal, "Bound to Follow? Leadership and Followership in the Gulf Conflict," *Political Science Quarterly* 46, no. 3 (1991): 391–410. See also Nye, J.S. Jr. *The Paradox of American Power: Why the World's Superpower Can't Go It Alone* (Oxford: Oxford University Press, 2002).

7. R. O'Brien, A.M. Goetz, J.A. Scholte, and M. Williams, *Contesting Global Governance* (Cambridge: Cambridge University Press, 2000).

8. Ibid., 208.

9. J. Pérez de Cuéllar, *Exposición del Presidente del Consejo de Ministros y Ministro de Relaciones Exteriores*, Embajador Javier Pérez de Cuéllar, ante el Consejo del la Republica. Lima. December 2000, www.rree.gob.pe/cdioea/perzdecuellar.htm.

10. M. Rodríguez Cuadros, "Promotion and Consolidation of Democracy," Commission on Human Rights: Sub-Commission on the Promotion and Protection of Human Rights, Fifty-fourth session, Item 6, E/CN.4/Sub.2/2002/36, June 10, 2002.

11. *Carta Democrática InterAmericana*, ed. E. García Calderón (Lima: Transparencia, 2001), and Intervención del Dr. D. García Sayán, Ministro de Justicia del Perú, in "Conferencia sobre el papel de las organizaciones regionales y multilaterales en la defensa y protección de la democracia," OEA, Washington, DC, February 21, 2001.

12. At this latter forum the impression of speed (cutting further into the entrenched image of the OAS and the wider inter-American system as a "talking shop") was reinforced by a number of factors. On the wider context see Andrew F. Cooper, "The Quebec City 'Democracy Summit,' " *The Washington Quarterly* 24, no. 2 (Spring 2001): 159–171.

13. OAS, "Peru Submits Democratic Charter Proposal for OAS Charter Proposal for OAS General Assembly Dialogue of Ministers," press release, E-089/01, April 18, 2001.

14. Not only was there an explicit linkage between the implementation of the clause and participation in the Summit of the Americas process but there was the potential at least to deny access to any Free Trade Area of the Americas under the clause. There was no actual mention of the FTAA in the clause as it appeared in the Quebec Declaration. For the Peruvian contribution see *Carta Democrática InterAmericana*, ed. E. García Calderón (Lima: Transparencia, 2001).

15. Paul Knox, "Democracy clause questioned," *Globe and Mail* [Toronto], June 2, 2001.

16. J. Pérez de Cuéllar, Exposición del Presidente del Consejo de Ministros y Ministro de Relaciones Exteriores.

17. OAS, *Inter-American Democratic Charter (2001)*, September 11, 2001, OAS oc.OEA/Ser.P/AG/ RES.1, XXVLLL-E/01, articles 11–16, www.oas.org/charter/docs/resolution1_en_p4.htm.

18. Ibid., Chapter 6.

19. Cynthia McClintock, "Room for Improvement," *Journal of Democracy* 12, no. 4 (2001): 137–140.

20. Robert A. Pastor, "A Community of Democracies of the Americas in the Americas: From Phrase to Reality" (Paper presented at the Inter-American Cooperation Beyond Free Trade conference, Quebec, April 18, 2001).

21. Kathryn Sikkink, "Restructuring World Politics: The Limits and Asymmetries of Soft Power," in *Restructuring World Politics: Transnational Social Movements, Networks, and Norms*, ed. S. Khagram, J.V. Riker, and K. Sikkink (Minneapolis: University of Minnesota Press, 2002), 312–313.

22. J. Pérez de Cuéllar, *Exposición del Presidente del Consejo de Ministros y Ministro de Relaciones Exteriores*.

23. Martha Finnemore and Kathryn Sikkink, "International Norm Dynamics and Political Change," *International Organization* 52, no. 4 (1998): 887–917.

24. On the concept of epistemic communities see Peter Haas, "Introduction; Epistemic Communities and International Policy Coordination," *International Organization* 46, no. 1 (1992): 1–35. On networks in Latin America see Kathryn Sikkink, "Human Rights, Principled Issue—networks, and Sovereignty in Latin America," *International Organization* 47, no. 3 (1993): 411–441; Kathryn Sikkink, "Nongovernmental Organizations, Democracy, and Human Rights in Latin America" in *Beyond Sovereignty: Collectively Defending Democracy in the Americas* ed. T. Farer (Baltimore: Johns Hopkins University Press, 1996): 150–168; and M.E. Keck and K. Silkkink, *Activists Beyond Borders: Advocacy Networks in International Politics* (Ithaca: Cornell University Press, 1998).

25. Audie Klotz, *Norms in International Relations: The Struggle Against Apartheid* (Ithaca: Cornell University Press, 1995), 140.

26. P. Hakim, "The Uneasy Americas," *Foreign Affairs* 80, no. 2 (2001): 46–61.

27. T. Catán, "The Sins of Montesinos," *Financial Times Weekend* [London], July 22, 2003.

28. Ibid.

29. D.E. Sanger, "Bush Will Press Free-Trade Issue at Quebec Talks," *New York Times*, April 21, 2001.

30. J. McCoy, "Comments on the Inter-American Democratic Charter," *Summits of the Americas Bulletin* 1, no. 4 (2001): 3.

31. *Carta Democrática InterAmericana*, ed. E. García Calderón (Lima, Peru: Transparencia, 2001).

32. For background see *Venezuelan Politics in the Chávez Era: Class, Polarization, and Conflict*, ed. S. Ellner and D. Hellinger (London: Lynne Rienner, 2003); and Sylvia and Danopoulos, 2003. On the Venezuela–U.S. relationship see J. Kelly and C.A. Romero, *The United States and Venezuela: Rethinking a Relationship* (New York: Routledge, 2002).

33. E. Lagos and T.D. Rudy, "The Third Summit of the Americas and the Thirty—First Session of the OAS General Assembly," *The American Journal of International Law* 96, no. 1 (2002): 173–181.

34. OAS, "Working Group to Study the Draft Inter-American Democratic Charter, Comparative Table on the Draft Inter-American Democratic Charter (Rev. 7) with the Proposals, Amendments, and Comments Submitted by Member States," GT/CDI-6/01 (Presented by the Chair of the Working Group to Study the Draft Inter-American Democratic Charter, Permanent Council of the OAS, August 14, 2001).

35. John W. Graham, "A Magna Carta for the Americas: The Inter-American Democratic Charter: Genesis, Challenges and the Canadian Connections" *FOCAL Policy Paper 02–09*, September 2002.

36. F. Pérez Roque, Minister of Foreign Affairs of the Republic of Cuba, "Address to the National and Foreign Press" (press conference, The Foreign Ministry, April 11, 2002).

37. T. Rogers, "OAS Meet Ends with Optimism," *The Tico Times* [San José], June 11, 2001.

38. Graham, "A Magna Carta for the Americas."

39. Paul D. Durand, *Reflections on the Inter-American Democratic Charter: A Canadian Perspective* (Washington, DC: Mimeo, August 2001).

40. The Inter-American Agenda and Multilateral Governance: The Organization of American States; A Report of the Inter-American Dialogue Study Group on Western Hemisphere Governance, Washington, DC: April. This dynamic sacrificed an internal democratic structure for effectiveness. On this point see Sikkink, "Restructuring World Politics," 311.

41. Graham, "A Magna Carta for the Americas."

42. Rogers, "OAS Meet Ends with Optimism."

43. Warren Allmand, President, Rights & Democracy, "Submission to the OAS," on the *Inter-American Democratic Charter*, August 10, 2001.

44. J. McCoy, "Comments on the Inter-American Democratic Charter," *Summits of the Americas Bulletin* 1, no. 4 (2001): 3.
45. OAS, *Draft Resolution Inter-American Democratic Charter (2001)*, May 30, 2001, OEA/Ser.P, June 3, AG/doc.4030/01, San José, Costa Rica.
46. Warren Allmand, "Submission to the OAS."
47. Rogers, "OAS Meet Ends with Optimism."
48. OAS, doc.OEA/Ser.P/AG/doc.4042/01, June 5, 2001.<http://www.oas.org/main/main.asp?sLang=E&sLink=http://scm.oas.org/Reference/english/english.htm>
49. *Carta Democrática InterAmericana*, ed. E. García Calderón (Lima: Transparencia, 2001).
50. Ibid.
51. Sikkink, "Restructuring World Politics: The Limits and Asymmetries of Soft Power," 312–313.
52. OAS, *Inter-American Democratic Charter (2001)*, September 11, 2001, OAS Doc.OEA/Ser.P/AG/RES.1, XXVLLL-E/01, www.oas.org/charter/docs/resolution1_en_p4.htm.
53. Maxwell A. Cameron, "Strengthening Checks and Balances: Democracy Defence and Promotion in the Americas" (paper presented at The Inter-American Democratic Charter: Challenges and Opportunities conference, Liu Institute for the Study of Global Issues, University of British Columbia, November 12–13, 2002).
54. P. Greste, BBC, "Democracy Pact for Americas: Peruvians Feel Their Democracy was Hijacked by Fujimori," September 11, 2001.
55. On the bureaucraticization of diplomacy see G.R. Winham, "Negotiation as a Management Process," *World Politics* 30, no. 1 (1977): 87–114.
56. On the capacity of secondary powers for the promotion of ideas see Richard Higgott, "Issues, Institutions and Middle Power Diplomacy: Action and Agendas in the Post–Cold War Era," in *Niche Diplomacy: Middle Powers after the Cold War*, ed. A.F. Cooper (London: Macmillan, 1997).
57. R. O'Brien, A.M. Goetz, J.A. Scholte, and M. Williams, *Contesting Global Governance* (Cambridge: Cambridge University Press, 2000), 207.
58. Andrew F. Cooper and Brian Hocking, "Diplomacy and the Re-Calibration of State-Societal Relations," *Global Society* 14, no. 3 (2000): 361–376.

Chapter 6   Passing the (First) Test?
The Venezuelan Coup of April 11, 2002

1. Domingo E. Acevedo and Claudio Grossman, "The Organization of American States and the Protection of Democracy," in *Beyond Sovereignty: Collectively Defending Democracy in the Americas*, ed. Tom Farer, 132–149 (Baltimore: Johns Hopkins University Press, 1996); Andrew F. Cooper and Thomas Legler, "The OAS Democratic Solidarity Paradigm: Questions of Collective and National Leadership," *Latin American Politics and Society* 43 (Spring 2001): 103–126.
2. OAS, *The Situation in Haiti*, CP/RES. 806 (1303/02), January 16, 2002.
3. John W. Graham, "A Magna Carta for the Americas. The Inter-American Democratic Charter: Genesis, Challenges, and Canadian Connections," *FOCAL Policy Paper* (FPP-02–09), September 2002.
4. On the *Puntofijo* political system, see *The Unraveling of Representative Democracy in Venezuela*, ed. Jennifer L. McCoy and David J. Myers (Baltimore, MD: Johns Hopkins University Press, 2004). On the political economy of *puntofijismo* and the importance of its oil wealth underpinnings, see Terry Lynn Karl, *The Paradox of Plenty: Oil Booms and Petro-States* (Berkeley: University of California Press, 1997).
5. See Charles Ameringer, "The Foreign Policy of Venezuelan Democracy," in *Venezuela: The Democratic Experience*, ed. John D, Martz and David J. Myers (New York: Praeger, 1977), 335–358.

6. This discussion provides only a partial overview of the crisis and demise of the *Puntofijo* system as an entry into the analysis of the OAS's role in Venezuela. For more complete treatments, see *The Unraveling of Representative Democracy in Venezuela*, ed. McCoy and Myers; *Venezuelan Politics in the Chávez Era: Class, Polarization, and Conflict*, ed. Steve Ellner and Daniel Hellinger (Boulder, CO: Lynne Rienner, 2003); Daniel H. Levine and Brian F. Crisp, "Venezuela: The Character, Crisis, and Possible Future of Democracy," *World Affairs* 161, no. 3 (Winter 1999): 123–165; Brian F. Crisp and Daniel H. Levine, "Democratizing the Democracy? Crisis and Reform in Venezuela," *Journal of Inter-American Studies and World Affairs* 40, no. 2 (Summer 1998): 28–61.

7. David J. Meyers, "The Normalization of Punto Fijo Democracy," in *Unraveling of Representative Democracy in Venezuela*, ed. McCoy and Myers, 29.

8. Daniel Hellinger, "Political Overview: The Breakdown of *Puntofijismo* and the Rise of *Chavismo*," in *Venezuelan Politics in the Chávez Era: Class, Polarization, and Conflict*, ed. Ellner and Hellinger, 31.

9. See Kenneth M. Roberts, "Social Correlates of Party System Demise and Populist Resurgence in Venezuela," *Latin American Politics and Society* 45, no. 3 (Fall 2003): 35–57.

10. On *chavismo*, see the collection of essays in *Venezuelan Politics in the Chávez Era: Class, Polarization, and Conflict*, ed. Ellner and Hellinger. See also Margarita López Maya and Luis E. Lander, "Refounding the Republic: The Political Project of Chavismo," *NACLA Report on the Americas* 33, no. 6 (May/June 2000).

11. Jennifer L. McCoy, "Chávez and the End of 'Partyarchy' in Venezuela," *Journal of Democracy* 10, no. 3 (July 1999): 64–77. The term partyarchy was originally coined by Michael Coppedge. See Michael Coppedge, "Venezuela: The Rise and Fall of Partyarchy," in *Constructing Democratic Governance: South America in the 1990s*, ed. Jorge I. Domínguez and Abraham F. Lowenthal, (Baltimore, MD: Johns Hopkins University Press, 1996), 3–19 .

12. María Pilar García-Guadilla, Ana Mallén, and Maryluz Guillén, "The Multiple Faces of Venezuelan Civil Society: Politization and Its Impact on Democratization," (paper prepared for the 2004 Congress of the Latin American Studies Association, Las Vegas, NV, October 7–9, 2004); Jennifer McCoy, "The Referendum in Venezuela: One Act in an Unfinished Drama," *Journal of Democracy* 16, no. 1 (January 2005): 109–123.

13. On the fragmentation of the two-party *Puntofijo* system, see Hellinger, "Political Overview: The Breakdown of Puntofijismo and the Rise of Chavismo," in *Venezuelan Politics*, ed. Ellner and Hellinger, 27–53.

14. "Venezuelan Business and Labor Groups Bring Country to a Halt," *NACLA Report on the Americas* 35, no. 4 (January/February 2002).

15. "Groups Bring Country to a Halt," *NACLA Report*, 2002; Steve Ellner and Fred Rosen, "*Chavismo* at the Crossroads: Hardliners, Moderates and a Regime Under Attack," *NACLA Report on the Americas* 35, no. 6 (May/June 2002).

16. Andres Canizalez, "Venezuela: Chávez Under Pressure," *NACLA Report on the Americas* 35, no. 5 (March/April 2002).

17. See Ellner and Rosen, "*Chavismo* at the Crossroads," *NACLA Report*, 2002.

18. Omar G. Encarnación, "Venezuela's 'Civil Society Coup,' " *World Policy Journal* 19, no. 2 (Summer 2002): 42.

19. See Luis Lander and Margarita López-Maya, "Venezuela's Oil Reform and *Chavismo*," *NACLA Report on the Americas* 36, no. 1 (July/August 2002).

20. Gregory Wilpert, "Coup and Countercoup: An Eyewitness Account," *NACLA Report on the Americas* 35, no. 6 (May/June 2002).

21. Margarita López-Maya, "Venezuela 2001–2004: Actores y Estrategias," *Cuadernos del CENDES* 21, no. 56 (May–August 2004): 113–114.

22. OAS, *OAS Secretary-General Calls on Venezuelans to Defend Democracy* (E-027/02). February 8, 2002, http://www.oas.org/OASpage/press2002/en/Press2002/february2002/027-020802.htm.

23. Rio Group. *Declaración del Grupo de Rio sobre la Situación en Venezuela*. San José, Costa Rica, April 12, 2002.

24. Larry Rohter, "Uprising in Venezuela: Fear of Loss of Democracy Led Neighbors to Aid Return," *New York Times*, April 15, 2002.

25. On the U.S. role in the coup, see Peter Hakim, "The World, Democracy, and U.S. Credibility," *New York Times*, April 21, 2002; Katty Kay, "Bush Team Met Chávez Coup Leaders," *The Times*, April 17, 2002; Michael Shifter, "Democracy in Venezuela, Unsettling as Ever," *Washington Post*, April 21, 2002; "Tales from a Failed Coup," *Economist*, April 25, 2002; Arturo Valenzuela, "Bush's Betrayal of Democracy," *Washington Post*, April 16, 2002; Fred Rosen, "Venezuela: Washington Suffers a Setback," *NACLA Report on the Americas* 35, no. 6 (May/June 2002); Peter Slevin, "Chávez Provoked His Removal, U.S. Officials Say," *Washington Post*, April 13, 2002; Karen DeYoung, "U.S. Seen As Weak Patron of Latin Democracy," *Washington Post*, April 16, 2002; Paul Krugman, "Losing Latin America," *New York Times*, April 16, 2002; Christopher Marquis, "Bush Officials Met With Venezuelans Who Ousted Leader," *New York Times*, April 16, 2002.

26. OAS, *Statement of the OAS Secretary-General on the Situation in Venezuela* (E-078-02), April 11, 2002, http://www.oas.org/OASpage/press2002/en/Press2002/april2002/078—041102.htm.

27. OAS, *Situation in Venezuela*, OEA/Ser.G CP/RES 811 (1315/02). April 13, 2002.

28. Steve Ellner and Fred Rosen, "The Remarkable Fall and Rise of Hugo Chávez," *NACLA Report on the Americas* 36, no. 1 (July/August 2002); Encarnación, "Venezuela's 'Civil Society Coup,' " *World Policy Journal*, 2002, 43.

29. For accounts of the events that led up to Chávez's return to power, see Juan Forero, "Uprising in Venezuela: Homecoming. Relief, Exhaustion, and Joy as Backers Greet Chávez," *New York Times*, April 15, 2002; Scott Wilson, "Chávez Reclaims Power in Venezuela," *Washington Post*, April 15, 2002.

30. For good contextual analyses of the events surrounding the coup within Venezuela, see Ellner and Rosen, "*Chavismo* at Crossroads," *NCLA Report*, 2002; Moisés Naím, "Democracy Dictates Latin America's future," *Financial Times*, April 26, 2002; Encarnación, "Venezuela's 'Civil Society Coup,' " *World Policy Journal*, 2002.

31. OAS, *Report of the Secretary-General of the Organization of American States, César Gaviria, Pursuant to Resolution CP/Res. 811 (1315/02) Situation in Venezuela*, OEA/Ser.P AG/doc.9 (XXIX-E/02), April 18, 2002.

32. Luis Alfonso Dávila, *Discurso del Señor Canciller Luis Alfonso Dávila ante la Asamblea General Extraordinaria de la OEA* (speech, OAS General Assembly, Washington, DC, April 18, 2002). http://www.oas.org/speeches/Speechother02/2002/spa/VE_041802Canciller.htm.

33. Colin L. Powell, *Remarks of the Secretary of State Colin L. Powell to the Special Assembly of the Organization of American States* (speech, OAS General Assembly, Washington, DC, April 18, 2002). http://www.oas.org/speeches/Speechother02/2002/eng/041802-Colin_Powell_VE.htm.

34. OAS, *Support for Democracy in Venezuela*. OEA/Ser.P AG/RES. 1 (XXIX-E/02), April 18, 2002.

35. OAS, *The Inter-American Commission on Human Rights Concludes Its Visit to the Bolivarian Republic of Venezuela*, Press Release No. 23/02, May 10, 2002, http://www.cidh.oas.org/Comunicados/English/2002/Press23.02.htm.

36. OAS, *The Current Situation in Venezuela* (presented by the delegation of Venezuela, Permanent Council meeting, Washington, DC, May 28, 2002) OEA/Ser.P CP/doc.3616/02.

37. OAS, *Report of the Permanent Council on the Situation in Venezuela* (presented pursuant to resolution AG/RES. 1 (XXIX-E/02) and adopted by the Permanent Council, Washington, DC, May 28, 2002), OEA/Ser.P AG/doc. 4131/02, May 29, 2002.

38. OAS, *Declaration on Democracy in Venezuela* (adopted at fourth plenary session of the General Assembly, Bridgetown, Barbados, June 4, 2002), AG/CG/doc.16/02, http://www.oas.org/xxxiiga/english/docs_en/docs_items/AGcgdoc16_02.htm.

39. For a good analysis of the conditions under which OAS member states can successfully advance their agenda multilaterally against U.S. interests, see Carolyn M. Shaw, *Cooperation,*

Conflict, and Consensus in the Organization of American States (New York: Palgrave MacMillan, 2004).

40. Alexandra Olson, "U.S. Embassy Warns Against Attempts to Oust Venezuelan Government," *Associated Press*, September 18, 2002.

Chapter 7   In Between Club and Networked Multilateralism: The Quest for a Solution to the Venezuelan Political Crisis

1. See Jimmy Carter, *Statement of Former President Jimmy Carter at the Conclusion of His Trip to Venezuela* (Atlanta: The Carter Center, July 9, 2002) http://www.cartercentre.org/doc1040.htm.
2. See OAS, *Apoyo al Proceso de Diálogo en Venezuela*, OEA/Ser.G CP/RES. 821 (1329/02), August 14, 2002, http://www.oas.org/OASpage/esp/Documentos/CPres821_02.htm.
3. See OAS, *Síntesis Operativa de la Mesa de Negociación y Acuerdos* (Caracas: OAS, November 7, 2002) http://www.oas.org/OASpage/eng/Venezuela2002_Negocia.htm.
4. Jimmy Carter, *A Proposal to Restore Peace and Harmony in Venezuela* (Atlanta: The Carter Center, January 22, 2003) http://www.cartercenter.org/printdoc.asp?docID=1157&submenu=news.
5. Jennifer McCoy. "Chávez and the End of Partyarchy in Venezuela," *Journal of Democracy* 10, no. 3 (July 1999): 64–77.
6. On recent trends in Venezuelan civil society, see Luis Salamanca, "Civil Society: Late Bloomers," in *The Unraveling of Representative Democracy in Venezuela*, ed. Jennifer L. McCoy and David J. Meyers, (Baltimore: Johns Hopkins University Press, 2004) 93–114; María Pilar García Guadilla, "Civil Society: Institutionalization, Fragmentation, Autonomy," in *Venezuelan Politics in the Chávez Era*, ed. Steve Ellner and Daniel Hellinger (Boulder, CO: Lynne Rienner, 2003) 179–196; María Pilar García-Guadilla, Ana Mallén, and Maryluz Guillén, "The Multiple Faces of Venezuelan Civil Society: Politization and Its Impact on Democratization," (paper prepared for the 2004 Congress of the Latin American Studies Association, Las Vegas, Nevada, October 7–9, 2004); Rosa Amelia González de Pacheco, "Las Organizaciones de Ciudadanos en Venezuela: ¿Ser O No Ser Actores Políticos?" (paper presented to the XXIV International Congress of the Latin American Studies Association, Dallas, Texas, March 27–29, 1993); Margarita López Maya, "Venezuela 2001–2004: Actores y Estrategias," *Cuadernos del CENDES* 21, no. 56 (May–August 2004): 105–128.
7. On the Group of Friends of Venezuela, see OAS, *Press Release: Group of Friends of the OAS Secretary-General for Venezuela*, E-020/03, January 31, 2003, http://www.oas.org/library/mant_press/press_release.asp?sCodigo=E-020/03; OAS, *Group of Friends to Support Secretary-General in His Facilitation Efforts in Venezuela* (Washington, DC: Organization of American States, January–February 2003). http://www.oas.org/oasnews/2003/Jan_Feb/English/art7.html.
8. César Gaviria, *The OAS in Transition: 1994–2004* (Washington, DC: Organization of American States, 2004): 55.
9. OAS, *Declaración de Principios por la Paz y la Democracia en Venezuela* (Washington, DC: Organization of American States, September 13, 2002) http://www.oas.org/library/mant_press/press_release.asp?sCodigo=VEN; OAS, *Síntesis Operativa de la Mesa de Negociación y Acuerdos* (Caracas: Organization of American States, November 7, 2002) http://www.oas.org/OASpage/eng/Venezuela2002_Negocia.htm; OAS, *Secretario General de la OEA Informa Sobre Declaración de Principios por la Paz en Venezuela*, Press Release C-203/02, October 16, 2002,

http://www.oas.org/library/mant_press/press_release.asp?sCodigo=C-203/02; see also OAS, *Síntesis Operativa*, 2002.

10. Jimmy Carter, "A Proposal to Restore Peace and Harmony in Venezuela," (Atlanta: The Carter Center, January 22, 2003) http://www.cartercenter.org/printdoc.asp?docID= 1157&submenu=news.

11. See the discussion in OAS, *Report on Facilitation Efforts of the Secretary-General in Venezuela*, OEA/Ser.P AG/doc.4231/03 add. 1 (Santiago: Organization of American States, June 7, 2003).

12. See *Preliminary Agreement Between the Representatives of the Government of the Bolivarian Republic of Venezuela and the Political and Social Groups Supporting It and the Coordinadora Democrática* (presented to the media by Fernando Jaramillo, Caracas, April 11, 2003) http://www.oas.org/OASpage/eng/Venezuela/Agreement-041103.htm.

13. Group of Friends of the Secretary-General of the OAS for Venezuela, *Comunicado do Grupo de Amigos do Secretário-Geral da OEA para a Venezuela sobre acordo entre o Governo e a Coordenadora Democrática*, Caracas, April 15, 2003.

14. See *Agreement Between the Government of the Bolivarian Republic of Venezuela and the Political and Social Groups Supporting It, and the Coordinadora Democrática and the Political and Civil Society Organizations Supporting It* (Caracas: Organization of American States, May 23, 2003) http://www.oas.org/OASpage/eng/Venezuela/Agreement052303en.htm.

15. Gaviria, *OAS in Transition*, 2004, 61–62.

16. Gaviria, *OAS in Transition*, 2004, 65.

17. Carter Center, *Democracy and Dialogue: Venezuelan Election Q&A* (Atlanta: The Carter Center, February 26, 2005).

18. On the "existential struggle," see García-Guadilla, Mallén, and Guillén, "Faces of Venezuelan Society," 2004; See also Jennifer McCoy, "The Referendum in Venezuela: One Act in an Unfinished Drama," *Journal of Democracy* 16, no. 1 (January 2005): 109–123.

19. International Crisis Group, *Venezuela: Headed Toward Civil War?* (Quito/Brussels: International Crisis Group, May 10, 2004).

20. For a critical treatment of the CNE's role during the recall referendum process, see Miriam Kornblith, "The Referendum in Venezuela: Elections Versus Democracy," *Journal of Democracy* 16, no. 1 (January 2005): 124–137.

21. See Fernando Jaramillo, *Carta de Fernando Jaramillo, Jede de Misión de la OEA en Venezuela, al Presidente del Consejo Nacional Electoral de Ese País* (Caracas: March 19, 2004).

22. McCoy, "Referendum in Venezuela," *Journal of Democracy*, 2005: 115; Carter Center, *Observing the Venezuela Presidential Recall Referendum: Comprehensive Report* (Atlanta: The Carter Center, February 2005), 16.

23. Carter Center, *Observing the Venezuela Presidential Recall Referendum: Comprehensive Report* (Atlanta: The Carter Center, February 2005), 28.

24. On the opposition's main allegations of fraud, see McCoy, "Referendum in Venezuela," *Journal of Democracy*, 2005: 109–123; Jennifer McCoy, "What Really Happened In Venezuela?" *Economist*, September 2, 2004.

25. See the Carter Center and the OAS, *Audit of the Results of the Presidential Recall Referendum in Venezuela* (Caracas: August 26, 2004).

26. "Venezuela: Extent of Pro-Chávez Victory Becomes Apparent," *Latin American Weekly Report*, November 9, 2004.

27. "Opposition Alliance Breaks Up," *Latinnews Daily*, September 22, 2004; "Deepening Opposition Split Over Elections," *Andean Group Report*, October 5, 2004.

28. On political opportunity structure analysis, see Sydney Tarrow, *Power in Movement*, 2nd ed. (Cambridge: Cambridge University Press, 1998); Charles Tilly, *From Mobilization to Revolution* (Reading, MA: Addison-Wesley, 1978).

29. See "Why Did the Venezuelan Opposition Get It So Wrong and What Will It Do Next?," *Latin American Weekly Report*, August 24, 2004.

30. For critical analysis of the Chávez government's reforms to the Supreme Court, see Human Rights Watch, *Rigging the Rule of Law: Judicial Independence Under Siege in Venezuela* 16, no. 3 (June 2004).

31. McCoy, "Referendum in Venezuela," *Journal of Democracy*, 2005: 114.

Chapter 8   Intervention without Intervening?

1. See Laurence Whitehead, "The Imposition of Democracy: The Caribbean," in *The International Dimensions of Democratization: Europe and the Americas*, ed. Laurence Whitehead (Oxford, UK: Oxford University Press, 2001), 59–92.

2. On hard versus soft forms of intervention, see Fernando Tesón, "Changing Perceptions of Domestic Jurisdiction and Intervention," in *Beyond Sovereignty: Collectively Defending Democracy in the Americas*, ed. Tom J. Farer (Baltimore, MD: Johns Hopkins University Press, 1996), 29–51.

3. On soft power, see Joseph Nye, "Soft Power," *Foreign Policy* 80 (Fall 1990): 153–171.

4. Charles Sampford and Margaret Palmer, "Strengthening Domestic Responses," in Morton H. Halperin and Mirna Galic, eds., *Protecting Democracy: International Responses* (Lanham, MD: Lixington Books, 2005), 195–196.

5. See the two *mesa* agreements: *Declaración de Principios por la Paz y la Democracia en Venezuela*, September 13, 2002. <www.oas.org/library/mant_press/press_release.asp?sCodigo=VEN>; *Declaración Contra la Violencia, por la Paz y la Democracia*, Caracas, February 18, 2003.

6. While the Haitian crisis is not part of the present study, it is illustrative of the power of the OAS' selection prerogative. The dialogue promoted by the OAS there gave voice and by extension, influence and international attention, to anti-Aristide elites who had little actual popular support.

7. On political pacts and democratization, see Terry Lynn Karl, "Dilemmas of Democratization in Latin America," *Comparative Politics* 23 (October 1990): 1–21; Terry Lynn Karl, "Petroleum and Political Pacts: The Transition to Democracy in Venezuela," in *Transitions from Authoritarian Rule: Latin America*, ed. Guillermo O'Donnell, Philippe C. Schmitter, and Laurence Whitehead (Baltimore, MD: Johns Hopkins University Press, 1986), 196–219.

8. Karl, "Dilemmas of Democratization in Latin America," 13.

9. The notion of external validation is taken from Thomas M. Franck, "The Emerging Right to Democratic Governance," *American Journal of International Law* 86, no. 1 (January 1992): 46–91.

10. John Ikenberry distinguishes between three types of international leadership: structural, institutional, and situational. Situational leadership refers to "actions and initiatives . . . that induce cooperation quite apart from the distribution of power or the array of institutions." See G. John Ikenberry, "The Future of International Leadership," *Political Science Quarterly* 111, no. 3 (Autumn 1996): 385–402.

11. See Annette Hester, "The Eagle's Talons Loosen," *Globe and Mail*, June 14, 2005; Joel Brinkley, "Latin American Nations Resist Plan to Monitor Democracy," *New York Times*, June 6, 2005.

12. Joel Brinkley, "Latin American Nations Resist Plan to Monitor Democracy."

13. On the limits of U.S. power over the OAS, see Carolyn Shaw, "Limits to Hegemonic Influence in the Organization of American States," *Latin American Politics and Society* 45, no. 3 (Fall 2003): 59–92; Carolyn Shaw, *Cooperation, Conflict, and Consensus in the Organization of American States* (New York: Palgrave, 2004).

14. See Peter Hakim, "Is Washington Losing Latin America?" *Foreign Affairs* 85 (1) (January/February 2006); Michael Shifter and Vinay Jawahar, "The Divided States of the Americas," *Current History* (February 2006): 51–57.

15. See the Carter Center, "President Carter Delivers Keynote Speech to OAS Lecture Series of the Americas," January 25, 2005 <www.cartercenter.og/doc1995.htm>; Friends of the Democratic Charter, "It's Taboo to Say Our Democracies Are Weak," *Miami Herald*, May 2, 2005.

16. Martha Finnemore and Kathryn Sikkink, "International Norm Dynamics and Political Change," *International Organization* 52, no. 4 (Autumn 1998): 887–917.

17. See Tom J. Farer, "Collectively Defending Democracy in the Western Hemisphere," in *Beyond Sovereignty: Collectively Defending Democracy in the Americas*, ed. Tom J. Farer (Baltimore, MD: Johns Hopkins University Press, 1996), 1–25; Fernando Tesón, "Changing Perceptions of Domestic Jurisdiction and Intervention"; Arturo Santa Cruz, *International Election Monitoring, Sovereignty, and the Western Hemisphere: The Emergence of an International Norm* (New York: Routledge, 2005).

18. Whitehead, "The Imposition of Democracy: The Caribbean."

19. Sampford and Palmer, "Strengthening Domestic Responses"

20. For more in-depth analysis of the sovereign limits of OAS multilateralism for democracy, see Thomas Legler, "The OAS Promotion of Democracy and Changing Sovereignty Practices in the Inter-American System," Paper presented at the 45th Annual Convention of the International Studies Association, Montreal, Quebec, March 17–20, 2004.

INDEX

The Welfare Experiments

Politics and Policy Evaluation

ROBIN H. ROGERS-DILLON

CABRINI COLLEGE LIBRARY
610 KING OF PRUSSIA ROAD
RADNOR, PA 19087

Stanford Law and Politics
AN IMPRINT OF STANFORD UNIVERSITY PRESS
STANFORD, CALIFORNIA
2004

*#54079886

Stanford University Press
Stanford, California
www.sup.org

© 2004 by the Board of Trustees of the Leland Stanford Junior University.
All rights reserved.

Library of Congress Cataloging-in-Publication Data

Rogers-Dillon, Robin.
    The welfare experiments : politics and policy evaluation / Robin H. Rogers-Dillon.
      cip:Includes bibliographical references and index.
      ISBN 0-8047-4730-X (cloth : alk. paper)—ISBN 0-8047-4746-6 (pbk : alk. paper)
      1. Public welfare—United States.   2. United States—Social policy—1993–
3. United States—Politics and government—1993–2001. I. Title.
  HV95.R58 2004
    361.6'0973'09049—dc22   2004001027

Printed in the United States of America on acid-free, archival-quality paper.

Original Printing 2004

Last figure below indicates year of this printing:
13 12 11 10 09 08 07 06 05 04

Designed and typeset at Stanford University Press in 10 / 12.5 Palatino.

Special discounts for bulk quantities of Stanford Law and Politics books are available to corporations, professional associations, and other organizations. For details and discount information, contact the special sales department of Stanford University Press. Tel: (650) 736-1783, Fax: (650) 736-1784